YALE ROMANIC STUDIES, SECOND SERIES 14

RONSARD'S SONNET CYCLES

A Study in Tone and Vision

DONALD STONE, JR.

New Haven and London

Yale University Press

1966

Library of Congress catalog card number: 66-12513

Published with assistance from the foundation established in memory of Calvin Chapin of the Class
of 1788, Yale College.

A la mémoire de mon père.

Preface

LITERARY CRITICISM, no less than literature itself, has tended to change its orientation over the years. Once philology dominated completely the study of medieval texts. The identification of sources occupied the life work of many a scholar, and interest in a writer's biography long forced itself upon the text to direct major questions of interpretation. French literature is no exception to these trends, and few of its great writers have been so continuously examined in the light of biography and sources as has Pierre de Ronsard.

Today, with the advent of "New Criticism," the text has come to occupy a place of honor it rarely, if ever, possessed, and whereas Baudelaire, Valéry, Rimbaud, and Verlaine, for example, quickly attracted new investigation, thought on Ronsard has moved only slightly toward a reevaluation through textual analysis. Henri Weber's thesis [1] affords some very challenging insights, but since Weber is interested primarily in themes, Ronsard appears as but one of many Renaissance poets in his work. The Desonay trilogy,[2] with its frequent return to questions of dates and the poet's biography, was clearly not designed to break entirely with the preoccupations of earlier critics of Ronsard. Gilbert Gadoffre's *Ronsard par lui-même*,[3] although stimulating in every respect, is extremely short and whets rather than satisfies the critical appetite. When he

1. Henri Weber, *La Création poétique en France au XVIe siècle* (Paris, 1956).
2. Fernand Desonay, *Ronsard, poète de l'amour* (Brussels, 1951–59).
3. Gilbert Gadoffre, *Ronsard par lui-même* (Paris, 1960).

writes, for example, "Pas plus que l'union mystique de l'Androgyne avec lui-même, la grosse béatitude charnelle n'est faite pour lui. . . . C'est peut-être cette insatisfaction fondamentale qui l'a poussé vers la magie blanche de l'art. Il reconstruit dans ses sonnets un paradis d'amours fictives où l'esprit parcourt voluptueusement la chair en l'enveloppant d'une sorte de conscience épidermique" (p. 63), the reader senses that this Ronsard of the "magie blanche de l'art" is no longer the catalogue of classical commonplaces which Paul Laumonier examined in his monumental thesis.[4]

We can only regret that Gadoffre, bound by the limits of the series for which he was writing, was not able to develop such ideas. In his bibliography, however, he does give a strong indication of his position by commenting on other studies of Ronsard. He writes of Laumonier's thesis, "Une mine de renseignements, mais sa contribution à l'intelligence de la poésie de Ronsard est faible, le goût et le sens littéraire de l'auteur n'étant pas au niveau de son érudition" (p. 187), and he insists that Chamard's *Histoire de la Pléiade*[5] was "malgré la somme des matériaux apportés, . . . déjà désuète dans sa conception de l'histoire comme dans sa méthode au moment où elle a été publiée" (p. 186).

I would perhaps not be so stringent with my predecessors, for Laumonier's critical edition of Ronsard's complete works and the source material there presented have advanced Ronsard scholarship immeasurably. Gadoffre's definite awareness of the importance of the poet's art above erudition and literary history points, nevertheless, to a new critical approach with which I am very much in sympathy. There is yet much to enjoy in the art of Ronsard's love poetry, however scant and unreliable the man's biography may be, and much to appreciate in the development of that

4. Paul Laumonier, *Ronsard, poète lyrique* (Paris, 1909).
5. Henri Chamard, *Histoire de la Pléiade* (Paris, 1939–40).

art, however extensive Ronsard's borrowings from other poets may be. Consequently, I have devoted my book entirely to an analysis of the art of Ronsard's love poetry and its development.

Because such analysis most often takes the form of *explications de texte*, the book will be useful not only to graduate students but to undergraduates as well. The undergraduate is relieved of the difficulties which arise when a vast background of reading is taken for granted, and both graduate students and undergraduates may find in these explications a new form of criticism to study and explore in the development of their own approach to literature. First and foremost, however, this book is intended for all students of poetry, and I sincerely hope they will experience in reading of Ronsard the same enjoyment and appreciation of his greatness which prompted me to undertake this study.

In quoting from Ronsard's poetry, I have used throughout the original text as published by Paul Laumonier in his edition for the Société des Textes Français Modernes. All spelling, punctuation, and capitalization of Ronsard's text follow this edition. Because of the completeness and competence of two recent bibliographies on the sixteenth century, A. Cioranesco, *Bibliographie de la littérature française du seizième siècle* (Paris, 1959) and Otto Klapp, *Bibliographie der französischen Literaturwissenchaft* (Frankfurt am Main) *1* (1956–58), *2* (1959–60), and *3* (1961–62), a further bibliography here did not seem necessary. All the works on Ronsard used extensively in writing this study appear, moreover, in the chapter notes.

I wish to thank Syracuse University Press for permission to use in Chapter 2 material which had appeared previously as an article in *Symposium*. P. Legrand's translation of Theocritus' "Le Bien-Aimé" is reproduced with the permission of La Société d'Edition "Les Belles Lettres."

To my professors at Yale, and in particular Jean Boorsch, Kenneth Cornell, Henri Peyre, Georges May, and Imbrie Buffum, I owe more than space allows me to relate here; without their guidance and generosity this book could not have been. To the library of the Ecole Normale Supérieure for many bibliographical services rendered, and to Elizabeth Humez and especially Wayland Schmitt for editorial direction, I wish to acknowledge special debts as well. But it is to my fellow Ronsard scholar, Miss Susan Walsh, that I acknowledge my deepest appreciation. Few know as does Miss Walsh the rewards of studying Ronsard or how to inspire others with these rewards.

D. S., Jr.

Kirkland House
Cambridge, Mass.
August 1965

Contents

RONSARD'S SONNET CYCLES

Introduction: Love and a Poet's Evolution

SPEAK of Pierre de Ronsard to any student of literature, and he will quote immediately from "Mignonne, allon voir" and "Quand vous serez bien vieille." He may also have read "Comme on voit sur la branche," but he will be familiar with little else. Anthologies have long persisted in presenting only an Epicurean Ronsard—the lover of beauty and nature, whose poetry ever laments the passing of all that is beautiful and advocates a philosophy of "Gather ye rosebuds while ye may." The selections have become so uniform, indeed, that Marcel Françon, reviewing Gilbert Gadoffre's *Ronsard par lui-même*, remarked: "The poems which Gadoffre quotes, or on which he comments, are seldom those customarily included in anthologies, and it is a welcome surprise to find so many pieces of poetry which now seem to be much more meaningful and beautiful than we were used to considering them to be." [1]

Evidence that Ronsard's work offers more to appreciate than most anthologies suggest does not come from Gadoffre alone. Some years before his book, the studies of Albert-Marie Schmidt and Frances Yates [2] had already brought added dimensions and meaning to Ronsard's hymns, prose works, *Bergeries*, and ballet verse. Since none of these critics took a primary interest in Ronsard's love verse, however, the Epicurean Ronsard of the anthologies has remained a traditional portrait, unchallenged and unex-

1. *Modern Language Quarterly, 24* (June 1963), 220.
2. Albert-Marie Schmidt, *La Poésie scientifique en France au seizième siècle* (Paris, 1938); Frances Yates, *The French Academies of the Sixteenth Century* (London, 1947).

amined. We are still invited to believe that Ronsard composed "Mignonne, allon voir" to win over a reluctant young girl.

Nevertheless, now that certain critics have been willing to search—with success—for new qualities and meanings in Ronsard's poetry, there is every reason not only to include his love poetry within such effort, but also to accord it a most prominent place. Love poetry was the heart of Ronsard's fame during his lifetime; it was to love that he devoted his sonnets, transforming, as a result, a difficult and foreign genre into a vehicle for personal expression and one of the pillars of French poetry. Moreover, since love was the subject he pursued most assiduously through his life, his love poems provide the greatest continuity in a career that spans more than thirty years of constant productivity.

To realize the value of this continuity in appraising Ronsard's development as a love poet, it is not necessary to go beyond the traditional anthology pieces. Even there, despite the air of sacrosanct authority which anthologies have acquired, the attentive reader can find new possibilities for interpretation and analysis to demonstrate how stultifying and misleading the Epicurean image of Ronsard can be. Here is the text of Ronsard's best-known ode, first published in 1553:

> Mignonne, allon voir si la rose
> Qui ce matin avoit declose
> Sa robe de pourpre au soleil,
> A point perdu, cette vesprée,
> Les plis de sa robe pourprée,
> Et son teint au vostre pareil.
> Las, voiés comme en peu d'espace,
> Mignonne, elle a dessus la place
> Las, las, ses beautés laissé cheoir!
> O vraiment maratre Nature,
> Puis qu'une telle fleur ne dure

Que du matin jusques au soir.
Donc, si vous me croiés, mignonne:
Tandis que vôtre âge fleuronne
En sa plus verte nouveauté,
Cueillés, cueillés, vôtre jeunesse
Comme à cette fleur, la viellesse
Fera ternir vôtre beauté.   (5 196–97) [3]

This may be contrasted with his most famous sonnet, from
Sonnets pour Hélène, first published in 1578:

Quand vous serez bien vieille, au soir à la chandelle,
Assise aupres du feu, devidant & filant,
Direz, chantant mes vers, en vous esmerveillant,
Ronsard me celebroit du temps que j'estois belle.
Lors vous n'aurez servante oyant telle nouvelle,
Desja sous le labeur à demy sommeillant,
Qui au bruit de Ronsard ne s'aille resveillant,
Benissant vostre nom de louange immortelle.
Je seray sous la terre, & fantaume sans os
Par les ombres Myrtheux je prendray mon repos.
Vous serez au fouyer une vieille accroupie,
Regrettant mon amour, & vostre fier desdain.
Vives, si m'en croyez, n'attendez à demain:
Cucillez dés aujourdhuy les roses de la vie. (sonnet II/24)

Both poems are exhortations to enjoy life, and in each the
theme arises naturally from a portrait of time's nefarious
effect: the death of a rose, the passing of Hélène's beauty.
There are, of course, certain differences in the elaboration
of the central theme: the ode is concerned with flattering
the young girl, while the sonnet makes ample mention of
the poet, his fate, and his fame. However, it is the word
"cueillez" and its connotations which must predominate in
any exegesis of the two poems.

3. All citations of Ronsard's works are to the *Oeuvres complètes*, ed.
Paul Laumonier (17 vols. Paris, 1919–60). Each quotation will be identified either by the number given to the particular sonnet in the Lau-

A compliment and an invitation, the ode has long been presented as the Renaissance prototype of one of the most enduring themes of love poetry: the comparison of the woman's beauty to that of a flower. And this interpretation is not without its justification. The poet, while he recounts the rose's story, never ceases to compare the flower and his companion. The rose possesses, he tells her, a "teint au vostre pareil." After a glance at the dead blossom, he returns to both the girl and the loveliness of the flower by remarking that she, too, is at the moment of full bloom: "Tandis que vôtre âge fleuronne/ En sa plus verte nouveauté." And, finally, in the last breath of exhortation, he closes his work by reminding her: "Comme à cette fleur, la vieillesse/ Fera ternir vôtre beauté." The invitation "Cueillés, cueillés," is present in the poem, but viewed as a whole, the ode is presented as a didactic lesson rather than a compliment or an invitation.

Its initial emotion—"allon voir"—is one of enthusiasm, but the imperative is in no way qualified by words that might suggest a love situation. The enthusiasm is, rather, a simple note of happiness: the poet, alone with his beautiful beloved, is excited at the prospect of enjoying a scene of beauty enhanced by her presence. By the first "Las," the mood of excitement has disappeared in the face of destruction. The expectation dies as the poet is filled with exasperation. The flower's beauty has not even been permitted to last beyond its birth.

From this bitter observation, Ronsard passes to what traditional criticism has defined as a *carpe diem* ending. But this interpretation of Ronsard's concluding verse is predicated on the view that a priori Ronsard's accent is on love. It is perhaps only natural to infer that the narrator, pronouncing his imperative to a girl whom he addresses by the

monier edition or, in the case of unnumbered poems, by the volume and page number where it appears.

affectionate "mignonne," had ulterior motives, but the poem itself spends no time expanding such thoughts. It does not contain the word "love," and the enunciation of its ideas is terse and implacable. While it is admittedly a poem of compliment, in terms of the strictest adherence to the text, it is a poem not of love but of philosophy, the final point of which can best be defined by the rational notation "Q.E.D."

Despite the complimentary material surrounding the lady and the rose, the movement of the poet's thought is amazingly linear. It never deviates from the central theme, and the transition from awareness of the meaning of the rose's withering to a formulation of the poet's reaction is significantly effected by the word "donc"—"therefore"— which transforms the walk and the sight of a wilted rose into an experiment's "if" or "given": "If we go looking for the rose, alas, we find . . . Therefore. . . ." The rigidity of composition—"allon . . . Las! . . . Donc"— creates a solemn air that dilutes any lyric abandon latent in the comparison of the two beauties. By making his compliment through a series of similes, Ronsard adroitly avoids any clash between compliment and narrative development.

Furthermore, the shift from first to second person in the poem's imperatives accentuates Ronsard's serious didactic purpose. If the poem begins with the narrator and the lady together, the moment of discovery breaks the intimacy, and the narrator now points out to the lady the results of his experiment. He has become her teacher, and in the final stage of instruction, beginning with "Donc," he imposes this new relationship, insisting on his superiority by the addition of "Si vous me croiés" ("If you accept my observations, then the obvious conclusions are the following:"). And, of course, the didactic attitude continues through the final imperative, again the second person, "Cueillés." The experiment having been performed, the observations hav-

ing been made and the results recorded, the poet-philoso-
pher rests his pen.

A superficial glance at the sonnet "Quand vous serez
bien vieille" might suggest a similar development in
thought. The opposition between the youth of the woman
and the image of her lonely and aged self regretting the
joys lost through "fier desdain" corresponds to the beauty
of the rose and its rapid death, and again Ronsard is
prompted to suggest a philosophy of "Cueillez, cueillez."
Yet the implications in the final line of the sonnet are not at
all equivalent in meaning to the imperative of the ode,
where the separation between the speaker and "mignonne"
gradually takes place as it becomes clear that the poet
knows in advance the outcome of their walk and has
arranged the stroll in order to advise his companion. This
development gives the ode's philosophy a universal application, to the speaker as well as to the woman, but in the
Hélène sonnet no such community of interests is created,
for the narrator attempts to isolate himself from the
woman. The image of the first tercet is explicit in itself, almost cruel in its self-complacency, as it opposes the aged
Hélène, still suffering the travails of this life, to the poet
who is at rest, free from his earthly ties and body. He has
advice to offer, and if she adheres to his philosophy, she
may be able to change her future regrets into happy
memories; but Ronsard is clearly just as interested in
presenting an image of his immortality to coexist with
Hélène's unhappy end. With or without Hélène's love,
Ronsard will be famous. At her pronouncement, "Ronsard
me celebroit du temps que j'estois belle," the servant will
react "au bruit de Ronsard." It is through Ronsard that
Hélène's name will continue to be sung.

The freshness of the verse in "Mignonne, allon voir,"
where the poet was, after all, pitting his talent against a

theme already almost exhausted by antiquity, and the vividness of Hélène's portrait in the candlelight and dimness of advancing age are qualities that have for generations assured the fame of Ronsard. If the literary value of these texts has never been seriously doubted, it is nonetheless significant, however, that they may be appreciated even more fully when the valuable lessons and information they provide about Ronsard are recognized. Even from my brief remarks, it should be evident that a definite distinction can be made between Ronsard the lover and Ronsard the poet. To call either the ode or the sonnet simply a "love poem" reduces the work to dimensions incommensurate with its content. The observation that "Mignonne" possesses a beauty like that of the rose and that her loveliness is also subject to death at the hands of "maratre Nature" is central to the structure of the poem but only indirectly related to the interpretation of the poem as love verse. Ronsard is making a philosophical statement, and that it should have relevance within what can be inferred of the relationship between the narrator and the woman may attest to the poem's richness but does not follow from any element in it. Similarly, the very syntax of "Quand vous serez bien vieille," which forces Hélène and the reader to follow through the taunting comparison ("When *you* are old . . . *I'll* take my rest."), most effectively dispels any effort to romanticize the sonnet.

In the French Renaissance, as throughout French literature, love is above all a theme, a tradition, and bound as such to further themes and traditions. Ronsard undoubtedly may have fallen in love during his lifetime, but these poems witness that he rarely if ever chose to write of love without the awareness that he was writing poetry. Despite all the tales that have been told to explain the *Amours*, the texts demonstrate that Ronsard is more than a frivolous courtier, a *bon vivant*, or a preromantic lover of nature.

Like the narrator of "Mignonne, allon voir," he is a serious craftsman of words, forms, and ideas.

Furthermore, the differences between these poems, written approximately at the chronological poles of Ronsard's career, offer a precise touchstone for the development of this craftsman. The philosophical change evidenced by the way in which "Quand vous serez bien vieille" reworks a familiar theme in order to express quite a different thought indicates that Ronsard has moved far away from the world of "Mignonne, allon voir" and the feeling of insecurity before the forces of nature toward an assurance of immortality which separates him from the woman. At the same time, since such a statement about his assurance of a "repos" in Elysium is inseparable from a sense of security about his own poetry, the evidence of a literary development from doubt to assurance cannot be ignored.

In a very important way, Ronsard himself was the first to underline the existence of an evolution in his poetry when, aware that his ideas had changed, he repeatedly rearranged the contents of his sonnet cycles and produced over the years a stunning quantity of variants for the poems. A famous sonnet to Pontus de Tyard contrasts the style of the first cycle of the *Amours* with that of the *Continuation,* and Ronsard's constantly shifting interests in literary taste and trends and the many women he sang provide clear evidence that his was a talent in perpetual development. Each aspect of his life and work—the variants, the succession of mistresses, the recourse to classical writers and contemporaries as models—has provided critics with a useful, if not entirely satisfactory, measure of the poet's development.

Because the variants seem to represent in essence Ronsard's reworking of his own earlier material, for example, it is not surprising that in recent years critics have debated such questions as: Did Ronsard's style really evolve? Did he improve the early poems by changing them in successive years? Did the changes represent true aesthetic advancement? [4] Henri Weber's article on Ronsard's changes in the *Amours* of 1552 demonstrates the complexity of these issues and has the distinct merit of stating at the outset, in very succinct terms, the basic (although perhaps misunderstood) problems involved in the conflicting pronouncements concerning Ronsard's style: "Le débat peut-il se résumer dans l'opposition d'un goût classique, qui met en avant l'élégance, l'harmonie, la logique et l'équilibre des images, à un goût baroque, qui exalte à la fois le désordre lyrique, la véhémence, le pittoresque et la surprise?" [5] In his very phraseology, Weber suggests that he is not a partisan of this opposition, but other critics have not hesitated to declare their preference for either the early verse with its baroque disorder or the late poetry of *Sonnets pour Hélène*, classic in its elegance, harmony, and equilibrium.

The two poems just examined represent these two distinct periods in Ronsard's career and point up the critical impasse which the single criterion of style can produce in an attempt to understand Ronsard's evolution. [6] Though they do reflect different attitudes toward a familiar theme, it does not seem completely fair or true to see in one of them a more developed sense of "élégance," for example, than in the other. The poems vary because their themes differ, and Ronsard has adapted his style to conform to the particular nature and development of each theme. Because "Mignonne, allon voir" is impersonal and philosophical, the

4. See, for example, F. Desonay, "Ronsard autocorrecteur," in *Ronsard, poète de l'amour*, 2 (Brussels, 1954), Ch. 5.

5. Henri Weber, "Les Corrections de Ronsard dans les *Amours* de 1552," *Studi in onore di Vittorio Lugli e Diego Valeri*, 2 (Venice, 1961), 989.

6. Even in regard to a comparison of sonnets I would have reservations about the application of style alone as a criterion; see p. 202.

comparison between the beauty of the lady and that of the rose always remains on the second plane, so to speak, while the narrator's experiment, through which Ronsard makes his statement, dominates the poem's development and style. The Hélène poem is far more sinuous because, by permitting the double theme of the woman's fate and his fate to intermingle throughout, the poet succeeds all the more forcefully in emphasizing his own destiny. The brusque opening of the ode places the reader immediately within the context of the experiment, while the use of a subordinate clause to begin the sonnet furnishes an intricate comparison without excluding the possibility of an elaboration of the woman's portrait and the role of the servant: that is, without reducing the poem to the terse development of the ode. It is no exaggeration, then, to say that the basic differences between these poems is not stylistic.

"Véhémence," "harmonie," "baroque," and "classique" are all terms which in the last analysis are difficult to use in discussing the evolution of a poet who lived in the sixteenth century. Before Boileau and Romanticism, style was less a question of school than of author: one wrote like Petrarch, like Vergil, like Pindar or Marot. After author came technique. The Pléiade liked to emphasize the concept of inspiration as a veritable demonic "fureur" which possessed them at the moment of creation. Yet even a casual glance at any preface or *art poétique* they wrote reveals that when "talking shop," these poets inevitably stressed not divine inspiration but models and technique, spelling, prosody, and vocabulary. On the other hand, the self-portrait of "Quand vous serez bien vieille" suggests that by the end of his life Ronsard had acquired such insights into the transcription of the poetic élan that he felt his place in Elysium was assured. But, by definition, such insights must embrace the choice and interpretation of themes; they cannot depend on variations in style alone, nor on events in the poet's life, nor on what he culls by imitating others. Ronsard's relation to earlier and contemporary literature, the facts of his life, and the history of the times, all may have played roles in the changing character of his work, and they must of course be considered when they are directly pertinent, but the essence of his evolution as a craftsman of poetry must be sought in the themes and attitudes of his texts conceived as poetic artifacts.

This is, I realize, a slightly unorthodox position, for the general emphasis in Ronsard studies has long been upon questions of biographical import and literary history. But there is no attempt here to denigrate what has already been accomplished by earlier investigators; rather, this study continues their work and draws its inspiration, in part at least, from their own discoveries, from that renewed importance they themselves have given to the text.

Now that we have become increasingly aware of the vast extent of Ronsard's borrowings,[7] we are more than ever challenged to confirm or reject Ronsard's reputation as a poetic genius, and critical confrontation rather than identification of source and text will prove sufficient to that task. In addition the repeated discovery of Ronsard's insincerity and infidelity to the supposed mistresses, as evidenced by the arrangement and rearrangement of his love poems, forces us to probe beneath the old discussions concerning a concordance between the titles of certain cycles and the mistresses Ronsard appeared to be addressing, in order to deal with the works as poetic artifacts rather than biography, for if we may judge by his own treatment of the texts, Ronsard himself evidently conceived of them in this way. Finally the facts of a poet's life, even when they are irrefutable evidence, form only a point of departure for an analysis of his art. If critics offer little speculation about the

7. See, for example, Isidore Silver, *Ronsard and the Hellenic Renaissance in France* (St. Louis, 1961).

genesis of the cycles written between 1556–60 because Marie and Sinope remain unknown, the identification of Hélène de Surgères has by no means brought to an end all study of the composition of the last cycles. On the contrary, the problem of creation can be more immediately discerned in *Sonnets pour Hélène* because the historical point of departure and its poetic transformation can be more fully analyzed than in the case of poems addressed to unknown women.

Though few of Ronsard's contemporaries acknowledged that Cassandre was the woman Ronsard described or that the affair was one of the heart,[8] his friends nevertheless were one in acclaiming him the greatest poet of his time.[9] Such men, many of them poets themselves, were not interested in historical references and probably had little awareness of the stylistic trends we today term neoclassical, mannerist, or baroque, but they did know how to judge a Renaissance love sonnet. Concerned with the sheer craft of poetry, they could easily recognize a Petrarchistic conceit and could judge whether it had or had not been skillfully adapted.[10] In brief, they were able to laud Ronsard not as a

8. See André Berry, *Ronsard* (Paris, 1961), pp. 72–73, for a summary of contemporary views on Cassandre. Brantôme was sure the name was a fiction; others, that she was of humble origin. Claude Binet, in his *Vie de Ronsard*, ed. Paul Laumonier (Paris, 1909), p. 15, states that Ronsard was "amoureux seulement de ce beau nom, comme luy-mesmes m'a dit maintesfois."

9. "Qui est-ce qui me convertira tout en voix et en langues . . . pour aller announcer que le grand Pan est mort." Du Perron, "Oraison Funèbre," in Ronsard, *Oeuvres complètes*, ed. Vaganay (7 vols. Paris, 1924), 7, 55.

10. Modern usage of the adjectives "Petrarchan" and "Petrarchistic" varies greatly both in critical writing and in dictionaries which still seek to define the terms. To avoid confusion about my use of these adjectives, let me distinguish immediately between "Petrarchan," which is used to refer to the poetry of Petrarch, and "Petrarchistic," which refers, in its largest sense, to any imitation of Petrarch's poetry but, most precisely, to lyric poetry of the fifteenth and sixteenth century directly or indirectly inspired by Petrarchan love verse.

historical figure but as a poet, and, above all, as a poet of love.

Because so much of Ronsard's poetry is dedicated to the theme of love, it was necessary, in order to provide a focus here, to restrict analysis essentially to those sonnet cycles presented by the poet as the story of his own adventures in love. It would be difficult to find a more striking continuity of effort throughout Ronsard's long career, since the period from 1552 (the first book of the *Amours*) to 1578 (*Sonnets pour Hélène*) embraces the years of Ronsard's most significant production in general as well as the disappointments, experiments, and literary vicissitudes that accompanied the advances of his talent within a specific genre. Moreover, possibly because these poems of love were presented as personal stories, the poet's effort toward perfection is especially concentrated in the sonnet cycles. Here Ronsard shows most conspicuously how the elements of imitation, philosophy, and the dictates of his own talent had to be molded together if he was to achieve the originality of which he boasted—and which was to insure his immortality.

Of the two elements that reveal most pointedly the essence of Ronsard's artistic development—tone and vision —the former is perhaps the more central and more important consideration. Whatever the tone may be—rapture, bantering, bitterness, sensuality, or a combination of some of these—it is truly the most precise means of establishing the poet's intent, and it is then but a short step to an examination of his success or failure in carrying out that intent. I am using the word "tone" here, and throughout this study, to mean the poet's attitude toward his subject. The term seems preferable to "style" because its connotation of mood and temper permits clear differentiation between the poet's choice and arrangement of words and the more general interplay of style and intent. As we have already seen, the full message of "Mignonne, allon voir" combines compliment and admonition as Ronsard simultaneously offers an appreciation of the lady's beauty and a general remark about the precarious state of beauty in the world and man's reaction to this work of fate. Yet the intimations of a love element in the word "mignonne" and the similes which link lady and rose have long dominated analysis, although they are ultimately very difficult to reconcile with the "givens" of the poem's structure. Such stylistic evidences are misleading and confusing here unless recognized eventually as subservient elements in a structure whose intent can be found only in such pivotal words as "allon" and "Las!" and in the weight which the poem's development gives to these words. An attempt to appreciate the poem in terms of the interaction of style and mood reveals much more clearly the exceptional quality of Ronsard's most famous ode than would any analysis in terms of style alone.

The word "tone" also seems most appropriate because, as we shall see in examining Ronsard's cycles between 1555 and 1560, critics have often unnecessarily falsified the character of the poetry and its development by attaching importance only to stylistic innovations when, in fact, the poet's tone is basically unchanged. In the domain of sixteenth-century love poetry, after all, the poet had little choice between the Petrarchistic world of adoration and lament and the patently sensual bantering of the *esprit gaulois* tradition. His task was further complicated by a marked tendency to fuse the concepts of tone and style, given the prevailing notions that only through Petrarchistic verse could the poet effectively convey his adoration of the woman and an appreciation of her beauty and that a more physical reaction to love must be communicated through the optic of a misogynous, licentious poetry. The shifting character of Ronsard's love cycles does, in fact, reveal that for many years the poet made a noticeable attempt to seek in the love poetry of others, and especially in their style, a means to vary such "given" tones and to obtain more satisfactory or more personal expression. Later, however, Ronsard passed beyond this stage of experimentation and engaged in a searching contemplation of what I term his vision of the love experience. By "vision" I understand essentially the value and significance the poet attaches to his subject: the more general, yet personal, implications behind his words. Every Petrarchistic sonnet cycle is essentially a narrative of which the individual sonnet relates an isolated event or attitude. In the sixteenth century, adopting either a Petrarchistic style or the tone of the *esprit gaulois* meant also commitment to a particular narrative and vision of the love story. Naturally, as long as a poet was willing to offer these external portraits as the true facts of his personal life, no problem existed. But what was he to do if his private feelings did not coincide with either of these traditions? Just as a close examination of the texts in terms of tone can reveal the significant shifts in technique and thought regarding individual episodes in the love story, so a consideration of the total narrative—the vision of the cycle—exposes the movement and evolution of the poet's personal philosophy of love. The reader must not be surprised to find among the many analyses of poems in this study a continuous attempt to define Ronsard's *état d'esprit* at each important turning in his career. Through tone the critic reaches the craftsman of words; through vision, he finds the craftsman of ideas.

Since Ronsard eventually formulated outside the sonnet his thoughts on love, poetry, and existence, we shall have to move occasionally beyond the sonnet cycles to develop a total picture of Ronsard's evolution. Only after the growing complexity and personal nature of the poet's vision of love have been seen, can the way in which his tone and style have matured be appreciated. There can be no doubt that the creator of *Sonnets pour Hélène* is a consummate artist, but the attainment of this artistry required a new appreciation of the meaning of love as well as changes in tone and style.

This general evolution in the vision and tone of Ronsard's love cycles developed slowly after 1552, passing through various styles and drawing on and discarding many sources. Gradually the personal vision of *Sonnets pour Hélène* was developed, and the poet was able to demonstrate a mastery of his material, a forceful style that communicates his feelings, and a technique in manipulating his sources that does not belittle his own inventiveness but attests rather to that sense of the demands of poetry which assures his position among France's greatest poets.

1. The Traditional Love Worlds

PETRARCH

WHEN Ronsard turned to the example of Petrarch to compose *Les Amours de P. de Ronsard*,[1] the Italian poet had already been adapted to French in Du Bellay's *L'Olive*. Attached to the *Deffense et Illustration de la Langue Françoyse* (1549), the cycle by Du Bellay was originally a meager 50 sonnets; the following year, after attacks by Sibilet and others, it was augmented to a total of 115. Du Bellay had opened the door to criticism of his lack of invention by admitting in 1549: "Vrayment je confesse avoir imité Petrarque, & non luy seulement, mais aussi l'Arioste & d'autres modernes Italiens: pource qu'en l'argument que je traicte, je n'en ay point trouvé de meilleurs."[2] In his enlarged, highly polemical preface to the 1550 edition he attempted to counter his critics by stressing that even translation demands a heavy dosage of art: "Et puis je me vante d'avoir inventé ce que j'ay mot à mot traduit des aultres."[3] Research by Chamard and Vianey has

---

1. The initial sonnet cycles pose a problem of titles. Ronsard called the sonnets of 1552–53 simply *Les Amours de P. de Ronsard;* the sonnets and other poems of 1555–56 he entitled *La Continuation* and *La Nouvelle Continuation des Amours*, and only in 1560 did Ronsard refer to *Les Amours* of 1552–53 as *Le Premier Livre des Amours*, as he had retitled the works of 1555–56 *Le Second Livre des Amours*. For the sake of clarity, the edition of 1552–53 is called here *Amours I*. The edition of 1560 is called *Amours II*, and the works of 1555–56 retain their original titles.

2. Du Bellay, *Oeuvres poétiques*, ed. Henri Chamard (6 vols. Paris, 1908), *1*, 8.

3. Ibid., p. 19.

demonstrated, however, that the role of imitation, even to the extent of skillful translation, is immense in *L'Olive*,[4] and the evidence of the text shows Du Bellay's confession, not his polemic, to be closer to the truth.

More important for the study of Ronsard than the admission of borrowing, however, is Du Bellay's remark that Petrarch and the Italians had no peer. Like Horace or Pindar and the other models of the *Deffense*, Petrarch was chosen for his mastery of a particular form. The commitment to Petrarch and the Petrarchistic tradition influenced the love poetry of all the Pléiade.

After *L'Olive*, however, Du Bellay himself strayed far from the Petrarchistic form of love verse. Though his poems of praise to Ronsard might seem to indicate that he quietly abandoned the love sonnet before the superior genius of Ronsard, his subsequent career demonstrates that he had little intention of abandoning the love theme, and in later life he published a great quantity of love poetry in Latin, the *Poemata*. In this evolution there is a noteworthy commentary on Ronsard's own development, for the chief of the Pléiade was also tempted by the Graeco-Latin tradition (and in particular by the non-sonnet forms of Marullus and Theocritus). But Ronsard ultimately returned to the sonnet and Petrarch, where he accomplished what Du Bellay failed to produce, a personal sonnet cycle of love in the Petrarchistic manner.

Ronsard's triumph touches upon a basic question that must be borne in mind throughout an examination of Ronsard's career—the impetus behind his borrowings. Morris Bishop once voiced a judgment that is both true and false: "[Ronsard] had no scruples on the score of originality. According to his doctrine, to recast in French the thought of the godlike Greeks was the poet's noblest task. Originality is a vain purpose. If a thought has never been thought

4. See Henri Chamard's notes to Du Bellay, *1*.

or uttered, it is not worth uttering now. . . . The poet's labor should be put on form not substance, for the poetic substance must be forever the same." [5] Though, in the domain of his love verse, Ronsard did imitate many authors all his life "without shame," there are clear waves of imitation—Petrarch for *Amours I*, Marullus for the *Nouvelle Continuation*, Theocritus for *Amours II*,—which correspond to changes in attitude and experimentation in style resulting from a noticeable desire to increase control of his material. Such straining to master form and content is hardly in keeping with a view of originality as "a vain purpose." Ronsard was in fact a weak innovator, and it is true that the term "originality" had a very different connotation in the sixteenth century, when everyone felt free to copy the same works and one another, but the express meaning of Du Bellay's "je n'en ai point trouvé de meilleurs" cannot be ignored. The sixteenth century's attitudes toward imitation did not exclude an appreciation of the art of the model, nor of the difficulty in reproducing this art, and it is extremely unfair to interpret Ronsard's recourse to Marullus and Theocritus as a frivolous search for new ideas or to call originality a senseless pursuit when, judging by the *Deffense*, such imitation may well be an indication of how much Ronsard, like Du Bellay, "had found none better." Moreover, the sixteenth-century conception of originality was not without its complexities and difficulties. In skillfully reusing recognizable forms and conceits, the poet knew instantly with whom he would be compared; to vaunt his talent he had to repeat yet change, copy yet animate—a far more difficult task than that of the poet who bases his fame on being different. Finally, as we have seen in "Quand vous serez bien vielle," Ronsard's texts themselves indicate a distinct goal beyond the skillful manipula-

5. Morris Bishop, *Ronsard, Prince of Poets* (New York, 1940), p. 80.

tion of models: immortality. The victory he claimed in this
late work, calmly and without the brash overtones of
earlier poems, must stand as proof of his prolonged effort
to develop a true and lasting originality.

Ronsard showed immediately in *Amours I* the quality
of "judgment" with which Du Bellay credited him in the
preface of 1550: "Je n'osay bien avanturer de mettre en
lumiere mes petites poësies: apres toutesfois les avoir
communiquées à ceux que je pensoy' bien estre clervoyans
en telles choses, singulierement à Pierre de Ronsard, qui
m'y donna plus grande hardiesse que tous les autres, pour la
bonne opinion que j'ay tousjours eue de son vif esprit, ex-
acte sçavoir & solide jugement en nostre poësie françoise." [6]
Such judgment is especially apparent if one compares Ronsard's work with *L'Olive*. If many of his poems contain
numerous Petrarchistic conceits, few, if any, of his sonnets
attain the word-for-word translation that Du Bellay did
not hesitate to employ so liberally. Ronsard had no confession to make, and his poetry, not a preface, answered his
critics.

Nevertheless, Ronsard did not emerge from his first
sonnet cycle as a great love poet. If he had, he might never
have been attracted to other traditions. But the Petrarchistic tradition, to which *L'Olive* and the first cycle of the
Amours belong, was the product of a long evolution
beginning with Petrarch's *Rime*, and contained certain pit-
falls which Ronsard and Du Bellay could not anticipate, or
perhaps understand. By the sixteenth century few Petrarchistic poets imitated Petrarch faithfully or exclusively,[7] and
most, including Ronsard, found inspiration as often in the
minor epigones of Petrarch's poetry as in the *Rime*. They

6. Du Bellay, *1*, 13.
7. Cf. Ernest Hatch Wilkins, *Studies in the Life and Works of
Petrarch* (Cambridge, Mass., 1955), p. 280.

certainly knew Petrarch, however, and the fact that they did not distinguish sharply between direct recourse to his works and imitation of imitators provides an important insight into the psychology of their approach. Despite his evident desire to be compared with Petrarch, the writer of Petrarchistic verse did not seek out the intrinsic value of the earlier poet's expression or experience in love and the relationship between the two. He looked instead for conceits, situations, antitheses, and a recognized vocabulary, the skillful use of which could suffice to reveal his own talent. In judging the success or failure of such a technique in Ronsard's case, we might first look at two of Petrarch's poems and observe the master's craft.

In "Chiare, fresche e dolci acque," for example, the opening apostrophes to nature provide a typical description of Petrarch's Laura:

> Chiare, fresche e dolci acque,
> Ove le belle membra
> Pose colei che sola a me par donna;
> Gentil ramo, ove piacque
> (Con sospir mi rimembra)
> A lei di fare al bel fianco colonna;
> Erba e fior che la gonna
> Leggiadra ricoverse
> Co l'angelico seno;
> A'er sacro sereno,
> Ove Amor co' begli occhi il cor m'aperse;
> Date udïenza insieme
> A le dolenti mie parole estreme.[8]

The description is characteristic primarily because of its brevity and its choice of features for description ("belle membra," "fianco," "seno," "occhi"). Not only is Laura seen very little in the *Rime*, she is repeatedly seen in the

8. Petrarch, *Rime*, ed. G. Carducci (Florence, 1899), pp. 183–84.

same way; only the blond tresses are necessary here to make the usual portrait complete. It is essential to realize, however, that Petrarch specifically indicates that he is working within the realm of memory ("Con sospir mi rimembra"), and he refers only to Laura's most distinctive aspects, those which have survived in time. Memory may also account for the lack of variety in the adjectives used to describe Laura ("belle," "bel," "angelico," "begli"). The description is not intended as a *tour de force* but as an example of the poet's effort to capture the intensity of Laura's beauty—that single fact he remembers most vividly and renders so faithfully with the repetition of the adjective "bel." Such beauty marks him both in itself and in its effect on whatever it reaches. "Colei che sola a me par donna," he calls her, showing how much she has transformed his judgment of other women. At the same time, since she has enriched all of nature that has known her presence, every natural object addressed is linked to Laura in the poet's memory and springs to mind as he reconstructs a scene of beauty. The description of the woman seems thin only when the reader looks for the physical presence of a woman in a poem that expresses the sheer force of her beauty and although the apostrophes may encourage the reader to concentrate on the natural objects, none of them is invoked without an immediate reference to Laura. In a later passage in the poem,

> Da' be' rami scendea,
> (Dolce ne la memoria)
> Una pioggia di fior sovra 'l suo grembo;
> Et ella si sedea
> Umile in tanta gloria,
> Coverta già de l'amoroso nembo.
> Qual fior cadea su 'l lembo,
> Qual su le treccie bionde,

Ch'oro forbito e perle
Eran quel dí a vederle;
Qual si posava in terra, e qual su l'onde;
Qual con un vago errore
Girando parea dir—Qui regna Amore—.[9]

the sense of this force, "tanta gloria," is rendered explicit
—at just the moment, one might add, when the fusion of
nature and Laura, who is now covered with flowers, also
reaches a climax. It should be no surprise that it is here that
the poet chooses to summarize the essence of his memory
by using the word "Love" ("Qui regna Amore").
Petrarch has woven memory, Love, nature, beauty, and
Laura together in a pattern of true poetic richness. Taken
alone, each element is deceptively poor in value, for the
poem is more than the sum of its parts; it is the sum of their
interrelationships, of all these elements seen in depth and
transformed by the ideas with which each is associated, by
the "gloria" of Laura.

The following sonnet is a characteristic description, not
of Laura, but of the poet:

Pien di quella ineffabile dolcezza
Che del bel viso trassen gli occhi miei
Nel dí che volentier chiusi gli avrei
Per non mirar già mai minor bellezza,
Lassai quel ch'i' più bramo; et ho sí avezza
La mente a contemplar sola costei,
Ch'altro non vede, e ciò che non è lei
Già per antica usanza odia e disprezza.
In una valle chiusa d'ogni 'ntorno,
Ch'è refrigerio de' sospir miei lassi,
Giunsi sol con Amor, pensoso e tardo.
Ivi non donne, ma fontane e sassi,

9. Ibid., pp. 185–86.

E l'imagine trovo di quel giorno
Che 'l pensier mio figura ovunqu'io sguardo.[10]

The poet is alone in the solitude of the Vaucluse. (Note the
pun in verse 9, "valle chiusa.") Separated from his Laura,
he is sad ("sospir miei lassi"); still the valley is his comfort,
for as has been true from the moment of the *innamoramento*,[11] his inward eye transforms the outer world into
images of Laura, who alone is the object of his emotions
("Quel ch'i' più bramo"). In its simplest terms, the poem is
a faithful rendering of the bittersweet quality of Petrarch's
love experience. Solitude is regret; yet, through memory,
it is no less a communication with Laura's "ineffabile
dolcezza." Even before his departure, this sweetness had
captured and filled him. But it filled him with desire, and
from other poems we know that this desire no less than the
solitude produced deep sighs, for Laura was cruel. And his
love remained unrequited. Presence, absence, love, regret
—all the basic Petrarchan antitheses are here, but not
necessarily as they will appear in the Petrarchistic tradition.
I quote this poem in particular among Petrarch's love
sonnets because, in addition to containing all the representative emotions of the poet, the sonnet reveals his ability to
develop antitheses in such a way that the poem reproduces
a fullness of emotion rather than a simple juxtaposition of
contrary reactions. The quatrains, for example, retell the
innamoramento ("Nel dí che . . .") and announce the
separation ("Lassai . . ."). But the events are less important than their psychological effect, which forms the true

10. Ibid., pp. 166–67.
11. The Italian word *innamoramento* means literally "the falling in
love." In the Petrarchistic tradition, the *innamoramento* is a central
moment which includes the attack by the woman's eyes, their wound-
ing of the poet and his immediate pain. When the word *innamoramento*
appears in the text, it is used to include this network of events and
emotion which no one English word could render.

content of the poem. When Petrarch left, he was "Pien di quella ineffabile dolcezza." As with the comparison between Hélène and the poet in "Quand vous serez bien vieille," where Ronsard uses the syntax of the quatrains to heighten the contrast in their destinies, the opening lines of this Petrarchan sonnet place the interior, sustaining, and un-dying portrait of the woman before the past experience of meeting, when desire began and would have closed the poet's mind to all but Laura. If in the tercets Petrarch is alone and sighing, he is yet alone with her image in that same attitude of exclusive concentration produced by the initial meeting upon his mind.[12] Through present and past the focus on Laura remains firm. The near-closed eyes and the closed valley, with this image of Laura forever in the center, afford a parallel in structure and a continuity of thought that effectively counterbalance the antitheses. As in "Chiare, fresche e dolci acque," the poem grows out of the exploitation of its parts. The poem is neither of sighs nor burning nor "dolcezza." It is of them all and repro-duces their relationship as it exists within the poet's mind. Because Petrarch understands within himself the interplay of regret and desire, loneliness, and contemplation of Laura, he produces a work of fluid interaction among these basic lyric sentiments, and on reading this account of shift-ing emotions, we are tempted to say of him, using his own words, "Qui regna Amore."

Here, now, is the way in which Ronsard presents the cause of his happiness and his torment in *Amours I:*

> Quand au premier la Dame que j'adore
> Vint embellir le sejour de noz cieulx,
> Le fils de Rhée appella tous les Dieux,

12. My analysis and interpretation of this poem owes a great debt to David Kalstone's remarks on Petrarch in his article, "The Trans-formation of Arcadia: Sannazaro and Sir Philip Sidney," *Comparative Literature*, 15 (Summer 1963), 234–49.

Pour faire encor d'elle une aultre Pandore.
Lors Apollin richement la decore,
Or, de ses raiz luy façonnant les yeulx,
Or, luy donnant son chant melodieux,
Or, son oracle & ses beaulx vers encore.
Mars luy donna sa fiere cruaulté,
Venus son ris, Dione sa beaulté,
Peithon sa voix, Ceres son abondance.
L'Aube ses doigtz & ses crins deliez,
Amour son arc, Thetis donna ses piedz,
Cleion sa gloyre, & Pallas sa prudence.   (sonnet 32)

The sonnet is especially interesting because it does not choose to develop the antithesis of happiness and torment (though Mars' gift was "fiere cruaulté"). The poet devotes the entire sonnet to a description of the woman. The word "description" cannot be taken too literally, however, since the woman is neither named nor seen except as a composite of gifts, indiscriminately abstract ("beaulté") and concrete ("piedz"). The same phenomenon occurs repeatedly throughout the sonnets of 1552, where the marble thighs, the golden hair, the ivory breasts form an equally composite picture of the poet's lady.

One of the Petrarch poems just analyzed, "Chiare, fresche e dolci acque," is also a description of the lady, and its opening lines proceed by an enumeration of traits, much like the list of gifts here. The choice of physical features—"membra," "seno," "fianco"—while not found in this particular sonnet, is equally preponderant in Ronsard's portrait of his love. Yet, despite so many parallels between these poems, how different they are! The meaning of Petrarch's apostrophes, their relation to Laura, and a sense of the total mnemonic experience emerge only slowly as Petrarch invites the reader to commune with a selected nature and a most angelic woman until Laura's "gloria" is fully rendered. For Ronsard's poem, no such effort is needed to recognize his central interest. He wants to describe the lady's qualities, and his enumerations *are* his description. There is no further level of discovery or complexity to the poem. It is no accident, moreover, that the numerous apostrophes at the beginning of Petrarch's poem are the least significant aspect of his intention. They are not the woman; they serve merely to usher the reader into the presence of the woman and the atmosphere she creates. The degree to which Ronsard's poem of description simplifies Petrarch's procedure can be seized immediately through the poets' respective use of a word that appears in both poems: "glory" ("gloria" and "gloire"). In "Quand au premier. . ." "gloire" presents just one more attribute, like "beauté" or "piedz." There is no progression or intensification leading to this word. Each quality receives the same emphasis as the others. The Petrarchistic poet has severed the lyric ties between the Petrarchan conceit and the Petrarchan vision. While supposedly omnipresent in the cycle, Ronsard's lady remains strangely absent, just as she is really absent from "Quand au premier. . . ." She is an abstraction, veiled in symbol or allegory. She is reflected in nature's every object; but Ronsard lists only the reflection, not the reality:

> Je ne voy pré, fleur, antre, ny rivage,
> Champ, roc, ny boys, ny flotz dedans le Loyr
> Que peinte en eulx, il ne me semble voyr
> Ceste beauté qui me tient en servage.
>   (sonnet 28, vv. 5–8)

And the same poem continues by evoking her presence in his dreams, but only through the symbolic form she takes:

> Ores en forme, ou d'un foudre enflammé,
> Ou d'une nef, ou d'un Tigre affamé,
>   Amour la nuict devant mes yeulx la guide.
>   (vv. 9–11)

When "Quand au premier . . ." furnishes a "description"
that conveys a sense of beauty, virtue, and perfection exclusively, when even the lady's physical traits are absorbed
by these abstractions in becoming gifts of the gods, Ronsard makes very evident that he does not see the "dame" as
anything but that amalgam of perfect features which
accounts as well for the marble, the ivory, the golden
tresses. There is no interplay between reality and abstraction, between the exposition of her presence and the
development of this fact through both the physical reality
of the woman and the psychology of the narrator. The
reproduction of the individual elements of the Petrarchan
description, whether physical or moral, alone and detached
from the other considerations of memory, nature, and
"gloria," does not succeed in creating poems in the manner
of Petrarch. But this is not all to be learned from "Quand
au premier. . . ."

At the moment of the lady's birth the gods assembled to
fete her, Ronsard writes, and the reader is made to note
with the gifts the impressive list of gods and goddesses
present at the gathering. By insisting as much upon the
dazzling array of deities as upon the lady's description,
Ronsard betrays his full intent. His description is a compliment. Again, his procedure is eminently Petrarchistic, but
not Petrarchan. However beautiful Petrarch said Laura to
be, however much he arranged his nature description to
accentuate her "gloria," few poems of the *Rime* make
compliment their sole aim. Compliment in Petrarch is the
handmaiden of that suffering and introspection which
make his poems so much denser than Ronsard's sonnets of
1552. Compliment to the French poet is its own aesthetic.
Compliment is fitting only for what is perfect, and flattery
for what is perfect can only be hyperbolic. Compliment
demands abstraction and white lies which, in truth, make
no claim to veracity but seek rather new heights. Even the

antitheses, so fundamental for "Pien di quella ineffabile dolcezza" and the elaboration of Petrarch's psychology, reappear in the Petrarchistic texts in very simplified terms. The innumerable reversals—the suffering poet who finally accepts his condition because of its source; the call upon death which is useless because the poet has already succumbed to the lady's charms—are parallel variants on the theme of compliment, since they are noticeably created to permit the poet his "pointe"—an epigrammatic surprise ending. The reader is at no time invited to appreciate the depth of emotion expressed but, rather, the poet's cleverness and, from the woman's point of view, the *beau geste* of the capitulation. Elsewhere, each time the poet paints his condition, he reiterates his homage, acknowledging the force of the woman's beauty. He once calls her "ma seulle Endelechie" (sonnet 56) and "ma Circe enchanteresse" (sonnet 65). But homage need not be love, and compliment alone does not have the force of lyric introspection. Still, Ronsard held to this option for compliment over lyricism, and compliment is the most important aspect of his understanding of Petrarchism in 1552.

Yet, Ronsard rarely succeeds in transmitting the sentiment of love when the woman is an abstraction and his tone, a mere compliment. The first quatrain of sonnet 32 hastily sets the stage for the gift giving, and the rest of the poem has no other pretension than to enumerate the god's presents and complete the compliment. There is no emotion expressed save the verb "adorer"; when the poet has an opportunity to exalt the woman's being, he chooses to condense all in the obvious "embellir." The poem is emotionally arid. Nothing transpires as the possibilities for exploitation—his love, her effect—are exhausted not only in two lines but actually in two words. The evocative weakness of "adorer" and "embellir" is evident, but the choice of words is quite in keeping with the complimentary intent.

The adoration underscores the woman's superior position, while "embellir" pays homage to her charms. In sonnet 32, at least, there can be little doubt that the lady is more complimented than loved.

Little by little a conflict had to arise between this lack of lyricism and the necessity to depict the love story as a personal experience of deep consequence. As long as the poet remained within the context of compliment, he risked diluting the force of his vocabulary through terms such as "adorer" and "embellir" as well as deadening the force of the situation by rushing to the flattering phrase. To counteract this tendency, the Petrarchistic tradition offered its second portrait, the lover and his lament:

> Ciel, air, & vents, plains & montz descouvers,
> Tertres fourchuz, & forestz verdoyantes,
> Rivages tortz, & sources ondoyantes,
> Taillis razez, & vous bocages verds,
> Antres moussus à demy front ouvers,
> Prez, boutons, fleurs, & herbes rousoyantes,
> Coustaux vineux, et plages blondoyantes,
> Gastine, Loyr, & vous mes tristes vers:
> Puis qu'au partir, rongé de soing & d'ire,
> A ce bel oeil, l'Adieu je n'ay sceu dire,
> Qui pres & loing me detient en esmoy:
> Je vous supply, Ciel, air, ventz, montz, & plaines,
> Tailliz, forestz, rivages & fontaines
> Antres, prez, fleurs, dictes le luy pour moy.
>   (sonnet 57)

This is in many ways reminiscent of sonnet 32. Again the poet's message has been reduced to a minimum, and enumeration accounts for more than half the sonnet's content. A cascade of apostrophes instead of gifts now fills the form, whose central idea is as rapidly dispatched as the content of the first quatrain in sonnet 32. What is different, of course, is the object described: the poet, not the woman. Ronsard sets the general mood of the description in line 8 by speaking of his "tristes vers." The speaker is "rongé de soing & d'ire"; the woman keeps him "en esmoy"; and his demand of nature is meant to be a supplication: "Je vous supply." The portrait is not unlike the "sospir miei lassi" of Petrarch's self-analysis. The separation from the lady, the natural objects which form a setting for lament recall "Pien di quella ineffabile dolcezza," and yet again resemblances afford only a deeper insight into basic differences between Petrarch and Ronsard.

In a similar situation Petrarch draws from his antithetical attitudes the fullness of his despair and his inspiration. In the Ronsard poem, even the idea of antitheses disappears. The poet insists only on his lament, and it is most revealing that to the emotionally arid portrait of the woman, Ronsard should add a lament of emotional hyperbole. Such terms as "de soing & d'ire" are naturally of the purest Petrarchistic nature; and Ronsard used this vocabulary, as he used the complimentary conceits, in complete accord with its place in the Petrarchistic love tradition. If the lover's personal sentiments were to match the nature of his compliments, the entire cycle had to move to a plane of excess. Fiction could be enhanced only with fiction; and, needless to say, between hyperbolic compliment and emotional hysteria, the sound of lyricism was lost. Thus, whether or not Ronsard did meet and fall in love with a Cassandre Salviati or some other woman of the period, his poetic transcription of the relationship in 1552 systematically transformed lady and lover into mere abstractions: she, of beauty, he, of exaggerated pain. And one could easily add the dimension of pain to the "pointes," the marble, and the abstract qualities as further proof that Ronsard's lady was well complimented.

Some critics (Desonay in particular) would take exception to the view that *Amours I* does not portray any true emotion, insisting as they do that the first sonnet cycle teems with one very recognizable emotion: sensuality. Chronologically speaking, Ronsard was proving his taste for love verse of anti-Petrarchistic ideals even as he wrote these sonnets. (The *Folastries* appeared in 1553.) But such pronouncements as Desonay's "La veine érotique court d'un bout à l'autre du recueil, avec, de-ci, de-là, des affleurements plus brûlants d'un sang plus âcre" [13] are excessive. The preceding pages have shown how intimately Ronsard worked within the Petrachistic, not the Petrarchan, vision. The abstract woman and the tortured lover remain faithful to a tone of compliment that offered little place to such an erotic vein as Desonay perceives in the cycle. It is significant that Ronsard eventually removed from the cycle the few sonnets of 1552 which are patently sensual (numbers 67, 100, 101, and 102), so great is the moral distance between them and the rest of the poems. The other sonnets contain a number of words ("flanc," "aiguillon," "sein," "ulcere," "furie"), borrowed from Petrarch and used by Desonay and Laumonier before him to prove the existence of sensuality in *Amours I*.[14] In "Chiare, fresche e dolci acque," we have already seen some of these words, some of the more "sensual" ones, in fact. Yet one would not be tempted to call this famous canzone of Petrarch a poem of "la veine érotique." In addition, when these words are examined in context, their Petrarchis-

13. Desonay, *Ronsard, poète de l'amour*, *1*, 107.
14. See Paul Laumonier, *Ronsard, poète lyrique* (Paris, 1909), pp. 507–09.

tic value becomes clear. Sonnet 86, for example, explains in
detail the meaning of "ulcere":

> Amour archer d'une tirade ront
> Cent traitz sur moy, & si ne me conforte
> D'un seul espoir, celle pour qui je porte
> Le cuoeur aux yeulx, les pensers sus le front.
> D'un Soleil part la glace qi me fond,
> Et m'esbays que ma froydeur n'est morte
> Au feu d'un oeil, qui d'une flamme accorte
> Brulle mon cuoeur d'un ulcere profond.
>
> (vv. 1–8)

The burning heart, rather than suggesting unbridled passion, derives its justification from the basic Petrarchistic
conceit of the woman's eye resembling a flame or fire. The
"ulcere" is the sore inflicted by the eye. Even the insistence
on the great depth to which the lover has been struck need
not contradict this interpretation. We must remember that
the desire to compliment is rarely absent in *Amours I*. So
here, to render the image of complete allegiance, the poet
underscores the strength of the assault. He is wounded, not
superficially, but deeply enough to cause an "ulcere profond." Allegory and compliment also explain such terms as
"flanc" and "aiguillon," for example, in sonnet 1:

> Qui voudra voyr comme un Dieu me surmonte,
> Comme il m'assault, comme il se fait vainqueur,
> Comme il r'enflamme, & r'englace mon cuoeur,
> Comme il reçoit un honneur de ma honte,
> Qui voudra voir une jeunesse prompte
> A suyvre en vain l'object de son malheur,
> Me vienne voir: il voirra ma douleur,
> Et la rigueur de l'Archer qui me donte.
> Il cognoistra combien la raison peult

> Contre son arc, quand une foys il veult
> Que nostre cuoeur son esclave demeure:
> Et si voirra que je suis trop heureux,
> D'avoir au flanc l'aiguillon amoureux,
> Plein du venin dont il fault que je meure.

The opening lines underline the irrational and imposed nature of the poet's love. When the woman ensnares him, love binds his reason. Reduced to the pose of a slave engaged in a useless chase, he seems afflicted with madness. He is condemned to love while everything points up the futility of his actions. The closing is a return to these thoughts: "aiguillon" echoes "A suyvre en vain," and "flanc" takes up the image of the ensnared heart, "nostre cuoeur son esclave." [15] The return is justified by its complimentary value. Until the final tercet the poet has presented his love as a painful emotion, but to end the sonnet he adds "Et si voirra que je suis trop heureux . . . ," one of those numerous paradoxes designed to turn complaint to homage. Such a compliment has its own explanation within the Petrarchistic context and as such needs no extensive argument to refute its interpretation as a sensual expression.

Thus, in his portrait of the lady, his portrait of the lover, and even in a description of his desires, Ronsard remained essentially within the confines of the Petrarchistic tradition. Apart from the few poems in which he allowed sensuality to appear openly, he devoted sonnet after sonnet to the abstract woman and the complimentary lover, yielding repeatedly to the demands of the traditional clichés.

Elsewhere in the allegories of the *innamoramento*, the vocabulary is so well defined as to hinder any departure

---

15. Littré points out that in the French of past centuries "flanc" was often used to mean "sein." *Dictionnaire de la Langue Française* (Paris, 1863), *1*, 1691.

from the tradition. Number 20, "Je vouldray bien richement jaunissant," tells of the poet's desire to become, like
Jupiter, a shower of gold or a bull, and then a Narcissus if
his beloved were a fountain. The desires of Jupiter leave no
room for discussion, but the mention of Narcissus introduces a slight problem. He is the prototype of the unhappy
lover, languishing for the impossible, and this situation of
fruitless and impossible desire is also the prototype of that
of the Petrarchistic lover who loves without success and
sees in death alone the solution to his dilemma. The story
was admirably suited for a sonnet in 1552, but is it possible
that Ronsard mixed the active, lustful Jupiter and the
languid Narcissus without realizing the fundamental difference between their characters?

The poem itself presents the final answer. Its very
structure—each metamorphosis is introduced by "Je vouldroy"—places the transformations on an equal plane while
effecting a progression toward the image of Narcissus.
These metamorphoses meet at the common theme of possession, but nothing in the poem indicates that this possession is meant to be physical. In point of fact, by arranging
the series so that the Narcissus-fountain image is the last,
Ronsard devalues the physical overtones of the first two.
In introducing the final image, moreover, the poet places
the reader fully in the Petrarchistic context. The leitmotiv
"Je vouldroy" is repeated, typifying the subservient attitudes of the lover who is precisely the opposite of the
enterprising Jupiter. He declares neither, "I will," nor
"I have," but hazards a pale, "I should like." The verse
continues by giving a reason for the wish, "afin d'aiser ma
peine": again a Petrarchistic conceit. His "peine" comes
from the disdainful attitude of the woman, who refuses him
all attention (and certainly her body). The word "peine"
could be ambiguous out of context, yet the use of "aiser"
("ease"; after 1560 "alleger")—rather than a verb of satis-

fying or obliterating—indicates specifically that the act of possession here desired and imagined should not be given too narrow an interpretation.

This vagueness in the poet's attitude toward possession is even more evident in the particular form of union described in the final metamorphosis. If the woman should become a fountain, the poet-Narcissus would enter under the cover of night, and were the night eternal, he would never want to leave. We might compare this desire with "Pien di quella ineffabile dolcezza," for the woman's absorption of the poet is by no means outside the Petrarchistic tradition. Of course, Ronsard the poet *seeks* such union, and for those who insist on seeing sexual imagery in the water of the fountain, the poem may have its sensual overtones. But the context—the tormented lover's desire for unending union with the woman who gives him his being—has its own psychology, and a Petrarchistic one.

Until now, I have insisted upon those qualities of *Amours I* which reduce the richness of Petrarch's verse to the simplicity of overworked and unrelated conceits. Yet Ronsard's contemporaries criticized *Amours I* not for its simplicity, but for its learned complexity, its classical illusions, and its mythology.[16] The sonnet about Jupiter and Narcissus gives a good illustration of the cause of their bewilderment. If the attitude represented is basically Petrarchistic and closely related to "Pien di quella ineffabile dolcezza," no Jupiter myth, no Narcissus legend complicates Petrarch's verse. However rich the treatment of the subject may be, there are but two characters in the poem. Ronsard communicates the narrator's sentiments through an intermediary myth. He is not adverse to using the same technique to describe the woman as when he calls her "Endelechie" and "Circe." He wants us to appreciate the woman's effect

16. See the first sonnet of the *Continuation*.

upon her lover, but only through the most recondite allusions. Naturally, the technique results in the opposite of direct expression and intensity, and we may well sympathize with those contemporaries who expected a love story and encountered instead such perplexing erudition—erudition that must also be taken into account when judging the validity for *Amours I* of Desonay's expression "la veine érotique."

In a few instances Ronsard sought more forcefully to break the hold of the tradition. A poem will begin as a Petrarchistic work, only to veer away from the compliment toward a clearly sensual expression, as in sonnet 41 "Ha, seigneur dieu." It is useless to belabor the idea that this poem is meant initially to exalt the beauty of the woman. Verse 1 quickly refers to "que de graces écloses." But when the poet passes to the last image, the tone is quite different:

> . . . Hé, que ne sui-je puce!
> La baisotant, tous les jours je mordroi
> Ses beaus tetins, mais la nuit je voudroi
> Que rechanger en homme je me pusse.
> (sonnet 41, ed. 1553)

Despite the insertion of "beaus" and the preceding and preparatory allusion to Jupiter, whose actions are pardonable if occasioned by similar beauty (compliment again!), there is no denying the daring in these verses. In a reappraisal of the sonnet, Ronsard eliminated completely the image of the flea. He returned to the central theme of beauty and Jupiter to terminate the poem with yet another compliment, an implication of perfection:

> Sage tu pris le masque d'un toreau,
> Bon Jupiter, pour traverser les ondes.
> Le ciel n'est dit parfait pour sa grandeur.

Luy & le sein le sont pour leur rondeur:
Car le parfait consiste en choses rondes.
(variants, vv. 10–14)

Such changes have repeatedly been singled out to show
how Ronsard "purified" his work in later years. Perhaps
so—but more impressive is the intent of the correction:
first, to give the sonnet a new thematic unity by taking up
again the figure of Jupiter and, second, through its final
note of compliment, to create a tone in keeping with the
atmosphere of *Amours I.* Whatever personal inclinations
brought Ronsard to include these sensual notes in the
original edition of *Amours I,* as over the years his literary
sense developed, he could not escape an awareness of the
difference in style and tone between the few sensual out-
bursts and the Petrarchistic tradition. He had every reason,
therefore, to change his sonnets for considerations that
were literary, not moral. Petrarchistic poetry offered no
place for any tone save the hyperbolic, the paradoxical, and
the complimentary. The reality of desire could not coexist
with so conscious an effort to relate a love story between
two fictional characters of compliment and hyperbole.

The influence of compliment and hyperbole on the execution of these sonnets is no less great than that on the
poet's portrait of the woman and himself. Sonnets 32 and
57 possess a very basic similarity in their development:
enumeration. Of course, there is enumeration in "Chiare,
fresche e dolci acque," but Petrarch justifies the objects selected through their relationship to Laura and through
their role in directing his thought toward Laura's "gloria."
Nothing of this nature takes place in Ronsard. Though the
gifts have a complimentary role, they tumble forth as indiscriminately as the natural objects of "Ciel, air, & vents.
. . ." In both cases the extent to which Ronsard prolongs

his enumeration finds its primary and almost sole *raison d'être* in the necessity to fill out fourteen lines. The poems tacitly proclaim the poverty of the Petrarchistic tradition and, in a different context, the failure of the tradition to inspire great poetry through isolated Petrarchan conceits. The narrative element in these sonnets and even the conceits themselves do not run beyond a line or two, and the rest is padding.

All of *Amours I* reveal such padding and the limits of the Petrarchistic material, limits within which Ronsard turned about again and again to produce his most monotonous cycle. One would like to think that such monotony had its origin in some positive intent: Ronsard's attempt to reach the perfection of Petrarch through the Petrarchistic tradition, for example. But this very monotony seems to speak against such a purpose. Ronsard's determination to write love poetry of compliment and hyperbole remained firm with only occasional flashes of sensuality. The texts attest to great effort, but it is expended repeatedly about the already tried and trite.

No aspect of the execution of the sonnets of *Amours I* reveals more graphically the complexity of failure—both in the inadequacy of the tradition and the inadequacy of the young poet—than does Ronsard's handling of sources. Here, too, there is only padding, repetition of the conceits for their own sake, and little evidence that Ronsard appreciated the qualities of Petrarch or the skills of those who imitated him. By way of example, here is the Bevilacqua sonnet which influenced sonnet 57 of *Amours I:*

Herbe felici, et prato aventuroso
De l'alma abscinthia mia, ch'io sola chieggio,
Sovente grato e honorato seggio
Et al piu caldo Sol dolce riposo.
Candidi et varii fior, ch'a l'amoroso

Et casto seno accolti insieme veggio,
 Per chi omai sempre di dolor vaneggio
Et d'invidia et timor resto geloso:
Limpidi fonti, e voi liti beati,
Ch'ascoltate talhor i lieti accenti
 Di quella ch'ogni bel del ciel possede:
Schietti arboscelli e di fredd'ombre grati,
Poi ch'ella udir non pote i miei lamenti
Ditele voi per me, ch'amor vol fede.[17]

Since the borrowed elements are evident, it may be more
valuable to observe a quality toward which Ronsard shows
no inclination: the structure of the enumeration. Each of
Bevilacqua's apostrophes forms a separate thought and is
enclosed within a natural division in the sonnet. More important, each thought signals the poet's effort to draw his
objects into a central theme. One by one they are related to
the poet, to the woman, to both, so that the final lines,
where nature becomes the lover's spokesman, portray a triangle of characters which the beginning has established as
being of long standing. In Ronsard there is no such integration of elements, but simply the interminable list.

Elsewhere Ronsard seizes upon the conceits to pad the
poem, not through enumeration but by means of juxtaposition and addition of one borrowed element after another.
An interesting example is sonnet 88, "Bien que six ans,"
where the verse, "Endore, emperle, enfrange nostre temps"
(vs. 10) is obviously taken from a line in Petrarch's sonnet
"Stiamo, Amor" ("Vedi quant'arte dora e'mperla e'nos-
tra" [18]), though no other element from that poem reappears
in Ronsard's. After the recounting of the traditional *innamoramento*, with its capturing glance and sight of incom-

17. Quoted in Henri Weber, *La Création poétique en France au XVI*
siècle (Paris, 1956), p. 321.
 18. See Petrarch, pp. 277–78.

parable beauty, the second quatrain insures the poet his compliment:

> Si suis-je heureux d'avoyr veu la lumiere
> En ces ans tardz pour avoyr veu le trait
> De son beau front, qui les graces attrait
> Par une grace aux Graces coustumiere.

The poem must continue—we are only at line 8—but the reworking of conceits and compliment is a bit too contained and the second quatrain too final, as the "Si" indicates. As a result, Ronsard seeks out another conceit—one that can develop the idea of beauty now that he has exhausted the possibilities of the *innamoramento*—and it is at this point in the poem that he borrows the line from "Stiamo, Amor." Other examples of this sort might be quoted—notably sonnet 40, where, after an initial effort which continues through line 9 to paint the lady's beauty through flower imagery, Ronsard injects: "Que diray plus?" And to fill out the poem, he turns to the image of the lady's eye which calmed the skies. In both poems there is a vague similarity between the elements Ronsard juxtaposes. In sonnet 40, for example, the lady's beauty is also her power to calm the heavens, yet the movement of ideas is nonetheless abrupt, and Ronsard's "Que diray plus?" must be singled out as a maladroit transition that is itself an admission of ineptitude.

Whatever Ronsard admired in Petrarch and his epigones, he did not succeed in writing love poetry of the emotional, psychological, or lyrical excellence that is to be found in the Italian master. The reasons behind this failure are varied. The Petrarchistic tradition was itself weak and treacherous. A tradition of conceits and antitheses, of compliment and hyperbole, it was at the outset un-Petrarchan. But a look at Ronsard's manipulation of sources reveals that he, too, must share the blame. The repeated reduction of his material to enumeration and juxtaposition of conceits demonstrates a rudimentary and uninspired approach. Not all of *Amours I* is monotonous hyperbole: when Ronsard wrote,

> J'iray tousjours & resvant & songeant
> En la doulce heure, où je vy l'angelette,
> Qui d'esperance & de crainte m'alaitte,
> Et dans ses yeulx mes destins va logeant
>   (112, vv. 1–4)

his musical sense did not fail him. Yet here, as elsewhere, the poem was destined to relate a complimentary paradox. Though the odes he had already written and was writing at the time of *Amours I* prove that a great poetic talent was emerging, Ronsard was only too evidently incapable of effecting a fortuitous union between his poetic sense and his subject. Unimaginative handling of source material and inexperience with the Petrarchistic tradition provide simple answers, but the crucial problems are those of tone and vision.

Because the tone of *Amours I* is one of compliment, the cycle veers continually away from the lyrical and psychological. If the lover insists upon his unhappy state, most often his lament is designed to emphasize his lady's force and his allegiance to her beauty, even in suffering and death. In the attempts to communicate the image of the woman, there is no lyric appreciation of love as sentiment; there are only hyperbolic abstractions.

The problem of vision is even more immediate. The love poems of Petrarch demonstrate to what degree love is for this poet a psychological state: he literally cannot think, see, or remember without the intervention of love, and, as a result, the words related to these processes take on new density and meaning. Love in *Amours I*, however, is a pose: the poet suffers, praises, regrets, adores, but in a vacuum, so to speak, as no supplementary element intervenes to enrich the vocabulary and the devices. The main devices in Ronsard's style (the lady's "bel oeil," the gods' gifts, the natural objects) perforce seem dull or thin compared to their Petrarchan counterparts. In Petrarch the lady's eye is the source of "ineffabile dolcezza," and the poem explains in detail the importance to him of this "sweetness." Her "beaulté" in Ronsard's "Quand au premier . . . " is an abstract quality. As only one of many, this trait fails to strike the reader because the poet, unlike Petrarch, has endowed it with no more importance than her fingers or her feet. This fact reveals to its fullest extent the treacherous quality of the Petrarchistic tradition, which on the surface seemed a source of highly expressive poetry. Animated by a vision of compliment alone, it could mean no more than what compliment conveys—flattery, praise, exaggeration. Thus, however Ronsard might change his style in the years to come, he could not revolutionize his love poetry without altering its tone and vision. The need to find the missing elements of a lyric personality resides in tone and vision, not style.

MARULLUS

Ronsard's next attempt with the sonnet cycle he entitled "continuations"—the *Continuation des Amours* of 1555 and the *Nouvelle Continuation des Amours* of 1556. Because these cycles contain the aubade "Mignongne, levés-vous" and repeated reference to a "stille bas" which Ronsard contrasted with the style of *Amours I*, it is traditional to see in the *Continuations* a rupture with *Amours I*. In truth, not enough has been made of the titles Ronsard gave to these new cycles and of the literal meaning of "continuations." These titles prove that in Ronsard's mind there was no sudden rupture with what had preceded and that whatever style, vision, or tone Ronsard contemplated using in his new love verse, he meant to place them within a frame of reference he had created with *Amours I.* The texts, moreover, taken as a whole, show this to be the case.

Here is sonnet 48 of the *Continuation:*

Tu as beau, Jupiter, l'air de flammes dissouldre,
Et faire galloper tes haux-tonnans chevaus,
Ronflans deçà delà dans le creux des nuaus,
Et en cent mille esclats tout d'un coup les descoudre,
Ce n'est pas moi qui crains tes esclairs, ni ta foudre
Comme les coeurs poureus des autres animaus:
Il y a trop lon tems que les foudres jumeaus
Des yeus de ma maitresse ont mis le mien en poudre.
Je n'ai plus ni tendons, ni arteres, ni nerfs,
Venes, muscles, ni poux: les feux que j'ai soufferts
Au coeur pour trop aimer me les ont mis en cendre.
Et je ne suis plus rien (ô estrange meschef)
Qu'un Terme qui ne peut voir, n'oüyr, ni entendre,
Tant la foudre d'amour est cheute sus mon chef.

The use of mythology in the subject's presentation, the compliment behind the comparison (the lightning of the lady's eyes is more fearful than Jupiter's) show as do sonnets 14, 15, 31, 33, 34, 55, 57, and 61 of the 1555 edition and sonnets "J'ay cent mille tormentz" and "Mars fut vostre parein" of the *Nouvelle Continuation* that in many instances there can be little to distinguish between the poems of *Amours I* and the sonnets of the *Continuation.* The same lover complains about his lady's cruelty, predicts his death and recalls the fatal moment of the *innamoramento.* On the one hand, there is no reason to be surprised at this continuity: *Amours I* was Ronsard's first sonnet cycle and therefore his only proving-ground. In addition, the personal and public commitment to rival Petrarch had not been fully acquitted. Ronsard's reputation was still to be firmly rooted, and the title of France's Petrarch was a tempting springboard to fame. On the other hand, an analysis of *Amours I* has shown that Ronsard's adaptation of the Petrarchistic tradition proved unsuccessful in many aspects, enough certainly to warrant not continuity but change.

Unfortunately, there are no documents—letters, prefaces, or the like—to provide a clear statement of the author's position concerning his initial sonnet cycle. The critic is obliged to be most guarded in asserting that Ronsard may have sensed the failure of *Amours I* to equal Petrarchan poetry. However, despite the titles of "continuation" and the evident Petrarchistic imitation in the cycles of 1552 and 1555, two interesting texts, one from *Amours I* the other from the *Continuation*, suggest strongly that a definite malaise grew out of this Petrarchistic experiment.

Sonnet 19 to Cassandre, "Avant le temps tes temples fleuriront," contains this revealing prophecy addressed to the poet by the lady-prophetess: "De tes souspirs tes nepveux se riront" (vs. 8). The context is a prophecy concerning their relationship and its future. With the passage of time, Cassandre says, nothing will remain of the verse created by the poet for her, an idea quite contrary to the poet's usual claim of immortality. The derisive element in her prophecy is equally exceptional. Ronsard seems not only unsure about the lasting quality of the poetry in his first cycle, but uncertain about the impression his poems will make. Since the Middle Ages it was not uncommon in French poetry to muse on the fragility of human things, but the derision ("riront") suggests that his poetry will suffer a fate not contingent on the fortune of all things but rather on its very quality as love verse. Cassandre declares that his suffering will evoke only laughter and shows no compassion for the lover's sadness and pathos, as if there was a definite consciousness that the hyperbole and compliment could never be taken for true sentiment. Of course, the poet may have meant only to reveal in another context the cruelty of Cassandre, but the particular attempt here to turn Cassandre's powers of prophecy toward the question of poetry gives the poem a resonance not to be found in the usual portraits of the woman's unsympathetic attitude.

The text from the *Continuation* contrasts the spring season with the poet's own feelings:

> É que me sert, Paschal, ceste belle verdure
> Qui rit parmi les prés, & d'ouir les oiseaus,
> D'ouir par le pendant des colines les eaus,
> Et des vents du printems le gracieus murmure,
> Quand celle qui me blesse, & de mon mal n'a cure
> Est absente de moi, & pour croistre mes maus
> Me cache la clarté de ses astres jumeaus,
> De ses yeus, dont mon coeur prenoit sa nourriture?
> J'aimeroi beaucoup mieus qu'il fust hyver tousjours,
> Car l'hyver n'est si propre à nourir les amours
> Comme est le renouveau, qui d'aimer me convie,
> Ainçois de me hayr, puis que je n'ay pouvoir
> En ce beau mois d'Avril entre mes bras d'avoir
> Celle qui dans ses yeus tient ma mort & ma vie.
>
> (sonnet 27)

Spring has come, but the lover would prefer a return to winter. Spring traditionally calls us to love, while only self-hate arises in the poet from this change of seasons since he cannot hold his lady in his arms. On the surface, the poem offers no complexity or particular difficulty. Yet in its arrangement of ideas (spring and love—what is normal, contrasted with spring and hate—the actual circumstance; while love and winter best approximates his true situation), the poem provokes comments about Ronsard, love, and the Petrarchistic tradition.

The first quatrain describes the coming of spring. There

is laughter, the singing of birds, the "gracieus murmure" of the spring breezes. When Ronsard takes up his situation and his separation from the lady, the gay sounds disappear. The first tercet introduces the wish for winter; the second tercet, the idea of self-hate. Through the progression from spring music to winter and hate, Ronsard lays bare the inevitable progression in thought, and consequently in style, from what love is to what love becomes within the Petrarchistic sonnet. The very themes of hate and winter cannot be separated from a poetic transcription of the Petrarchistic situation. The objective analysis of the lover's plight perforce emphasizes the barren love and the sterile longing, so that the poem's opening line, "É que me sert, . . . ," could well be paraphrased, "What good to me are lyric lines and poetry of 'gracieus murmure'," since the Petrarchistic tradition demands sterile hate and no such lyric élan as can be equated with the coming of spring. I do not mean to imply that Ronsard had such a direct commentary of his poetry in mind when he wrote this sonnet. But, as with the Cassandre prophecy, in elaborating a love theme the poet betrays certain sentiments which can be linked most directly to his poetry although the context did not necessitate a given development. These sentiments bring to the fore the poet within the lover and a voice that is to be heard more and more as time passes.

The conflict of emotion—the desire to "continue" and the growth of dissatisfaction—takes two different forms in the *Continuations:* a gradual transformation of the cycles' composition and the introduction of new stylistic devices. *Amours I* contained 182 sonnets, grouped together and followed by a song of purest Petrarchism, an "Amourette" of the Marullus, Second tradition, and sonnets of praise written by friends of Ronsard. Thus, of the love verse only the "Amourette" lies outside the Petrarchistic tradition.

The *Continuation* of 1555 maintained this pattern. The sonnets, divided between those in alexandrines and those in decasyllabic verse, open the cycle and are grouped together. The other forms follow the sonnets. The similarity is nonetheless a bit deceiving. While the cycle begins with an exclusive use of the sonnet, the sonnets do not all treat of love alone. The first, for example, raises immediately the problem of style:

> Thiard, chacun disoit à mon commencement
> Que j'estoi trop obscur au simple populaire:
> Aujourd'hui, chacun dit que je suis au contraire,
> Et que je me dements parlant trop bassement.
>
> (sonnet 1, vv. 1–4)

Others relate his sentiments to his friends, and one (sonnet 5) praises his teacher Daurat. In sonnet 24 Ronsard censures Baïf's latest efforts with the love theme and continues in sonnets 27, 50, 51, and 64 to offer to others the portrait of his state. Use of the sonnet, therefore, no longer means a strict adherence to the theme of love. Through these extended conversations, Ronsard seems to want to provide the cycle as a whole with a certain relief from the single topic of love, and a brief glance at one of these sonnets can show how much such conversations did, in fact, alleviate many of the problems of the love sonnet.

> Peletier mon ami, le tems leger s'enfuit,
> Je change nuit & jour de poil & de jeunesse:
> Mais je ne change pas l'amour d'une maistresse,
> Qui, dans mon cueur colée, eternelle me suit.
> Toi qui es des anfance en tout savoir instruit,
> (Si de nottre amitié l'antique neud te presse)
> Comme sage & plus vieil, donne moi quelque adresse,
> Pour eviter ce mal qui ma raison détruit.
> Aide-moi, Peletier, si par philosophie,
> Ou par le cours des cieus tu as jamais apris

Un remede d'amour, di-le moi je te prie,
Car, bien qu'ores au ciel ton cueur soit elevé,
Si as-tu quelquefois d'une dame esté pris.
Et pour dieu! conte-moi comme tu t'es sauvé.

(sonnet 4)

The first quatrain, in addition to identifying the friend, presents the familiar situation of despair and discouragement mixed with continued fidelity. The second quatrain is devoted to Peletier. Ronsard reveals why he has addressed him and the tercets merely develop this theme (in a rather repetitious way, moreover, as there is really no difference in content between the two final parts of the sonnet). Thus, through this introduction of the friend, Ronsard has been able to write yet another sonnet around a very worn theme. The material pertinent to the particular friend Ronsard is addressing is ample enough so that the poet need only sketch the familiar theme to complete his sonnet.

At the end of the sonnet portion of the *Continuation*, though the general distinction in forms is maintained, there are further departures from *Amours I*. Poems by friends are still included, but the personal production is much increased. This section now contains thirteen poems by Ronsard, all (except the previously published "Gayetés" and two odes addressed to friends) preceded by titles or subtitles indicating that they are imitations and translations. The intention seems fairly evident. Just as Ronsard no longer wants to write sonnets dealing exclusively with the narrator-lover and the woman, so he does not want to devote his love cycles exclusively to the sonnet. He is anxious to show his superiority in the ode.[19] He salvages some

19. Here are the first verses of the first poem to follow the sonnets of the *Continuation*:

Verson ces Roses prés ce vin,
Prés de ce vin verson ces Roses

poems from the *Folastries* (the "Gayetés"); he borrows
overtly from Anacreon, and retranslates Daurat to close
the *Continuation* with a fine display of different forms and
styles, some Petrarchistic, some (the "Gayetés," for example) in the spirit of the *esprit gaulois*.

In the *Nouvelle Continuation* the division between the
sonnet and other genres disappears completely. Songs and
odes abound throughout; the proportion of sonnets is low
(twenty-five sonnets to twenty-one songs and eight odes).
The concept of a *sonnet* cycle has clearly been lost. Instead, Ronsard continues his production of sonnets but sur-
rounds them and counterbalances them with the forms that
in 1555 he still placed separately at the end of the cycle.
Thematically, too, the concept of a sonnet cycle suffers a
setback in the *Nouvelle Continuation*. While most of the
cycle's works do refer to love, Ronsard does not hesitate to
include the famous "Bel aubepin" and odes "Quand je dors
je ne sens rien" and "Celuy qui est mort aujourd'hui"
which Laumonier is certainly correct in linking to
"L'Hymne de la Mort," published just the preceding
year.[20] By 1556 Ronsard had moved farther and farther
from *Amours I* as a love cycle and a sonnet cycle, effecting
a steady betrayal of his original plan. The love cycle is
aerated, so to speak, with the fresher style of the odes and
relieved of its monotony by tales to friends and a variety of
themes and forms.

Insofar as "variety" suggests the juxtaposition of diversi-
fied elements rather than a clear structure of alternance, it

----

Et boyvon l'un à l'autre, à fin
Qu'au coeur noz tristesses encloses
Prennent en boyvant quelque fin. (7, 189.)

It is interesting to note, moreover, that while the narrator is addressing
his friend Aubert, as he addressed many friends in the love cycle, Ronsard effectively cuts this poem and the others following from the personal love story by giving it the subtitle "Imitation d'Anacreon."

20. Laumonier, 7, 283, n. 3.

aptly describes as well the new stylistic devices which comprise the second aspect of the *Continuations* to show the strain of continuity and dissatisfaction. In style, as well as in the arrangement of the poems, the cycle offers, sometimes within the same poem, increasing departures from the Petrarchistic tradition. "É que me sert, Paschal . . ." can serve again as an important example.[21] The dominant vision is Petrarchistic. Ronsard laments the absence of the lady as she is his being and without her there can be no thought of love, regardless of the season. The tone is complimentary and hyperbolic. Spring would stir him to love, but his feelings insist upon a reversal of the usual situation. He must react with self-hate, not love because the woman is absent. The style, too, scarcely deviates from the Petrarchistic vocabulary in describing the woman and her relationship to the poet: "Celle qui me blesse & de mon mal n'a cure . . . ," "la clarté de ses astres jumeaus," "Celle qui dans ses yeus tient ma mort & ma vie." But amid these conceits, verse 13, which alludes to the April season, slips significantly into a rather different tone, "En ce beau mois d'Avril entre mes bras d'avoir," a tone that is hyperbolic and complimentary only if desire be compliment. Of this tone of desire I shall say more later; but for the moment let us note in what way this verse, by its content, echoes obliquely the entire first quatrain and indicates not only the duplicity of tone but also of style in the sonnet. In contrasting the spring with his own sentiments, Ronsard opens the tradition ever so slightly to a new kind of love, one in tune with nature and not contrary to it, a kind of love that is itself laughter and music. The poet explains his wish "de [s]e hayr" through the woman's absence, but in truth the Petrarchistic tradition of itself repeatedly forced the poet to embrace such a pose in the absence of that sense of love's

---

21. See p. 48.

"gloria," which maintains throughout the Petrarchan verse a poetry of true élan. By juxtaposing the sterile lament and nature's "renouveau," Ronsard opposes not only styles but fundamental attitudes toward love.

In other poems, sonnet 17, for example, the juxtaposition is purely stylistic. Ronsard relates an allegorical dream which is traditional in Petrarchistic verse. The speaker chases an animal (the lady) but instead of catching it, is trapped himself in an unseen snare. Yet from the first lines:

> Le vintiéme d'Avril couché sur l'herbelette,
> Je vy, ce me sembloit, en dormant un chevreuil,
> Qui çà, puis là, marchoit où le menoit son vueil,
> Foulant les belles fleurs de mainte gambelette,
>
> (sonnet 17, vv. 1–4)

it is obvious that the poet is using another form of expression. The diminutives, the very movement of the animal, his games among the flowers, create within this rather complicated allegory-compliment a definite feeling of that "gracieus murmure" described in "É que me sert, Paschal. . . ." As the liminal sonnet of the *Continuation* suggests, Ronsard had certain reasons for this change, "Thiard, chacun disoit à mon commencement/ Que j'estoi trop obscure au simple populaire" (vv. 1–2), and it is easy to write off these verses of "gracieus murmure" as a simple attempt by Ronsard to placate critics of his obscurity. The reader would not be entirely unjustified in saying, to describe the *Continuation* of 1555, that Ronsard suppressed the denser allegories and the mythology in favor of a style that is lighter and more varied even though, as the title suggests, he did not alter the basic Petrarchistic tone and vision. And were it possible to conclude an analysis of variety in the *Continuation* of 1555 or its sister cycle of 1556 with such a description, this middle period in Ronsard's development would be a simple one to define. In reality, the period from

1552 to 1560 is undoubtedly the most confused in the long history of Ronsard's work with the sonnet form. Behind the main lines of Ronsard's effort—preservation of the Petrarchistic tradition with, nevertheless, a growing interest in forms other than the sonnet and in new material for the periphery of the Petrarchistic vision—lies the fact that this peripheral material, though primarily stylistic in nature, can undermine the traditional Petrarchistic vision. In "É que me sert, Paschal . . ." the poet's regret at the lady's absence, not only because he is removed from her sight but because he cannot hold her in his arms, gives the love story a complexity quite different from the traditional tone of compliment. Ronsard's depression is immediately linked with a concept of love as pleasure or excitement and the poetic associations which are set in motion within the poet's mind force him to transcribe this dichotomy between love and regret in terms which go beyond the normal love lament. The dichotomy embraces the seasons, that is, nature and the natural course of time and emotion, so that, finally, Ronsard produces a poem torn between two conflicting worlds: the world where love and nature are in harmony and the emotional winter of Petrarchistic self-hate. Before the cycles of "continuation" close, Ronsard will have juxtaposed in a similar manner most of the essential petrarchistic attitudes and a quite opposite vision of love.

Strains of sensuality have never been absent from Ronsard's love sonnets; traces appear even in *Amours I*.[22] But with the varied style and tone of the *Continuations*, the strains are more noticeable, although they still weave in and out of the conceits of the Petrarchistic tradition, which dominate and direct them. Sonnet 66 from the *Continuation* reveals the sensuality of the lover literally enclosed

22. See p. 34.

(by the first quatrain and second tercet) in a firm Petrarchistic framework of imposed chastity. The opening quatrain
states the poet's refusal to approach his lady again:

> J'ai l'ame pour un lit de regrets si touchée,
> Que nul, & fusse un Roy, ne fera que j'aprouche
> Jamais de la maison, encor moins de la couche
> Où je vy ma maitresse, au mois de May couchée.
>
> (sonnet 66, vv. 1–4)

The central part describes what the poet saw in the past:
the woman lying in "Un somme languissant." In her eyes
Cupid the archer lies in wait, and the Graces have made
their home in her hair. But beside these conceits exists the
evocation of a langorous beauty on her bed in the May
heat. Nothing is specifically sensual and the body is described only through the normal traits of eyes, mouth, and
hair. Yet the image of the second tercet, "J'en ai tel
souvenir que je voudrois qu'à l'heure/(Pour jamais n'y
penser) son oeil m'eust fait rocher," suggests too strong a
reaction within the poet to permit a wholly Petrarchistic
interpretation of the sonnet's tone. The Petrarchism leaves
its mark in the hyperbolic recoiling of the first quatrain or
this complimentary gesture at the end of the poem. The
poet remains faithful to the tradition by keeping his distance from the lady but underneath there is a motivation
no longer based on the acceptance of a subservient position
but rather on the tacit fear "(Pour jamais n'y penser)" of a
definable desire. The clash between Petrarchistic fidelity
and fidelity to desire is only one of many throughout the
Continuations. The nature of the woman to be loved, the
nature of their physical relationship and fundamental attitudes toward the love experience, each of these questions,
too, receives a distinct variety of reactions on the part of
the poet.

Again and again the poet declares his fidelity to the woman:

> Ma plume sinon vous ne scait autre suget,
> Mon pié sinon vers vous ne scait autre voiage,
> Ma langue sinon vous ne scait autre langaige.
> (sonnet 15, vv. 1–3)

> Je ne scaurois aimer autre que vous.
> (sonnet 28, vs. 1)

> Aultre (j'en jure Amour) ne se scauroit vanter
> D'avoir part en mon cueur, vous seule en estes dame.
> (7, 256)

Elsewhere (sonnet 68) he praises constancy through a dialogue with a bird whose companion has been lost. But to these eloquent pronouncements there can be added a similar number of complete rejections of such an attitude:

> Les hommes maladis, ou mattés de vieillesse,
> Doivent estre constans: mais sotte est la jeunesse
> Qui n'est point eveillée, & qui n'aime en cent lieus.
> (sonnet 9, vv. 12–14)

or, concerning the two Maries he loves, "tant ferme je suis/ Que pour en aimer une, une autre je n'oublie" (sonnet 40, vv. 7–8). He may be less categorical: "Je ne suis variable" he says in sonnet 25 and, already grey-haired, he has no desire so to become. But, then, too, he would sympathize with Helen's Paris and his like, for nothing is more ridiculous than to refuse a more beautiful prospect when it appears. This intermediate attitude is interesting to compare with Ronsard's ideas on the kind of woman one should prefer. First we encounter absolute contradiction. Some may love city women and country girls, but

> Tout ainsi qu'en amour le plus excellent bien
> Est d'aimer une femme, & savante, & gentille,

> Aussi le plus grand mal à ceuls qui aiment bien
> C'est d'aimer une femme indocte, & mal-habille.
> (sonnet 21, vv. 5–8)

Yet this did not stop Ronsard from writing an apologia for
a "maistresse un petit putain" (sonnet 62). Here, too, there
is an alternative. In "Aultre (j'en jure Amour)" the speaker
tells his beloved:

> Si vous n'estes d'un lien si noble que Cassandre
> Je ne scaurois qu'y faire, Amour m'a fait descendre
> Jusques à vous aymer, Amour qui n'a point d'yeus.
> (7, 256–57)

In both cases there are the absolute opinions and the exten-
uating circumstances; one is constant until one has a better
opportunity. The noble lady is the only true object for
love, but when Love intervenes, there are no more rules.
The confusion persists into the very details of their relationship. In sonnet 51 he refuses to touch her with the
mouth or hands but tells in another sonnet of his kisses and
fondling (see sonnets 3, 18, and 11). He can adopt an air of
near total detachment from the experience, as in sonnet 16
where, having been rebuffed, he openly rebels: "May God
give him patience, for before twenty years are past, he will
have his revenge by seeing her grow old." Yet in sonnet 42,
he affects a Petrarchistic pose of the most complete subjec-
tion to the woman. He sends her his heart and closes the
poem by remarking that should she reject his gift, he does
not want it back, detesting all that cannot please her. Further
quoting would only uncover similar situations. The point is
not difficult to see. Throughout the *Continuations* there is a
persistent appearance of non-Petrarchistic themes and ideas
attached to, or surrounded by, the tradition of *Amours I.*
The clashes are sporadic and unpredictable. They follow
no pattern and establish no movement in the cycles which
could be termed the "structure" of these cycles. In their

presentation and execution, the *Continuations* are the works of an unsettled style and vision.

All the material just discussed is from the sonnets of the *Continuations*. Since the traditional view of these cycles as a turning toward sensual love relies heavily in its interpretation on the presence of the numerous songs and odes, a comparison between this variety in attitudes in the sonnet and the content of the songs and odes seems warranted.

One name stands out in all commentaries of the non-sonnet material of the *Continuations:* Marullus. Even Alexander Micha, in his edition of *Amours II* (1951), "ne s'écarte guère de l'opinion traditionnelle: renoncement à Pindare et à Pétrarque, goût marqué pour Marulle et les érotiques latins et néo-latins, 'mignardises,' fraîcheur rustique, sensualité jouisseuse." [23] Not only do the songs and odes traditionally represent a movement away from Petrarch, the *rapprochement* Ronsard-Marullus is said to be a definite step toward sensual expression. Desonay's theories on the *Continuations* and *Amours II* attack principally the ideas of a "rustic" love (not applicable to a majority of the texts) and the sensuality "jouisseuse" (Ronsard shows rather a timid nature before Marie).[24] I do not disagree with Desonay, but there is more to criticize in the traditional views on the *Continuations* than the rustic or sensual quality of Ronsard's love. As Desonay's remarks themselves suggest, a movement toward Marullus need not represent a movement away from Petrarch, and indeed, it does not.

Of Marullus' life we know very little. He seems to have been of Greek origin but to have lived most of his life in Italy, where he died in 1500. Of his sources we know more. That he wrote all his works in Latin has no doubt contributed directly to the equating of Marullus (and Ronsard through him) with Graeco-Latin poetry. But, writing love

23. Desonay, 2, 7.
24. See ibid., p. 42.

poetry in fifteenth-century Italy, Marullus could not have
escaped Petrarch's influence. More impressive than the traditional pronouncements then, are the remarks of the scholars who have studied the texts. Augusto Sainati's *La Lirica
Latina del Rinascimento* [25] is a very modest work, but
even his most summary inquiry into Marullus' sources produced this statement: "In realtà egli subí molteplici influssi:
di Catullo, di Ovidio, dell'*Antologia* greca, del Petrarca
specialmente." [26] Moreover, there is no reason to be misled
by the names of Catullus and Ovid in this list. The close relationship of Ovid to courtly love and eventually to the Petrarchistic tradition is a fact too well established to be redem-
onstrated here. Sainati attributes the influence of Catullus
on the neo-Latin poet to the fact that both were what one
might call an "amante inquieto," a man who loves but fears
to lose whom he loves: "Il Marullo aveva, egli pure, pro-
vato le gioie, le amarezze, le delusioni dell'amore: niente di
più naturale quindi che si ispirasse al poeta che aveva saputo
cosí potentemente ritrarre condizioni spirituali non troppo
diverse dalle proprie. Catullo aveva in due versi famosi
dipinto il contrasto, che gli agitava l'animo, tra l'odio e l'a-
more." [27] This "contrasto" between love and hate needs
little reworking to become a basic Petrarchan and Petrarchistic antithesis. The presence of Ovid and Catullus
among Marullus' sources, therefore, is hardly proof that all
ties with Petrarch have been abandoned.

But perhaps the text should speak for itself. The following poem from Marullus' *Epigrammaton* was translated by
Ronsard in the *Nouvelle Continuation* as a "chanson,"

> Suaviolum invitae rapio dum, casta Neaera,
> Imprudens vestris liqui animam in labiis,

25. (Pisa, 1919).
26. Ibid., p. 76.
27. Ibid., p. 77.

Exanimusque, cum nec per se ipsa rediret
Et mora lethalis quantulacunque foret,
Misi cor quaesitum animam; sed cor quoque blandis
Captum oculis nunquam deinde mihi rediit.
Quod nisi suaviolo flammam quoque, casta Neaera,
Hausissem, quae me sustinet exanimum,
Hic dies misero, mihi crede, supremus amanti
Luxisset, rapui cum tibi suaviolum.

[While I, dear Neaera, stole a little kiss against your will,
Imprudently I left my life spirit upon your lips,
And I, long lifeless, since it would not of itself return
And delay, however small, would be fatal,
I sent my heart to seek my spirit; but my heart, too,
Caught by your alluring eyes, never thereafter returned to
me.
Thus, dear Neaera, unless by one small kiss,
I had drunk in the flame which sustains my lifeless self,
This day, believe me, would have been the last of this poor
lover
When I stole a little kiss from you.] [28]

Sainati's remarks concerning this poem are short and revealing as well as exact: "Platone, Catullo, il Petrarca hanno
fornito ciascuno qualche cosa al Marullo per questa com-
posizione delicata, ma alquanto artificiosa nel fondo." [29]
True, there is a kiss, but between the kiss and its justification, as expressed in the poem, there is no clear sensual
intent. Instead, and Sainati's observation makes this evident,
the poet envelops the act in a very unsensual and philosophical framework. His spirit has fled his body to live

28. *Epigrammaton*, II.IV, "Ad Neaeram." A good modern edition of
Marullus was done by Alessandro Perosa in 1951 for the series "The-
saurus Mundi." As I know of no available translations of Marullus, the
translation given here is my own.
29. Sainati, *Lyrica*, pp. 88–89.

within the lady—a basic Platonic idea. More important, he *must* kiss her to continue life as she alone sustains him—a basic Petrarchistic idea. While the poet does enjoy a certain physical contact, the poem is less concerned with the act of the kiss than the why's and wherefore's, and they have nothing to do with "sensualité jouisseuse" but with old conceits of Petrarchistic compliment. I reproduce Ronsard's poem here to show how thoroughly unimaginative is his paraphrase and how faithfully he translates the ideas of Marullus:

> Hyer au soir que je pris maugré toy
> Un doux baiser assis de sur ta couche,
> Sans y penser, je laissay dans ta bouche
> Mon âme, las! qui s'enfuit de moy.
> Me voyant prest sur l'heure de mourir,
> Et que mon ame amuzée à te suivre
> Ne revenoit mon corps faire revivre,
> Je t'envoiay mon coeur pour la querir.
> Mais mon coeur pris de ton oeil blandissant
> Ayma trop mieux estre chez toy, ma dame,
> Que retourner: & non plus qu'à mon ame
> Ne luy chaloit de mon corps perissant.
> Et si je n'eusse en te baisant ravy
> Du feu d'Amour quelque chaleur ardente,
> Qui depuis seule (en lieu de l'ame absente
> Et de mon coeur) de vie m'a servy,
> Voulant hyer mon torment apaiser,
> Par qui sans ame & sans coeur je demeure,
> Je fusse mort entre tes bras, à l'heure
> Que maugré toy je te pris un baiser.
>
> (7, 287–88)

One verse alone, "Voulant hyer mon torment apaiser," might conceivably constitute an addition by Ronsard, but it flows too naturally from Marullus' lines and situation to afford any significant basis for considering Ronsard's adaptation profoundly sensual. As is true for so many sonnets in 1555–56, the style is lighter than the purely Petrarchistic verse and free of mythology. The form and the kiss do recall the Latin tradition. Still, in its vision of a languid lover, dependent upon the woman and complimenting her through hyperbolic suffering and attachment, the poem represents no significant departure from Petrarchistic verse. As a result, whatever conclusion may come from a comparison of Ronsard and Marullus, it cannot state that Marullus represents the abandonment of Petrarch as a model of love verse. The poems derived from Marullus demonstrate rather the same phenomenon which characterizes the sonnets of the *Continuations:* slight changes in style at the periphery of the poet's vision while its core "continues."

There are varying degrees of continuity, of course. If "Hyer au soir . . ." belongs to *Amours I* in vision, "Bon jour mon cueur, bon jour ma doulce vie" and "Belle & jeune fleur de quinze ans" are directly inspired by Ronsard's desire to counteract the obscurity of his early sonnets. "Mais voyez, mon cher esmoy" tells how her beauties "[l]e brulent," but the normal Petrarchistic fire is now meant as physical passion since he burns "desirant par grande amour/En avoir la jouissance" (7, 245). But what do these varying degrees of continuation represent, if not the same gamut of attitudes prevalent in the sonnets! In style and vision the songs and odes of the *Continuations* form a striking parallel with the sonnets and define with precision the role of Marullus in the *Continuations.* The continuity of a Petrarchistic vision, the lighter style and wider range of emotions indicate not only that Marullus did not lead Ronsard far afield of the Petrarchistic tradition, but that Marullus corresponds quite fully to Ronsard's rather confused disposition of mind in the late fifties.

Marullus, far more than an inaugurer of a new Ronsard, serves to return the poet (and the critic) to a state of flux in Ronsard's thought and a decided variety in his style. Marullus is not a cause; he is an effect. Outside the sonnet, it is the choice of Marullus which abets this flux and supplies Ronsard with convenient material for the whole gamut of his "continuation." Whatever other critics have written about Marullus and the cycles of 1555–56, the strength of the title of "continuation" cannot be dismissed lightly nor the fact that in deviating from the strict Petrarchistic style as well as vision, Ronsard shows a marked preference for a lighter style and suggestion of sensuality that are nonetheless surrounded by a tone of humility, timidity and compliment vis-à-vis the woman—a far cry from a new vision of the love sonnet!

If the theory of a rupture between *Amours I* and the *Continuations* has so far proven unacceptable, it is also true that nothing has yet been said about such unorthodox poems as "Mignongne, levés-vous" and "A son Livre," or the precise value that should be ascribed to them. The first poem is a love scene which abandons Petrarchism indirectly by creating an intimacy between poet and lady unparalleled in the Italian tradition; the second, a personal attack by Ronsard against Petrarch. Both have their place in the flux and variety of 1555–56, and it is an important place. For they serve to define most directly Ronsard's reaction to *Amours I* as one of a fainthearted and confused rebellion. Just as he pursued the love theme and imitated Marullus in the songs and odes, yet clung repeatedly to the Petrarchistic tradition, so in "Mignongne, levés-vous" and "A son Livre" he effected a definite break with certain basic elements of the Petrarchistic tradition, only to find himself not closer to a conquest of the sonnet cycle, but decidedly farther from his goal.

Of all the poems in the cycles of 1555–56, none have

contributed so much to the creation of the sensual myth as
sonnet 23 of the *Continuation:*

> Mignongne, levés-vous, vous estes paresseuse,
> Ja la gaye alouette au ciel a fredonné,
> Et ja le rossignol frisquement jargonné,
> Dessus l'espine assis, sa complainte amoureuse.
> Debout donq, allon voir l'herbelette perleuse,
> Et vostre beau rosier de boutons couronné,
> Et voz oeillets aimés, ausquels avés donné,
> Hyer au soir de l'eau, d'une main si songneuse.
> Hyer en vous couchant, vous me fistes promesse
> D'estre plus-tost que moi ce matin evaillée,
> Mais le someil vous tient encor toute sillée;
> Ian, je vous punirai du peché de paresse,
> Je vois baiser cent fois vostre oeil, vostre tetin,
> Afin de vous apprendre à vous lever matin.

A simple comparison with a nearby sonnet, number 26, can
show how truly exceptional in the *Continuation* is "Mignongne, levés-vous." (Both sonnets relate a scene between
the lover and his lady. The reader sees them together and
feels the impact of the woman's presence on the man.) The
first line of sonnet 26, "C'est grand cas que d'aimer!"
(changed in 1578 to "Amour est un charmeur") establishes
to perfection the mood of each scene. (The poet is over-
joyed; he cannot hide that he has been "charmed" and
stirred.) Both poems capitalize on the antithesis between
movement and action-less poses. In sonnet 26 the contrast is
between the poet's listlessness before any woman other
than his lady and his eloquence before his beloved.

> Sans me forçer me vient
> Un propos dessus l'autre, & jamais je ne cesse
> De baiser, de taster, de rire, & de parler

he tells her, and as a result, he loses all sense of time. In
sonnet 23 (the awakened poet chides his mistress for sleep-

ing too long. The poem's opening quite successfully translates the poet's agitation—"levés-vous"—a note to which Ronsard returns in line 5, "allon," to give parallel movement to the quatrains, while the choice of adverbs, "Ja" used twice and "Debout," "donq" modifying "allon" conveys the urgency of the poet's voice. Ronsard has never been so alive in his love sonnets as here. But the source of the pleasure in these two sonnets is rather different. The lady in sonnet 26 is still the familiar Petrarchistic woman who imparts happiness by her mere presence, and the lover's excitement is still a direct compliment. There is no tone of compliment in "Mignongne, levés-vous." The woman has never been so willing, so anti-Petrarchistic, so much a woman. She is a partner in love, and the narrator addresses her in intimacy, not adoration. It is an intimacy, moreover, not only of style but situation (the awakening after a night of love). This is an important distinction, as the many songs and odes of the *Continuations* suggest endearment and intimacy—"Petite pucelle, Angevine . . ." (7, 238), "Belle & jeune fleur de quinze ans" (7, 248)— when in reality the woman remains "plus fiere & plus cruelle/ Qu'un roc pendu dessus la mer" (7, 239) and hides beneath her friendship "une jeunette mauvaitié" (7, 248). In the emotional and thematic kaleidoscope of the *Continuations* "Mignongne, levés-vous" offers through its portrait of the lovers a variant that is in every respect an exceptional one. It is not the vision of the majority of sonnets; it is not even comparable to the portrait of the songs and odes or other poems of excitement. It is far too special to typify the sonnets of 1555–56, yet, in its very specialness, this is a poem which demands to be appreciated, for it provides Ronsard with a lyric tone unknown to the Petrarchistic tradition.

Here alone the reader finds a lyric joy in love which returns to the love sonnet a form of the emotional richness so

eloquently captured by Petrarch. Devoid of compliment
and hyperbole, "Mignongne, levés-vous" makes use of its
various elements—the lark, the nightingale, the rose bush
—to evoke the morning freshness and awakening nature
which form an integral part of the poem and a striking contrast to the indiscriminate enumeration of "Ciel, air, &
vents . . ." It is hardly conceivable that Ronsard could
not have been aware of the new potential in this portrait of
the couple, and the poem's source suggests strongly that he
was. Editors frequently remind the reader that this sonnet
follows the tradition of the medieval aubade, a fact of
which there can be little doubt. As in the case of the
Marullus imitations, Ronsard possessed a fixed model to
copy for this further departure from the Petrarchistic tradition, and his decision to write this aubade in 1556 in con-
junction with a predominant interest in Marullus has never
failed to suggest to his critics that Ronsard was also about
to redefine his sonnet poetry in terms of the lyric possibilities rediscovered in this poem. Such an interpretation sur-
prises not only by its categorical nature but by its repeated
failure to consider the concluding work of the *Nouvelle
Continuation,* where Ronsard made a clear and uncompromising statement concerning his position in 1556.

   The poem, entitled "A son Livre," is composed of three
parts: an introduction addressing his book on the dangers
of leaving its creator; a charging of the book, now deter-
mined to face the world, to explain Ronsard's lack of fidelity to Cassandre; and a justification of this infidelity
through a portrait of women in general. The sonnets of
1555–56 have already shown how important the theme of
fidelity could be and how much Ronsard's repeated reviewing of this segment of the love story is an integral part of
the poet's fluctuating throughts in the *Continuations.* The
two poems of *Amours I* analyzed at length earlier in this
chapter reveal, moreover, the importance of fidelity to the

Petrarchistic tradition. Quite in keeping with its complimentary and hyperbolic tone, the poet loves and adores his lady, *despite* her cruel beauty. Despite his pain, he is her slave, and nothing can make him desist from this enslavement. The circle of ideas is a vicious one. Fidelity to the woman means an acceptance of suffering which is the zenith of Petrarchistic compliment, so that devotion to the lady was in fact tantamount to devotion to the tradition and to a single pose of adoration. Little wonder that the Petrarchistic cycles were static and monotonous, especially in comparison with their Petrarchan prototype. Petrarch's *Rime* progressed from "In Vita" to "In Morte" but a cycle like *Amours I* progressed not at all. The woman did not die, she did not change, and the poet's fidelity never waned—or nearly never. The *Continuations* offer an interesting agglomeration of ladies' names. Cassandre is present,[30] Marie predominates, in the *Nouvelle Continuation* especially,[31] but a Jeanne is also named.[32] Of course, the cycles relate the *Continuation des Amours*, but judging by "A son Livre," Ronsard did not complete the *Continuations* without realizing that a breach of fidelity had taken place, that the situation required a justification, and most important and revealing, a literary justification as well as a moral one.

In taking up the question of fidelity to Cassandre in "A son Livre," Ronsard's discussion is not abstract. He has a very particular argument in mind, to wit, that the example of fidelity given by Petrarch is a myth. "Should anyone reproach Ronsard his infidelity to Cassandre," the poet says to his book:

> Responds luy, je te pry, que Petrarque sur moy
> N'avoit authorité pour me donner sa loy,

30. See Laumonier, 7, p. 173, sonnet 56.
31. See ibid., p. 188, sonnet 70.
32. See ibid., p. 140, sonnet 25.

> Ny à ceux qui viendroient apres luy, pour les faire
> Si long temps amoureux sans s'en pouvoir deffaire.
> (7, 3 1 7, vv. 4 1–44)

No single word stands out more pointedly in this quotation than "authorité." The immediate context suggests that Ronsard is speaking of fidelity ("sa loy"), but the presence of this poem in the *Nouvelle Continuation* makes it clear that Ronsard is speaking about a literary tradition much more than any moral convention. And later in the poem, even when Ronsard takes up the moral question more directly, the discussion continually veers toward the literary aspect of the question. Ronsard insists that Cassandre was disdainful and uncooperative in love. For this reason he was justified in leaving her, and if Petrarch remained true to his lady, it is no doubt because she was reciprocating his attentions. The only alternative is to consider Petrarch extremely foolish:

> Il estoit esveillé d'un trop gentil esprit
> Pour estre sot trente ans, abusant sa jeunesse,
> Et sa Muse, au giron d'une seule maitresse.
> Ou bien il jouissoit de sa Laurette, ou bien
> Il estoit un grand fat d'aymer sans avoir rien.
> (7, 3 1 7, vv. 46–50)

But note that according to Ronsard, Petrarch's fidelity, if true, deceived not only his youth but his Muse. Fidelity of Petrarch's sort is not only contrary to human nature, it is contrary to the demands of poetry. "A son Livre" does not elaborate upon this point, but I shall return to it presently as there is no more important statement in "A son Livre" than this linking of poetry to the demands of nature.

The remainder of the poem presents a second justification for his infidelity: woman is unworthy of such attention. She is a "sotte beste" (7, 3 1 8, vs. 64), and she and all

her race "sçavent trouver mille faintes excuses/ Apres qu'el'
ont peché!" (7, 320, vv. 108–09). Here, too, the literary
question reappears, since before closing the poem, Ronsard
will define the true lyric style of love: "Il sufist qu'on
luy [Love] chante au vray ses passions (7, 324, vs.
178). Thus, whatever the moral implications of the poem's
subject, "A son Livre" remains essentially a document
about the writing of love poetry. When Ronsard repu-
diates the authority of Petrarch in the question of fidelity, deprecates the woman to such an extent that fidelity
becomes a meaningless term, and finally defines style in
terms of "passions," he is admitting that a tone of compliment and hyperbole does not succeed in transmitting the
emotion of love, a fact born out by an analysis of "Quand
au premier . . ." and "Ciel, air & vents. . . ." Like the
aubade world of "Mignongne, levés-vous," the love vision
of "A son Livre" is patently anti-Petrarchistic, and in
spurning Petrarch's fidelity in order to speak openly of
"passions," it returns to that very essential aspect of the
aubade, the correspondence between the excitement of love
and the poetic élan. Unfortunately, the emotions of the
narrator arise out of a situation that has no place in the Petrarchistic tradition. With its singular conception of the
woman, whether she be the companion of the aubade or
the "sotte beste" of "A son Livre," and this definition of
style as the true song of passion, the new vision of love
could only return Ronsard to a love poetry comparable to
the *Folastries*. This remark is not meant to deprecate either
the aubade or the *Folastries;* there is no denying that a definite richness of expression appears in "Mignongne, levés-
vous" in contrast with *Amours I.* The poet does succeed in
transmitting to the reader a decided emotional state which
is free of compliment. But the individual success of the
aubade cannot blot out the general problems of tone and
vision that Ronsard faced at this time with the sonnet

cycle. These problems persist and it is difficult to see in what sense either of the two anti-Petrarchistic poems represents a positive attack on the failings of *Amours I*. In the case of "Mignongne, levés-vous" Ronsard possessed the example of the aubade which he faithfully imitated, and one could argue that his success is not necessarily his own. There is no attempt elsewhere in the *Continuations* to attain the richness of the aubade using the traditional Petrarchistic elements.

A close examination of "A son Livre" suggests, in addition, that Ronsard most likely did not write the poem with the calm deliberation of a poet who has redefined his aesthetics. Throughout the text Ronsard betrays diverse emotions—frustration in particular—which render the poem an angry outburst and taunting criticism but hardly a carefully elaborated literary manifesto. The verses pertaining to Petrarch are very revealing in this aspect. "Petrarque sur moy/ N'avoit authorité pour me donner sa loy . . ." exudes the petulance of the poet who recognizes his model and yet cannot rise to his heights. Frustrated the imitator proclaims himself free, as if to compensate for his failings, just as the many songs and odes of the *Nouvelle Continuation* compensate for the inadequacies of the sonnets. One feels this rather blind reaction in Ronsard's analysis of the "true" relationship between Petrarch and Laura as well: "Il estoit esveillé d'un trop gentil esprit/ Pour estre sot trente ans." This accent on "sottise" is likewise a rapid, yet shallow, form of argumentation. It reappears later in the poem when Ronsard writes, "un homme est bien sot d'aymer si on ne l'ayme" (7, 323, vs. 168). By reducing the whole affair to a question of common sense, Ronsard is not obliged to demonstrate the slightest appreciation of the literary value of Petrarch's fidelity or the lyricism inherent in Petrarch's laments. Laumonier gives as a source for this verse Marullus' line: "nam miserrimum amare non amantem est." [33] If Laumonier is right, then even Ronsard's sources betray his flippancy, for "miserrimum" is scarcely equivalent to "sot." Finally, there is the feminine ideal offered by "A son Livre": "Humble, courtoise, honeste, amoureuse & gentille,/ Sans fard, sans tromperie" (7, 322, vv. 132–33). As is true of the *Continuations* in general, the entire portrait of the ideal is one of contradictions and confusion. The poet desires a woman "sans tromperie," a desire very comprehensible from the poet's previous description of the woman as a faithless creature. But, at the same time, "A son Livre" is the poet's justification of his own infidelity. Secondly, the adjectives describe a girl who is "humble" and "honeste." Marie, Ronsard would have us believe, was such a girl, and for this reason, too, he abandoned Cassandre:

> Marie, tout ainsi que vous m'avés tourné
> Mon sens, & ma raison, par vôtre voix subtile,
> Ainsi m'avés tourné mon grave premier stile,
> Qui pour chanter si bas n'estoit point destiné.
>   (sonnet 70, vv. 1–4)

But the woman is also required to be "courtoise" and "gentille," both words which in the sixteenth century were hardly divested of their medieval connotations of "genteel" and "well-born." [34] This portrait of the ideal *bien-aimée* is no more definite, no less confused, than all the declarations of position on love, ladies, and fidelity to be found in the *Continuations*. Like the cycles to which it belongs,

---

33. Marullus, I, "Ad Neaeram."

34. Littré, *Dictionnaire, 1,* 867, gives as the first meaning of "courtois" (the only one applicable to persons): "Gracieux dans ses discours et ses manières." Huguet gives as first and second meanings of "gentillesse" ("gentille" is not listed): "noblesse" and "noblesse morale," the only meaning possible in this context. *Dictionnaire de la Langue Française du Seizième Siècle, 4* (Paris, 1946), p. 303.

"A son Livre" repeatedly betrays an agitated but unsettled mind.

The "authorité" of Petrarch, so deeply felt and observed by Ronsard in *Amours I*, has become a perceptible annoyance. Ronsard's experience in writing the *Folastries*, published in 1553, brought him even closer to the antithetical *esprit gaulois* tradition, and it was only natural that these two aspects of Ronsard's works in the early fifties should come into conflict at the time of the *Continuations*. But the 1555–56 cycles show with what confusion this clash took place and how indecisive they are in their presentation of the literary problems involved. "Mignongne, levés-vous" and "A son Livre" together succeed in relieving the tension precipitated by the poet's recent activities with the divergent *esprit gaulois* just as the aubade (permitted Ronsard to write a love sonnet about love, not compliment,) and "A son Livre" allowed him to vent his feelings about Petrarchan fidelity. No genuine conquest of the traditional sonnet form or cycle could be found, however, in the free-loving, misogynist vision of the *esprit gaulois*. The repeated recourse to Marullus proves that consciously or unconsciously, Ronsard found it more often satisfactory to work with a Petrarchistic vision but non-Petrarchistic style than to pursue within the love cycle the tone of the *Folastries*.

The period of 1555–56 portrays a veritable moment of crisis, but a crisis unsolved. The vision vacillates, the style reveals definite experimentation, and yet the Petrarchistic tradition holds. The very poem of revolt signals its strength as do the songs and odes adapted from Marullus, for only a poet deeply committed in his own mind to the imitation of Petrarch could have written the spiteful lines of "A son Livre." This poem is as much a confession as a protest. Laumonier has called "A son Livre" "capitale pour l'étude de l'évolution du génie de Ronsard" (7, 325, n. 3). The poem does have its importance, but like the stylistic changes in the *Continuations*, it is primarily important because it makes clear where some of the problems lie (fidelity, conception of the woman, a definition of style), not because it solves any of them.

Over and over the critics write that the "stille bas" originated in Ronsard's contact with new traditions, notably the *Greek Anthology* [35] and the general Graeco-Latin love world. Ronsard himself hints at this by citing new models in "A son Livre": "Tibulle,/ L'ingenieux Ovide, & le docte Catulle" (7, 324, vv. 175–76). Yet if Marullus, and Ovid or Catullus through him, have affected Ronsard's style in 1555–56, there is no true overriding revolution or change in vision and tone.

What this contact with non-Petrarchistic traditions does produce, however, is Ronsard's realization that by remaining faithful to Petrarchism, he was "abusant sa jeunesse/ Et sa Muse." The commitment to Petrarch is accompanied by a confession that Petrarchism is not compatible with human nature (his nature at least) and poetry; his Muse was stifled in the compliments and the hyperbole. Some time will be necessary for these ideas to germinate, as Ronsard is still too noticeably preoccupied with traditions as traditions and not with the question of vision as it applies to his own talent and feelings about love. But it is nonetheless from this grain of philosophy—that a tradition which deceives "youth" and "Muse" must be rejected—that Ronsard's conquest of the sonnet form and cycle will come.

INTERLUDE

Between the *Nouvelle Continuation* and the first *Edition Collective* of his works (1560), Ronsard published in the *Second Livre des Mélanges* of 1559 a small group of

35. See Weber, *Création poétique*, p. 254.

Sonets amoureux addressed to a certain Sinope. Despite numerous theories, this lady still remains an unidentified figure. But the sixteen sonnets she inspired can be read, and appearing soon after the *Continuations* and immediately before the creation of *Amours II* (the great novelty of the *Edition Collective* of 1560), they have a singular value in themselves. If "Mignongne, levés-vous" and "A son Livre" mark a moment of unresolved crisis, the old problems of vision and of tone will reappear in these *Sonets amoureux.* If, on the other hand, a new program was indeed formulated in the *Continuations,* we may expect to see such a program implemented in 1559. A knowledge of Sinope's real identity could hardly shed any constructive light on this question of orientation, but the story and its presentation, especially in comparison with the preceding cycles, bear directly on a judgment of Ronsard's intent.

In the *Sonets amoureux,* Ronsard relates a definite plot of unrequited love, attraction, preference in the woman for another man, and finally denunciation of the whole affair. Because this range of events and emotions is covered in a mere sixteen sonnets, it is natural that there should be a definite variety in theme, but the poems to Sinope actually reveal a variety of tone quite in excess of the major developments in such a story. There is the lament of unrequited love:

> Vous me laissez tout seul en un tourment si gref,
> Que je mourray de dueil, d'ire & de jalousie:
> Tout seul je le voudrois, mais une compagnie
> Vous me donnez de pleurs, qui coulent de mon chef.
>
> (II, vv. 5–8)

but there is also personal bitterness:

> Je cognois bien que ta Sinope t'ayme,
> Mais beaucoup mieux elle s'ayme soy-mesme,

> Qui seulement amy riche desire.
> Le bonnet rond, que tu prens maugré toy,
> Et des puisnez la rigoreuse loy
> La font changer & (peut estre) à un pire.
>   (XVI, vv. 9–14)

When he speaks to her of love, it may be with playful bantering:

> Je sçay que je commets envers vous une faute,
> Mais la playe d'amour que je porte si haute,
> Et si parfonde au cueur, m'a l'esprit empesché.
> Ou bien ne soyez plus si gentille & si belle,
> Ou bien je ne sçaurois (tant que vous serez telle)
> M'engarder de vouloir faire un si beau peché.
>   (XI, vv. 9–14)

with passion:

> Quand je suis tout bessé sur vostre belle face,
> Je voy dedans vos yeux je ne sçay quoy de blanc,
> Je ne sçay quoy de noir, qui m'esmeut tout le sang,
> Et qui jusques au cueur de vene en vene passe.
>   (VI, vv. 1–4)

or with not too proper suggestiveness:

> Il ne faut dedagner le troupeau de l'Eglise,
> Pourtant s'il est gaillard, jeune, frais, & dispos,
> Sejourné, gros, & gras, en aise, & en repos,
> En delices confit, en jeux & mignardise.
>   (IX, vv. 1–4)

Thus between the monotony of *Amours I* and the variety of the *Continuations*, the sonnets to Sinope have conspicuously more in common with the latter. Moreover, while Ronsard relates the entire story through sonnets, in con-

trast with his use of songs and odes in 1555–56, traces of that
intermediate zone between pure Petrarchism and sensuality
supported by the Marullian adaptations keep appearing in
the Sinope poems (in sonnets VI and IX, for example), and
this perpetual movement in ideas penetrates even the construction of several of the Sinope sonnets. Whereas the
sonnets of *Amours I*, devoted in the main to the traditional
clichés, run on in a piecemeal construction of juxtaposed
conceits, these sonnets very often proceed in a peculiar,
jerking, thesis-antithesis, manner. The finest example is
sonnet XII:

> Sinope, baisez moy: non: ne me baisez pas,
> Mais tirez moy le cueur de vostre douce halene.
> Non: ne le tirez pas, mais hors de chaque vene
> Sucez moy toute l'ame esparse entre vos bras.
>
> (vv. 1–4)

Or sonnet VIII:

> Si j'estois Jupiter, Sinope, vous seriez
> Mon espouse Junon . . .
>
> . . .
> Mais je ne le suis pas . . . ,

sonnet III:

> Avant vostre partir je vous fais un present,
>
> . . .
> Sinope, c'est mon cueur . . .
>
> . . .
> Il vous sera fidele, humble & obeïssant.
>
> . . .
> Il est de toute amour, fors la vostre, delivre:
>
> Mais la vostre le tue, & taist le mal qu'il sent,

or sonnet II:

Sinope, de mon cueur vous emportez la clef,

. . .

Et toutesfois (helas!) je ne leur porte envye,

. . .

Vous me laissez tout seul en un tourment si gref,

. . .

Tout seul je le voudrois, mais une compagnie

Vous me donnez de pleurs, qui coulent de mon chef.

Like the kaleidoscopic movement of the *Continuations*,
these sonnets grow out of the poet's dialectic of adopting
or advancing one thought only to refute or nuance it with
another. Of course, thesis-antithesis as a psychology of love
exists already in *Amours I*, and in sonnet II the dialectic is
quite close to the usual Petrarchistic conceits of hate-love,
despair-adoration. In sonnets XII and VIII, however, the
constructions with "non" and "si" occupy the entire octave
and prepare the tercets so that theme and structure in the
sonnets are virtually inseparable. Even at the most minute
level of analysis, the poet's mind retains its predilection for
variety, but for a variety that penetrates more deeply than
the accumulation of forms or moral theorizing of the *Continuations*.

Within the poems themselves, the poet hypothesizes and
explores his emotions to such a degree that the critic must
contend with an even greater lack of focus than in the
1555–56 poems. Just as Ronsard created in the *Continuations* a gamut of potentially dominant tones—lament, detachment, adoration, desire, and bantering—that remain
distinct and disjointed, so in the cycle to Sinope the poet
now constructs his themes only to contradict them. As a result, the cycle as a whole proves incapable of uniting the
themes around so stark and rich a vision as the cohesive
force of "gloria" in Petrarch's "Chiare, fresche e dolci
acque" or the recurrent "imagine" of "Pien di quella

ineffabile dolcezza." Each sonnet with this particular dialectical structure is the formulation and destruction of a
separate vision. If "A son Livre" was the announcement of
a new program for the sonnet cycles, it is rather difficult,
then, to see this new program in the *Sonets amoureux* of
1559. There is a suggestion of passion; the woman's infidelity is revealed. At the same time, there can be no denying
the presence of adoration and lament, verbal antithesis and
compliment, all of which testify to Petrarch's continued
authority.

The texts themselves are not the only reason to dispel
any theory that the *Continuations* announce a complete
reorientation of Ronsard's poetry. The subsequent fortune
of these poems to Sinope also shows that the general confusion of the late fifties had failed to produce an independent
vision which could embrace Petrarchism and yet dominate
it. The year following the publication of these sonnets,
Ronsard removed them from the *Second Livre des
Mélanges* to rearrange the majority of them in *Amours II*
with the name of Sinope transformed to Marie. With the
change in the name of the woman, nothing remained to
group these sonnets or to distinguish them from the others
written to describe an unhappy love. In 1560, at least, looking over his most recent efforts with the sonnet, Ronsard
apparently saw no reason to segregate or accentuate certain
sonnets as representing a new direction in his poetry. He
very simply grouped together the sonnets which most re-
sembled each other: the poems to Sinope and those of the
Continuations.

The themes and the style of both cycles belie any profound evolution in the mind of the poet. All the love poems
published between 1555 and 1559 belonged in *Amours II*
because they were the products of a communal inspiration:
experimentation. The dominant trend of the late fifties is
not to be found in concerted effort with vision or style but

simply in the word "variety." Even the noticeable growth
in verse with sensual overtones (sonnets VI and IX) must
not be overemphasized. The sonnets to Sinope offer nothing in their bantering or suggestive verse that is not to be
found in the *Folastries* or even *Amours I.*[36] The most important innovation in these sonnets, moreover, has little or
nothing to do with sensuality at all.

The first poem of the group is the most successful,
stylistically and thematically:

> L'an se rajeunissoit en sa verde jouvence,
> Quand je m'espris de vous, ma Sinope cruelle:
> Seize ans estoyent la fleur de vostre age nouvelle,
> Et vos beaux yeux sentoyent encore leur enfance.
> Vous aviez d'une infante encor la contenance,
> La parolle, & les pas, vostre bouche estoit belle,
> Vostre front, & vos mains dignes d'une immortelle,
> Et vos cheveux faisoyent au Soleil une offense.
> Amour, qui ce jour là si grandes beautez vit,
> Dans un marbre, en mon cueur d'un trait les escrivit:
> Et si pour le jourdhuy vos beautez si parfaittes
> Ne sont comme autresfois, je n'en suis moins ravy:
> Car je n'ay pas egard à cela que vous estes,
> Mais au doux souvenir des beautez que je vy.

I quote the entire poem to give a full sense of the sonnet's
untrammeled movement. There is a complete absence of
the dialectic structure. The poem is one of declaration, not
hypothesis, "Car je n'ay pas egard. . . ." The theme, a
description of the woman through the poet's "doux souvenir," is a familiar one, for it defines the essence of "Chiare,
fresche, e dolci acque." Nevertheless, there is slight but all-
important variant in Ronsard's use of the theme. While Petrarch recreates in the present a past image which will
never fade in his mind, Ronsard makes quite specific that he

36. See p. 37.

is recreating an image that is past in time and in reality. The poem is a conscious rejection of the present in preference to the past, and in this fact the poem is not only the most successful but the most significant sonnet of Ronsard's continued experimentation with the sonnet form and cycle.

The *Continuations* in their various departures from the Petrarchistic tradition culminated in "A son Livre," which is so basically incompatible with the Petrarchistic tradition. In keeping with the experimentation of 1555–56, Ronsard created for Sinope a series of sonnets which embrace no less wide a gamut of attitudes. But he began with a theme that partakes exclusively of neither extreme. "L'an se rajeunissoit . . ." makes a statement about the poet's position vis-à-vis the woman much as "A son Livre" did, yet one that is far less radical. Its program advocates nothing concerning the relationship between sensuality, fidelity, and poetry and gives no definition of the woman. The poet adores her; he is faithful, and he is faithful to her as representing the exceptional beauty of every Petrarchistic lady. But all in the context of the past.

On the surface, this attitude may not be excessively striking. The poet is still talking about a Petrarchistic fidelity and a Petrarchistic beauty.

At the same time, however, Ronsard has made one notable advance in dealing with a fundamental problem in the Petrarchistic tradition. Over and over the tacit equation that love equals grief, tears, mourning, and death reappears in his love verse, even in 1559:

Je devois mourir lors sans plus tarder d'une heure.
Le temps que j'ai vescu depuis telle blesseure,
Aussi bien n'a servy, qu'à m'alonger la mort.
(II, vv. 12–14)

Les Roys ny les amans ne veulent point ensemble
Avoir de compagnons. Helas! je leur ressemble:

Plustost que d'en avoir, je desire la mort.
                          (V, vv. 12–14)

And as in *Amours I*, joy and regret form a cemented
whole:

Quand d'un baiser d'amour vostre bouche me baise,
Je suis tout esperdu, tant le cueur me bat d'aise:

                    .   .   .

Mais quand toute mon ame en plaisir se consomme,
Mourant de sus vos yeux, lors pour me despiter
Vous fuiez de mon col, pour baiser un jeune homme.
                          (X, vv. 2–3, 12–14)

Avant vostre partir je vous fais un present
(Bien que sans ce present impossible est de vivre),
Sinope, c'est mon cueur, qui brule de vous suyvre.

                    .   .   .

Il est de toute amour, fors la vostre, delivre:
Mais la vostre le tue, & taist le mal qu'il sent.
                          (III, vv. 1–3, 7–8)

The conceits are Petrarchistic clichés and the pale quality of the poetry reflects an old problem—Petrarchistic
over-simplification of the Petrarchan antitheses such as love
and hate, joy and despair. If the several sonnets just quoted
show that Ronsard found no means of capturing the psychological density of the Petrarchan antitheses or of separating joy and despair when describing his state in the
present, "A son Livre" has revealed that the desire to
render love as a joyful élan devoid of torment and languishing was, nonetheless, very much on his mind. Before
"L'an se rajeunissoit," the only sonnet of continued joy in
love was "Mignongne, levés-vous," and this was feasible
only at the expense of refashioning the vision beyond all
Petrarchistic limits. In 1559 Ronsard supplied himself with

an answer to this problem in discovering that the separation of joy and lament could be effected through a separation of past and present time.

Because this new means to convey continued excitement in love is far less radical than the solution of "Mignongne, levés-vous," it is not surprising that this innovation will dominate the forthcoming creation of *Amours II*. By refusing to accept the woman as she is *in the present*, Ronsard has provided himself and his poetry with the very lyric luxury of reproducing an image of the woman made impregnable by memory and independent of the reality of his unrequited passion: the reality of the present.

The full importance of this innovation in Sinope's sonnets will become evident only in the next section with an analysis of the role of Theocritus in the edition of 1560. But even without referring to this future effort, it is possible to sense the place of these *Sonets amoureux* in the evolution of Ronsard's poetry. These poems, like the *Continuations*, show a particularly double nature—both change from and continuity with the poetry of 1552–53. The presence in the poems of 1559 of yet another innovation after the "stille bas" proves that Ronsard was still in the throes of change, traversing an interlude in a long period of general experimentation. The nature of the innovation, so conciliatory with regard to Petrarchism in contrast with the general content of "A son Livre," bears witness to the continued hold of the Petrarchistic tradition noticed in the *Continuations* and shows that if Ronsard was not above venting his frustration openly or attacking his Italian master, there was no sweeping aside of the adored for a "sotte beste." Although he terminated the affair with Sinope rather bluntly, renouncing his fidelity with a logic reminiscent of "A son Livre," "C'est trop aymé, pauvre Ronsard, delaisse/ D'estre plus sot . . ." (sonnet XVI, vv. 1–2), the story of Sinope repeatedly skirts the Petrarchistic vision of admiration and lament.

Still the poet emerged from "A son Livre" with greater daring. He had a sharper focus on the relationship between poet and lady, and suddenly only sixteen sonnets are necessary to relate an adventure in fact more complete as a narration than *Amours I* or the *Continuations*. Most important, he replaced the moral break with Petrarchism outlined in "A son Livre" with the separation in time of "L'an se rejeunissoit. . . ." Within the Petrarchistic narrative, Ronsard has remained faithful to one idea of "A son Livre" and, insofar as this innovation is specifically aimed at separating the lyric tone of joy from the traditional disappointment and lament, it has decided poetic as well as psychological implications.

The poet's new and potent theme is not without its problems, however, especially if we try to understand to what degree this innovation meets the general difficulties Ronsard has faced with the Petrarchistic tradition. It should be clear, for example, that his rejection of the present solves little regarding a satisfactory definition of the love relationship since he is even more free than before to compliment his lady. (He refuses to see her as she is.) He has increased the possibility of a cycle without movement as he holds to a moment with no regard for the temporal context in which the affair can evolve. (Sinope's story is brought to an end despite sonnet I, not as a result of it.) Finally, it makes of the woman an even more perfect being and as thoroughly removed from the portrait of the partner in "Mignongne, levés-vous" as the normal Petrarchistic description. In short, Ronsard has found a more successful means of dealing with the theme of excitement, but it is still not the élan of "Mignongne, levés-vous." Like the poems imitated from Marullus, "L'an se rajeunissoit . . ." permits the poet a momentary innovation without announcing the far-reaching review of the Petrarchistic vision which *Amours I* proved so necessary.

The edition of 1560 provides many an insight concerning the importance of "L'an se rejeunissoit . . ." in this regard. The creation of *Amours II* and the poet's recourse to Theocritus close his initial period of effort with the love theme and epitomize its meaning and accomplishments.

THEOCRITUS

It is not possible to study Ronsard for very long without realizing to what degree he was a proud and jealous poet. In private life and in his poetry, self-effacement was never a virtue Ronsard sought to cultivate. He sang his own glory and his talent openly from the earliest period of his career. In *Amours I*, however, perhaps because of the force of his commitment to imitate Petrarch, Ronsard was profoundly professional and impersonal. The cycle devotes its attention quite exclusively to love and the voice of the poet as lover. The *Continuations* present a rather different picture. Beginning with the opening sonnet to Pontus de Tyard concerning style, the voice of the poet *qua* poet begins to be heard, expressing not only the familiar themes of immortality and love of nature, but themes which have little or no relation to love. Ronsard chastizes the Loir for trying to overturn his boat when, he, a great poet, has celebrated the river so eloquently (sonnet 19). He writes a touching sonnet to the Muses without whom he would die (sonnet 12), not saying, however, whether the inspiration he draws from them is necessarily one of love. To this list could be added the numerous adaptations and translations at the end of the *Continuation* and "A son Livre" at the end of the *Nouvelle Continuation:* all poems which indicate again that the period following *Amours I* is one of crisis. In the cycles of 1552–53, the desire to follow Petrarch subordinated the poet to his poetry. Now, engaged in the examination as well as the execution, of his poetry, Ronsard watches himself as he writes, including among the love poems the voice of the poet as himself, aroused to greater consciousness by the problems of the moment, and writing about many subjects other than poetry or love.

Of all the poems originally published in the *Continuations* which do not treat of love, the most famous by far is "Bel Aubepin":

> Bel aubepin verdissant,
> Fleurissant
> Le long de ce beau rivage,
> Tu es vestu jusqu'au bas
> Des longs bras
> D'une lambrunche sauvage.
>
> Deux camps drillantz de fourmis
> Se sont mis
> En garnison soubz ta souche:
> Et dans ton tronc mi-mangé
> Arangé
> Les avettes ont leur couche.
>
> Le gentil rossignolet
> Nouvelet,
> Avecque sa bien aymée,
> Pour ses amours aleger
> Vient loger
> Tous les ans en ta ramée:
>
> Dans laquelle il fait son ny
> Bien garny
> De laine & de fine soye,
> Où ses petitz s'eclorront,
> Qui seront
> De mes mains la douce proye.

> Or' vy gentil aubepin,
> Vy sans fin,
> Vy sans que jamais tonnerre,
> Ou la congnée, ou les vens,
> Ou les tems
> Te puissent ruer par terre.
>
> (7, 242–44)

The poem is perhaps most readily appreciated as a description of the hawthorn and a statement of desire that the tree may live forever in view of its many services. In detail, however, the poem is complex and poses certain problems not easily solved. In the description, for example, while the tree is originally depicted as "verdissant/Fleurissant," Ronsard also writes that its branches are covered with a wild vine and its bark infested with ants. Later on, though the tone has been one of admiration and appreciation before the selfless hospitality of the hawthorn, the poet does not hesitate to insert himself into the poem as stealing from the branches the small birds which the tree has protected and fostered, as if suddenly this admiration were in fact but greedy opportunism. Finally, the poet's concluding exhortation, "Vy sans fin" ("Live forever"), is gradually tempered by the verses that follow. When he writes, "May the tree live on" in spite of the natural elements which might fell it, it is as if, again, the poet has changed his orientation, so that instead of indicating "Live forever," he really meant "Live on, to suffer not a violent and premature death, but rather the normal course of existence."

Of these three problematic aspects, the second is the least difficult to analyze. When Ronsard speaks of the birds as his "proye," he qualifies the word with the adjective "douce" ("sweet"), which I would interpret to mean "source of sweetness." He is stealing a nightingale not with the predatory, destructive intent of a hunter, but rather with the distinctly poetic desire for sweetness and beauty, represented here by the music of the bird. For all its harshness, then, the word "proye" is the most significant word in the poem, for it defines in itself (seizing) and in its context (stealing an object of sweetness) the poem's inspiration as well as what may be termed the nexus of Ronsard's relationship to the hawthorn and to nature in general. The hawthorn, the rose, the Loir, the Gâtine forest, each in its way offers the poet something to seize, a very sweet grist for the poetic mill. The word "proye" remains, nevertheless, a strong, uncompromising word. Perhaps Ronsard chose it because of the rhyme; I should like to think, however, that it was the word "proye" and not its rhyme "soye" which occupied the poet's attention. It is, after all a word for which there was no substitute, whereas the use of "soye" (material with which the nest is constructed) permits many more possibilities. That "proye" was very likely of such importance is suggested, moreover, by the remaining questions concerning the state of the hawthorn and the sense of "Vy."

There exists in all three cases a common thread of thought: the idea of death. The hawthorn, for all its generosity (indeed because of it), nurtures elements which literally live from its flowering. The birds it protects cannot be protected from the poet, who, like the ants and vines, uses the tree to his advantage and, by robbing it, betrays its selflessness. Little wonder, then, that the poet's conclusion turns about the tree's existence. For, in addition to the tree's parasites, and man, there are the natural elements of wind and lightning to beset this source of sweetness. "Bel Aubepin" in its totality is a profound commentary on life and beauty, their continuity and fate. In this light the opposition between "verdissant/Fleurissant" and the "lambrunche" or the "fourmis" is no unconscious slip of the pen, but essential to the poem's meaning, as essential as the harshness of "proye." Whether we are reading "Mignonne,

allon voir," "Comme on voit sur la branche . . ." or "Bel
Aubepin," the beauty and freshness of natural objects are
inseparable in Ronsard from their fateful opposites. And as
regards the poet's qualification of "Vy sans fin," I would
suggest that Ronsard does propose a quiet death and not
eternal life. He recognizes as in the "Cueillés" of "Mignonne, allon voir," that there is no ultimate escape from the
workings of "maratre Nature," but hopes for a full existence of pleasure, whether it be the joy of love or the creation of beauty, beyond the accidents of fortune and the
violence of fate.

"Bel Aubepin" adds quite another dimension to the
poet's preoccupations with himself and his art by showing
to what extent the *Continuations* can stray from the subject of love into the realm of philosophy, and that new
dimension bears an important resemblance to the innovation of the *Sonets amoureux* of 1559. It is truly remarkable
that soon after a period of confusion and indecision about
his work coupled with a pronounced preoccupation with
death,[37] Ronsard should follow "Bel Aubepin" with an
innovation in his love poetry that shuns the realities of the
present and holds love to a remembered image which never
changes. In each case the poet expresses a desire for
permanence in the face of discontinuity and difficulty. May
the hawthorn live on, though its life is predestined to be in-
vaded by man, its parasites, and the elements. Let his image
of his lady be attacked by time, he will blot out all but the
reality of a memory. Both statements mark in slightly
different contexts the same malaise and crisis of Ronsard's
love verse. His experimentation with new themes, his frustration before the "authorité" of Petrarch: all this must be
seen finally in a total picture of search and realization
which brought Ronsard to an eventual awareness of the

37. In addition to "Bel Aubepin" he composed during this time
"L'Hymne de la Mort" (1555) and the ode "Quand je dors" (1556).

eternal problems of life as well as love. The desire for stability encompasses the two worlds, and it is in response to
the problems of each that in 1560 Ronsard constructed his
new cycle of *Amours II*.

Amours II is an attempt toward stability, both in the
organization of a sonnet cycle and in the formulation of a
vision of love. To the lapse in effort to create such a cycle
in 1555 and 1556, when Ronsard moved farther and farther
from the sonnet to flood the cycles with songs and odes,
the poet reacts by suppressing from further love cycles
most of the poems such as "Bel Aubepin" which were not
written in the sonnet form and do not deal directly with
the subject of love. In addition, while he willingly used
most of his love sonnets written between 1555 and 1559 to
form *Amours II*, Ronsard excluded all the sonnets addressed to patrons and important personages, of which the
Nouvelle Continuation contained a long series. *Amours II*
was to be truly a cycle of sonnets, and truly a cycle of love.
The few songs Ronsard retained break the monotony of
the sonnets but in no way duplicate the variety of the
Continuations. For this newest love story Ronsard also
created a structure, placing at the beginning, middle, and
conclusion of the cycle three long poems of discussion and
analysis concerning the affair. The first poem is an old
friend, "A son Livre," whose presence in *Amours II* must
be interpreted with care. It could suggest, for example, that
Ronsard was still insistent on rejecting Petrarch's authority
in favor of a philosophy in keeping with the *esprit gaulois*
tradition. In truth, the two other poems in *Amours II*
written especially for this cycle, "Voyage de Tours" and
"Elégie à Marie," find their inspiration in a source quite
different from the vision of "A son Livre." This source,
however, is also not Petrarchistic, and for this reason, the

principal value of placing "A son Livre" at the beginning
of *Amours II* I would interpret to be the continued announcement that the poet is free of Petrarch, free to select
his inspiration and vision where he wants. "Voyage de
Tours" and "Elégie à Marie," are both, like "A son Livre,"
long poems in rhymed couplets. The choice of this verse
form for the new poems of 1560 is rather paradoxical if we
assume that Ronsard is now anxious to place the sonnet in a
dominant position again. But this paradox, the particular
vision of *Amours II*, the structure of the cycle, and the relation of all these aspects to Ronsard's search for stability
can be explained through Ronsard's conscious recourse to
the poetry of Theocritus.

Of Theocritus we know only that he lived somewhere
between 300 B.C. and 260 B.C. and was influenced by the
Alexandrian poetry of the period.[38] This school, in react-
ing against the epic and tragedy of ancient Greece, favored
shorter genres and a very artificial and erudite poetry.
Modern criticism of Theocritus, though recognizing his relation to Alexandrian poetry, has not always agreed that he
participated fully in this cult of the artificial. As A. S. F.
Gow cogently remarks, Theocritus "has often been looked
on as an unsophisticated singer of the countryside, immortalizing the artless ditties of his rustic friends." [39] And
it seems certain that to the Pléiade Theocritus was, indeed,
this "unsophisticated singer of the countryside." Not Ronsard, but Baïf among the "brigade" was the first to discover
the verse of Theocritus and imitate him extensively in his
poetry, a fact Ronsard willingly admitted in 1558 to the
Cardinal of Lorraine:

38. See A. S. F. Gow, *The Greek Bucolic Poets* (Cambridge, 1953)
and Legrand's introduction to Théocrite, *Bucoliques grecs* (Paris, 1925).
39. Gow, p. xxiii.

Et le docte Baïf qui seul de noz Poëtes
A fait en ton honneur bourdonner ses Musettes,
Te sacrant ses pasteurs, que d'un gentil esprit
En France il a conduit des champs de Theocrit.

(*9, 69*)

The singling out of "pasteurs" and "champs" shows that
for Ronsard the essence of Theocritus was in his pastoral
setting, not the particular quality of his verse. Miss Alice
Hulubei, in her study of the eclogue, suggests that Ronsard
was attracted to Theocritus and the eclogue in general because of the greater facility it provided the poet in develop-
ing his themes, especially praise and flattery.[40] *Amours II,*
however, shows that Ronsard also perceived the value of
the eclogue in a love context, and Baïf's adaptation of
Theocritus in his pastoral love poems may well explain
Ronsard's return to the sonnet cycle in 1560. Whatever the
chain of events, Ronsard was firm in his choice of Theocritus as a model for the new poems of *Amours II,* so firm
that while on the one hand he suppressed from the *Continuations* nearly all the poems which were not sonnets, he
wrote for the new cycle no new sonnets but two long
poems of the eclogue-Theocritus tradition introduced by
Baïf.

The following poem by Theocritus, entitled "Le Bien-
Aimé" in Legrand's translation, is a fine example of The-
ocritus' style, and its great influence on the "Elégie à
Marie" makes it of particular interest in understanding
Ronsard's appreciation of Theocritus' poetry.

> Tu es venu, cher enfant!—tu es venu, avec la troisième
> nuit et la troisième aurore! Ceux qui soupirent vieillis-
> sent en un jour. Autant la belle saison est plus douce
> que l'hiver, autant la pomme que la prune sauvage,

40. Alice Hulubei, *L'Eglogue en France au XVI*ᵉ *siècle* (Paris, 1938),
p. 402.

autant la toison de la brebis est plus épaisse que celle de son agneau, autant la vierge l'emporte sur la femme trois fois mariée, autant la biche est plus légère que la génisse, autant le rossignol à la voix harmonieuse est prince du chant parmi tous les oiseaux, autant tu m'as réjoui en paraissant, et j'accourus, comme sous l'ombrage d'un chêne un voyageur lorsque le soleil brûle.

Puissent les Amours sur nous deux souffler d'un souffle pareil! Puissions-nous, pour tous ceux qui vivront après nous, devenir un sujet de chant: "Ils furent, chez les hommes d'autrefois, un couple de mortels divins: l'un qu'appellerait *eispnèlos* [41] celui qui parle la langue d'Amyclées; et l'autre que, d'accord avec le Thessalien, il appellerait *aïtès*.[42] Ils s'aimèrent l'un l'autre également sans que penchât la balance. Certes, c'était alors de nouveau l'âge d'or, quand l'aimé aimait en retour!" Puisse-t-il en être ainsi, auguste fils de Cronos! puisse-t-il en être ainsi, Immortels qui ne vieillissez point! Puisse, dans deux cents générations d'ici, quelqu'un venir me dire aux bords de l'Achéron d'où l'on ne ressort pas: "L'amour qui t'unissait à ton charmant bien-aimé est maintenant sur les lèvres de tous, principalement dans le monde des jeunes gens."

Mais, là-dessus, les dieux fils d'Ouranos aviseront comme ils veulent. Pour moi, je puis faire ton éloge, bel enfant, sans risquer que sur la pointe de mon nez poussent des boutons de mensonge. Car, s'il t'arrive de me faire de la peine, aussitôt tu guéris la peine que tu m'as faite; tu me donnes deux fois plus de joie; et je m'en vais ayant plus que mon compte.

Habitants de Mégare Niséenne, qui excellez au maniement des rames, vivez heureux chez vous, vous qui avez honoré par dessus tous les autres l'hôte venu

41. Gow translates as "Inspirer."
42. Gow translates as "Hearer."

d'Attique, Dioclès le tendre amant. Chaque année, au début du printemps, les jeunes garçons en foule autour de son tombeau luttent pour emporter le prix du baiser; et celui qui a, sur des lèvres, imprimé plus suavement ses lèvres, retourne à sa mère chargé de couronnes. Heureux qui est, au milieu des enfants, l'arbitre de ces baisers! Sans doute il invoque instamment Ganymède aux yeux de lumière pour avoir une bouche comme la pierre de Lydie, avec quoi les changeurs véridiques reconnaissent si l'or n'est pas mauvais.[43]

Neither of the modern scholars who have edited Theocritus shows an extended interest in this poem, which does lend itself to several criticisms. The organization, for example, is rather fluid. The poem advances in small blocks—the comparisons, the desire to be sung as a perfect couple, the kissing games—which bear only the slightest relation to each other, and Theocritus has not tried to provide the poem with transitional passages to introduce each of these sections. The Alexandrian penchant for recondite expressions appears in the names of various gods and the geographical allusions, as well as the poet's evident pleasure in introducing two words of dialect. The tone of the poem does not remain entirely constant as Theocritus moves from section to section. While the beginning portions depict an exalted lover, the section introduced by "Mais, là-dessus . . . ," with its rather unaesthetic image concerning the man's sincerity, marks the beginning of a movement toward a less exalted tone. The concluding section shares the tone of neither. The description of the love games leads not to the exaltation of love, but an appreciation, much more sensual, of the judge's role. Yet Ronsard found the poem very useful and imitated in 1560 both the story of the love games and the lover's desire to be sung.

43. Théocrite, *Bucoliques*, pp. 82–83.

It is a sign of the times that Ronsard shows no interest in reproducing the many hyperbolic comparisons found in Theocritus' introductory section. Ronsard was serious when he put "A son Livre" at the beginning of *Amours II*. He could now do without such complimentary hyperbole. The kissing contest, however, was intriguing. It was quite in keeping with the simple, pastoral vision of the Golden Age which Theocritus evoked. The scene suggests nothing of the orgiastic but rather unabashed, unconscious play —an image which Ronsard could well appreciate after the complexities and complexes of the Petrarchistic tradition. It is Ronsard's interest in the section "Puissent les Amours . . . ," however, which brings his affinity for Theocritus most clearly into focus. Long before 1560 Ronsard shared with Theocritus the desire to be sung and immortalized, but he did not express himself in the special way in which Theocritus develops the theme in "Le Bien-Aimé." The speaker goes so far as to write the song himself and create, therefore, a fictitious but happy story of love. Like "L'an se rajeunissoit . . . ," the result is a poem that consciously prefers to ignore the actual relationship in favor of the portrait of love as it was in the Golden Age.

From this pastoral world Ronsard fashioned his love vision in 1560. He made it the conscious poetization of his story, the creation of a progressively Never-Never world of fictional happiness. There, if nothing was real, nothing could be ephemeral and unstable, and through the gradual movement of the cycle's narrative into this world, the story at last attained a structure.

"Voyage de Tours" relates a trip taken by two young men, Perrot and Thoinet, to attend a wedding. When they arrive, they come upon their *bien-aimées*, Marion and Francine. Each man addresses a long discourse to his girl, and these speeches form the substance of the poem.

Thoinet begins. There are two distinct parts to his speech. The first recounts his meeting with Francine: "C'estoit au mois d'Avril, Francine, il m'en souvient," he says. And the act of remembering brings forth a complete repetition of the theme of the first sonnet to Sinope:

> Il y a bien six ans, & si dedans l'oreille
> J'entens encor' le son de ta vois nompareille,
> Qui me gaigna le coeur, & me souvient encor
> De ta vermeille bouche & de tes cheveus d'or,
> De ta main, de tes yeus: & si le tems qui passe
> A depuis dérobé quelque peu de leur grace,
> Si est-ce que de toi je ne suis moins ravy
>
>   * * *
>
> Car je n'ay pas égard à cela que tu es,
> Mais à ce que tu fus, tant les amoureus traits
> Te graverent dans moy, voire de telle sorte
> Que telle que tu fus telle au coeur je te porte.
>   (*10*, 217–18, vv. 81–87, 91–94)

He seeks counsel in the occult powers of a certain Janeton and other means of knowing the future only to learn that "seulement la mort/ Dénoura le lien qui [l]e serre si fort" (*10*, 219, vv. 107–08)—a remark which seems to confirm the permanence of a love so independent of reality. But despite Ronsard's evident intent to prolong beyond the *Sonets amoureux* a simple and stable vision of the lover's situation, the second part of Thoinet's speech is quite different. Recalling the *innamoramento*, and still in its power, he longs to enjoy this love rather than to remember it. He pleads with Francine to end her cruel indifference and, in a conflict reminiscent of the confusion in the Sinope group, the speech is ultimately unable to separate love from despair despite the supposed security offered by memory. Like the traditional Petrarchistic lover, Thoinet is not really capable of effecting the shift to memory announced

in the opening verses of his speech. The perfection he remembers does not satisfy him, and the prophecy of an eternal love proves in the end a source of eternal lament. When
his speech is over, Thoinet falls into a faint and, significantly, in the poem's concluding scene immediately tries to
follow Francine upon regaining his senses, while Perrot re-
strains him and takes him away to find lodging. The portrait of Thoinet is from every aspect the description of the
Petrarchistic lover. The force of the introduction concerning memory is quickly nullified, and the final image of
Thoinet reveals a traditional hapless lover.

The same ending indicates that Perrot does not share
Thoinet's attitudes, and the speech Ronsard created for
him differs profoundly from Thoinet's. Ronsard has perhaps "arranged" the stage a bit. Before Perrot can talk to
Marion, her mother speeds her away in a boat. As a result,
Perrot's speech is scarcely the confrontation between lover
and lady of Thoinet's remarks. At Marion's departure, the
reality of river, boat, and woman passes quickly into a
poetic portrait. To the sight of the passing boat, Perrot
offers a "convoy" committing her person to the care of the
river and evoking a framework of nymphs and beautiful
flowers to accompany her on the journey. His initial remarks do explore the possibilities of reunion: "Que ne puis-
je muer ma resamblance humaine/ En la forme de l'eau qui
cette barque emmeine!" (*10*, 224–25, vv. 233–34). He
would be a water creature, a Glaucus, and win her with
Hippomenes' apples. Perrot is beginning to sound like
Thoinet and recalls him even more when, after the Glaucus
image, he says, "Or cela ne peult estre." The reader foresees despair and lament in the face of this impossible love.

Ronsard, however, has other intentions. Here is the full
verse and the verse following: "Or cela ne peult estre, & ce
qui se peult faire/Je le veus achever afin de te complaire"
(*10*, 226, vv. 253–54). The about-face is to be a positive

turning in the poem. The poet catches himself at the brink
of despair in his effort to be united with Marion; he rejects
the outlandish metamorphoses so common in *Amours I* [44]
and devotes his effort to "ce qui se peult faire."

He is referring to the creation of the pastoral portrait, a
world of peace amid nature:

> Je veus faire un beau lit d'une verte jonchée,
>
> .   .   .
>
> Je veus jusques au coude avoir l'herbe, & si veus
> De roses & de lis coronner mes cheveus.
>
> (*10*, 226, vv. 261, 267–68)

After the extravagance of the Glaucus image, this simple
scene is all the more striking, but it is also striking because
by selecting it over the Petrarchistic metamorphoses, Ronsard makes explicit the shift in vision we have had to observe by inference. "Or cela ne peult estre" is the basic
message of "A son Livre" regarding fidelity, adoration of
the woman, and, in a word, the entire complex of Petrarchistic conceits, while the assurance of "ce qui se peult
faire" is Ronsard's new-found security in Theocritus. It is
as if, after the *crise de conscience* of "A son Livre," after
all the vain hypothesizing of the *Sonets amoureux*, Ronsard
knew literally, "what could be done" with the love theme.

In so far as Theocritus and the pastoral vision represent
his new answer, "Voyage de Tours" exhibits a sometimes
fumbling execution. Perrot avoids the difficulties of
Thoinet, but in his formulation of the songs to be sung by
posterity—"Melchoir champenois et Guillaume manceau"
(*10*, 227, vs. 275)—relating his pastoral bliss, he includes
the real story:

> Comment, pour flechir ta rigueur,
> Je t'appellay ma vie, & te nommay mon coeur,
> Mon oeil, mon sang, mon tout: mais ta haute pensée
> N'a voulu regarder chose tant abaissée,

44. See p. 37.

Ains en me desdaignant tu aimas autre part
Un, qui son amitié chichement te départ.

(10, 227, vv. 279–84)

It is the old story of Sinope repeated, but now, instead of postulating and speaking of happiness as a condition contrary to fact ("Si j'estois Jupiter . . ."), he speaks in the present:

Ou bien, si tu ne veus, il me plaist de me rendre
Angevin, pour te voir, & ton langage aprendre,
Et là, pour te flechir, les hauts vers que j'avois
En ma langue traduit du Pindare Gregeois,
Humble je rediray en un chant plus facile
Sur le dous chalumeau du pasteur de Sicille.
Là, parmy tes sablons, Angevin devenu
Je veus vivre sans nom comme un pauvre incognu.

(10, 228, vv. 309–16)

It is hard to recognize the arrogant Ronsard in such a pose, but it is not difficult to appreciate the poetic release it furnished, the freedom to bypass the antitheses and the depression of unrequited love.

If Ronsard placed "Flégie à Marie" at the end of *Amours II,* it is because from every aspect this poem is the most successful adaptation of the Theocritus idyl. From the very beginning Ronsard defines his intention in such a way as to accentuate a concentration in effort:

Marie, à celle fin que le siecle advenir
De nos jeunes amours se puisse souvenir,
Et que vostre beauté que j'ay long tems aimée
Ne se perde au tumbeau par les ans consumée,
 Sans laisser quelque merque apres elle de soi,
Je vous consacre icy le plus gaillard de moi,
L'esprit de mon esprit, qui vous fera revivre
Ou long tems, ou jamais, par l'aage de ce livre.

(10, 238, vv. 1–8)

Not only is the poem written with the express intention of immortalizing Marie and establishing a poetic monument to her rather than a picture or résumé of their relationship, but Ronsard offers her "le plus gaillard de [lui]/ L'esprit de [s]on esprit."

This quintessence of talent takes the form of a quintessence of the idyllic vision. In "Elégie à Marie" Ronsard goes beyond the expression of a simple wish for a perfect love to give a full description of pastoral, agrarian settings which avoids completely the problems of relating in detail the poet and his lady in the present. He takes up a theme of "Le Bien-Aimé" to describe their love as perfect harmony:

> Je voudrois bien
> Qu'Amour nous eust conjoinct d'un semblable lien,
> Et qu'apres nos trespas dans nos fosses ombreuses
> Nous fussions la chanson des bouches amoureuses,
>
> . . .
>
> Et que ceus là d'Anjou disent tous d'une voix:
> Nostre belle Marie aima un Vandomois,
> Tous les deus n'estoient qu'un, & l'amour mutuelle,
> Qu'on ne voit plus ici, leur fut perpetuelle.
> Leur siecle estoit vraiment un siecle bien heureus.
>
> (*10*, 242–43, vv. 93–95, 101–05)

While "voudrois" and "qu'on ne voit plus ici" both suggest that the reality of the situation is quite different, it is noteworthy that Ronsard no longer mentions in the commemorating song Marie's preference for another. The rest of the poem, again borrowing heavily from Theocritus, enlarges upon this evasion by presenting Ronsard and Marion as local deities with a temple and games (kissing games, of course) to honor them.

This portrait of the couple as gods whose love the country celebrates not only moves the cycle far outside the reality that "Voyage de Tours" admits, it comes very close to creating a formal myth and marks the culmination of a structure that begins with the quarrel with Petrarch ("A son Livre"), proceeds to an express desire for a happiness that is belied ("Voyage de Tours"), and ends in "Elégie à Marie" with a pastoral fiction that moves toward the myth. Ronsard's attempt here to burst the impasse of fidelity to, yet dissatisfaction with the Petrarchistic sonnet even prompted a very frank expression of intent:

> Je veus en vous chantant vos louanges parfaire,
> Et ne sentir jamais mon labeur engourdi
> Que tout l'ouvrage entier pour vous ne soit ourdi.
>
> (*10*, 239, vv. 24–26)

These verses from "Elégie à Marie" contain, I think, yet another slap at Petrarch and a tradition which for so long had troubled Ronsard by not permitting him to "ne sentir jamais [s]on labeur engourdi." Theocritus may well have been an affected erudite Alexandrian poet, but Ronsard saw him as something else: a poet whose flight into the idyllic could permit him to perfect the lady's praises and lighten his efforts. We could not ask for a better expression of Ronsard's debt to Theocritus than these three lines. Through Theocritus' poetry, he knew he could accomplish the aims he outlined, leave behind the sonnet and its difficulties, and turn to happy, flowing verse.

From the point of view of Ronsard's intention, *Amours II* scored a singular victory, but it was a Pyrrhic victory. The sonnet is once again the dominant genre; the cycle has a definite structure; the poet has found a new vision to impart a joyful élan to his poetry. However, Ronsard did not write any new sonnets for *Amours II*. He embraced the

world of the elegy and the eclogue, too different in scope
and expression to be of much use to the sonnet form. As
for the story itself, the temple, the games, the songs to be
sung by future generations, none of this belongs to a personal portrait of emotion. It belongs to the man and to the
poet Ronsard, not the lover. When Ronsard describes in
"Voyage de Tours" the world he desires, he speaks little of
love but a great deal of poetry:

> Pour te flechir, les hauts vers que j'avois
> En ma langue traduit du Pindare Gregeois,
> Humble je rediray en un chant plus facile
> Sur le dous chalumeau du pasteur de Sicille.
>   (*10*, 228, vv. 311–14)

The appearance of the poet's voice in the sonnet cycle, beginning in the *Continuation*, has in the long run hindered
Ronsard's development of the sonnet cycle and the sonnet
form. He has escaped the difficulties of both by moving
away into happier, easier realms of pastoral bliss. The discovery of Theocritus facilitated the poet's task, but in
order to say "Je veus . . . / . . . ne sentir jamais mon
labeur engourdi," he had to avoid the problems posed by
Amours I, notably the description of the woman or the description of the lover's attitude, which in Ronsard's case
would have to include love and desire to be sufficiently in
accord with the poet's own sentiments.

His treatment of source material also attests to an external approach in these years. The song from Marullus
was scarcely altered. The same is true of the material Ronsard borrowed from Theocritus. The desire to be sung and
commemorated,

> O ma belle maistresse, & que je voudrois bien
> Qu'Amour nous eust conjoinct d'un semblable lien,
> Et qu'apres nos trespas dans nos fosses ombreuses
> Nous fussions la chanson des bouches amoureuses,
>   (*10*, 242, vv. 93–96)

is but a verse translation of "Puissions-nous, pour tous ceux qui vivront après nous, devenir un sujet de chant." [45] And the kissing game,

> Mais tous les jouvenceaux en païs d'alentour,
>
> . . .
>
> S'assembleroient au temple avecques leurs aimées.
>
> . . .
>
> Celui qui mieus seroit en ses baisers apris,
> Sur tous les jouvenceaus emporteroit le pris,
> Seroit dit le veinqueur des baisers de Cythere
> Et tout chargé de fleurs s'en iroit à sa mère,
> <div align="right">(<i>10</i>, 241–42, vv. 77, 80, 89–92) [46]</div>

are not significantly different from the games of Diocles,

> Chaque année, au début du printemps, les jeunes garçons en foule autour de son tombeau luttent pour emporter le prix du baiser; et celui qui a, sur les lèvres, imprimé plus suavement ses lèvres, retourne à sa mère chargé de couronnes.[47]

On the other hand, it is not necessary to go so far as Desonay, who called "Elégie à Marie," "la très littéraire conclusion d'une aventure amoureuse," [10] and who has said of "Voyage de Tours" that Ronsard did not create the poem "à l'intention de la fillette de Bourgueil, mais pour 'théocritiser' tout son saoul." [49] There can be no doubt that Desonay is right in interpreting these poems as conscious efforts to transcribe Theocritus into French. But it is equally obvious that the critic must see beyond the general

---

45. Théocrite, p. 82.
46. Ronsard does leave out the lover's envy of the judge, giving the segment a more unified tone. On the other hand, his verses are not to be considered any less sensual. Ronsard adds (vv. 82–83): "& qui mieus baiseroit,/ Ou soit d'un baiser sec, ou d'un baiser humide."
47. Théocrite, p. 83
48. Desonay, *2*, 177.
49. Ibid., p. 176.

question of borrowing and into the internal questions of Ronsard's position in 1560. Imitating Theocritus was more than a renewed flexing of the poetic muscles. What Desonay's remarks do not take into account is the inspirational value of the model. There is a distinct emotional side to the use of Theocritus in 1560, even if the élan remains an affair between the poet and his model and not between the poet and his subject: Theocritus afforded Ronsard a point of departure that was a true respite from the Petrarchistic tradition and yet another chance to fulfill the gnawing sentiment that love should engender a portrait of joy.

Whatever personal preferences may encourage the reader to praise Ronsard's initial cycle or more earthy poems of the *Continuations,* the period from 1552 to 1560 must remain, in retrospect, a form of apprenticeship for Ronsard in the art of the sonnet cycle, a period in which his effort to rival Petrarch has had to give way more and more to a painful recognition of many insufficiencies. At the end of repeated recourse to other poets, Ronsard is still not a master of the genre. He has seen certain basic difficulties ("A son Livre"); he has attempted innovations ("L'an se rajeunissoit . . ."), but in a spirit essentially of facilitating, not overcoming his problems ("Elégie à Marie").

In many ways, though the Thoinet of "Voyage de Tours" is meant to represent Baïf, and Perrot Ronsard, Thoinet's confused attitude toward Francine is actually much closer to the Ronsard of 1560. *Amours II* presented a love story that was pastoral and highly poetic, but in other poems of the edition of 1560, a more sensual, earthy voice was dominant. In an "Amourette" Ronsard invites his love, with the coming of spring, to "folastres jeux." He knows her resistance to be feigned, "Car toute fille, encor' qu'elle ait envie/ Du jeu d'aimer, desire estre ravie" (*10,* 121, vv.

25–26). This "Amourette" along with several other pieces of similar nature written later in the sixties was eventually to be included in *Amours II*, but in 1560 this poem was put with a general collection entitled simply "Poems." Ronsard was permitting no contamination of genres, no contamination of themes beyond the poems borrowed from Theocritus. The exclusion of this poem from *Amours II* resembles Perrot's restraint of Thoinet at the end of "Voyage de Tours" and the dialectical structure of so many sonnets to Sinope. In each case the poet has not been able to banish from his creation very conflicting views on love. We could not ask for more graphic evidence of Ronsard's unsettled poetic intentions throughout 1555–60 than this persistent doubling in attitudes toward love where the poet repeatedly innovates but rejects, experiments but avoids the principal issues. If Ronsard could escape to the future, he could not escape the fact that *Amours II* was a cycle built around eclogues and "continued" sonnets. To bring his poetry, his character, and his ambitions into harmony, new and broader soundings were necessary, and Ronsard did not fail to act.

2. The Emergence of a Personal Vision

A Philosophy

BETWEEN 1560 and 1578 Ronsard did not publish another sonnet cycle, nor did he publish any sonnets in significant numbers prior to 1569. The fact that his Pléiade contemporaries, too, abandoned the sonnet cycle during this period [1] points to a general lack of interest on the part of poets in this genre. In Ronsard's case, it has also been suggested that he simply had no more to say. Henri Chamard, upset at this charge that after 1560 Ronsard's inspiration had begun to wane, insists the lyric talent was there but that Ronsard was to make less and less use of it: "Mais l'heure allait sonner où, sans cesser d' . . . être [lyrique] encore, il devait cependant l'être de moins en moins." [2] He gives two reasons: exhaustion ("épuisement") of the lyric themes, "si bien doué que soit un poète, il ne peut indéfiniment, sous peine de se répéter, chanter le vin, l'amour, et même la nature," [3] and transformation of the status of the poet, who, after the death of Saint-Gelais (October 1558), succeeded to the post of official court poet. His duties, insists Chamard, drew Ronsard progressively into the realm of the encomiastic and, as the clouds of religious dissension gathered, into the polemic.

For us, who have been following closely the evolution of the poet's love cycles, Charmard's choice of arguments affords an interesting complementary analysis of the trends as we have seen them take form since *Amours I*. Ronsard's

1. See Henri Chamard, *Histoire de la Pléiade* (4 vols. Paris, 1939), 3.
2. Ibid., 2, 354.
3. Ibid., p. 354.

success at court not only meant new tasks, it meant that a good deal of the necessity for writing love poetry was removed. His talent was officially recognized. More important, however, is Chamard's comment on the exhaustion of the lyric themes—a revealing corollary of the impasse Ronsard faced in 1560. The sense of "épuisement" as I would use the term is slightly different from Charmard's, nevertheless. That Ronsard had exhausted his inspiration is a matter relative to the poetic possibilities he commanded. Since 1552 Ronsard had turned around and around the problems of the sonnet and the sonnet cycle, repeatedly escaping instead of meeting the basic problems he faced. This is the real "épuisement" of 1560: the incapacity of the poet to use in an original context the love themes and styles he had inherited.

The abandonment of the sonnet form at this time need not be interpreted as a decline of the lyric voice, however, for the poet's awareness of this relative "épuisement" and of the basic problems raised by the portrait of lover, lady, and their relationship as well as his desire to conquer the love sonnet, continue to play a role in Ronsard's writing long after 1560. But now Ronsard worked upon these problems in a different context, as if sensing that further experimentation within the love cycle could solve little. He needed a new vision of his amorous adventures, a vision which could bring the woman and the poet together, if not in sensual union, at least in an emotional bond that would revitalize the lover's song and the writer's verse. The answer came in 1563 with the hymns of the four seasons, in which a discussion of natural philosophy and poetic technique suddenly united the themes of love, nature, and poetry to form Ronsard's definitive vision of the love experience.

Few critics, in discussing Ronsard's views on the writing of poetry, have failed to quote the famous lines:

Je vins estre
Disciple de d'Aurat, qui long temps fut mon maistre,
M'aprist la Poësie, & me montra comment
On doit feindre & cacher les fables proprement,
Et à bien deguiser la verité des choses
D'un fabuleux manteau dont elles sont encloses.
                              (*12, 50,* vv. 77–82)

At the same time it is only the footnote which tells us that
this quotation is taken from the "Hymne de l'Autonne,"
one of four hymns to the seasons which Ronsard first published in the *Trois Livres du Recueil des Nouvelles Poésies*
(1563). Not only has little been said in general about the
content of these lines and a possible relationship between
them and the hymns, but the few comments occasioned by
these lines have alluded only to a fable of natural phenomena. "Dans ses hymnes saisonniers ce symbolisme
s'applique à des phénomènes physiques; mais ailleurs,
presque toujours, notre poète a vu dans les mythes païens
des symboles d'ordre moral, comme tout le moyen âge"
(*12, 50,* n. 2), is Laumonier's succinct judgment of the
symbolism of the seasonal hymns. Yet, the presence in these
hymns of a sustained discussion of the poet's art as evidenced by the passage "Je vins estre . . ." is by no means
accidental. The discussion of how poetry is written, like
Ronsard's reflections on the moral nature of the poet found
in the same hymn, is meant to expand his subject in such a
way as to orient the reader toward the multiple questions
—poetry, love, morality, and nature—which the poet will
make revolve about the central allegory of the seasons.

Of the four poems, two are preceded by long introductions concerning philosophy, the poet, his art, and his nature. The element unifying these themes is the idea of
work. Philosophy's function according to the introduction
to the "Hymne de l'Hyver" is to dissipate ignorance. But
its work of propagation is not direct:

Puis afin que le peuple ignorant ne mesprise
La verité cognue, apres l'avoir aprise,
D'un voile bien subtil (comme les paintres font
Aux tableaux animez) luy couvre tout le front,
Et laisse seulement, tout au travers du voile,
Paroistre ses rayons, comme une belle estoille,
A fin que le vulgaire ait desir de chercher
La couverte beauté, dont il n'ose approcher.

(*12*, 71–72, vv. 71–78)

and Ronsard immediately creates a parallel between this work and his own poetic effort in the hymns: "Tel j'ay tracé cet hymne, imitant l'exemplaire/ Des fables d'Hesiode & de celles d'Homere" (*12*, 72, vv. 79–80). In the same introduction Ronsard insists that poetry is work, a self-imposed discipline like philosophy's task of propagation. He depicts himself climbing to untrodden heights to capture his laurels: "Je veux avecq' travail brusquement y monter,/ M'esgraphinant les mains avant que l'apporter" (*12*, 68, vv. 5–6).

In the beginning of the "Hymne de l'Autonne," Ronsard explains what must comprise the moral and literary foundation for this work. The divine mysteries are transmitted only to virtuous, pious, and solitary souls and to this moral perfection the poet must add a knowledge of the art of poetry, how to disguise "la verité des choses," for example. Philosophy and poetry, then, are continually aligned. Philosophy is the knowledge of all things; poetry, the revelation of divine mysteries to a virtuous and dedicated man who in turn transmits these mysteries to other men. In each case the transmission of knowledge requires exceptional effort and great work, since philosophy's duty, like the poet's art, is to communicate knowledge in a veiled and hidden form.

These two introductions complement one another and

furnish the reader with a framework of rather elaborate ideas intended at the same time to prepare him for the myths of the seasons. This marriage of philosophy and poetry tells us that the poems to follow reveal in a poetic context certain truths about natural phenomena—that is, philosophical knowledge—and also underlines the poet's serious intent. He purposely calls attention to the subtlety of his art and to a special definition of the poet: one stereotyped in the sixteenth century to be sure, but surprising in a context supposedly reserved for natural phenomena. Further probing into the content of the hymns reveals the depth of this subtlety and the reasons for Ronsard's insistence on a special view of the poet: for each aspect—work, dedication, creativity—is reintroduced into the allegory in order to take the reader far beyond a simple metaphor of personifications into a world of exceptional and unexpected complexity.

The work motive which links the discussions of philosophy and poetry also joins the introductions to the allegory and appears in two striking passages from the "Hymne de l'Autonne," the same hymn which describes the difficulty of the poet's task. "L'industrieux Zephyre" catches Flora in his net:

> Ainsi qu'en nos jardins on voit embesongnée,
> Des la pointe du jour, la ventreuse Arignée,
> Qui quinze ou vingt fillets, comme pour fondement
> De sa trame future atache proprement,
> Puis tournant à l'entour d'une adresse subtile,
> Tantost haut tantost bas des jambes elle file,
>
> . . .
>
> Puis se plante au millieu de sa toille tendue
> Pour attraper le ver ou la mouche attendue.
>
> (*12*, 59, vv. 289–94, 297–98)

Ronsard's obvious admiration for this tenacious and tireless worker is soon followed by a description of the Palace of Nature. A hundred boys, a hundred nymphs attend to the work of Nature, and "à celle fin/ Que ce grand Univers ne preigne jamais fin," they watch over "les semans tous les ans d'un mutuel office . . ." (*12*, 62, vv. 351–53). The passage provides a fine insight into the context in which Ronsard has placed his seasons. They are all workers, "industrieux," and just as important, they are all engaged in an essential work: the preservation and creation of life. In the "Hymne de l'Hyver" some even take up arms to this purpose when Winter threatens the world with eternal cold and sterility. And once Winter is beaten, Jupiter is careful to stipulate: "Que tu la [Venus] traittes bien, pour voir apres Cybelle/ Se germer de leur veüe, & s'en faire plus belle . . ." (*12*, 85, vv. 383–84). The term "work" must be carefully defined, however.

It is of the utmost importance that the work of the seasons is presented here not as planting and harvesting, but as that supreme creation which was the coupling of natural forces to unleash the generative processes of all time. This essential element of the sense and significance of the hymns is of Ronsard's own invention. In other poems of the period, Pelletier's *Odes*, for example, the theme of work is rendered for each season by a long description of the actual labor associated with it, while the element of sexual activity is introduced only at the beginning with Spring, the season devoted to Venus. Even Folengo, the only likely source for Ronsard's hymns, and a very distant one at that, returns to Pelletier's presentation after describing the birth of the seasons. As a consequence of this special definition of "work," next to "travail" no expression is more important in Ronsard's hymns than "germer." Under the aegis of poetic dedication and surrounded by lesser figures devoted to their work, the seasons, Nature, Flora, Ceres, and Bacchus perform through sexual union the rites of preservation and creation. In all the hymns except that of Winter, the central story is the allegorical coupling of two divinities to bring forth life: first Flora and Spring, then Summer and Ceres, and last Autumn and Bacchus, the partners chosen, of course, to represent the particular seasonal production.

The attitudes and circumstances which provoke these acts are just as important as the acts themselves. In no sense could one call these hymns love tales. When Ceres finishes her speech to Summer,

> L'Esté tout soudain,
> De sa vive challeur luy eschaufa le sein,
> La prist pour son espouse . . .
> (*12*, 45, vv. 211–13)

The procedure is scarcely modified elsewhere. The characters are passionate beings, destined for the act which will fulfill their nature, and therefore incomplete without their partners. This is singularly evident in the "Hymne de l'Autonne." When Autumn arrives at the home of Nature, her mother, Nature cries:

> Tu perdras tout cela que la bonne froidure
> De l'Hyver germera, tout ce que la verdure
> Du Printemps produira, & tout ce qui croistra
> De mur et de parfait quand l'Esté paroistra.
> (*12*, 62, vv. 361–64)

Then, immediately, Autumn sees Bacchus, and Ronsard ends the hymn not on the note of her negative work, but with the image of Autumn "Maitresse du vaisseau que l'Abondance tient" (*12*, 66, vs. 447). Autumn alone and unfertile evokes the image of destruction; joined with Bacchus, she participates in the cycle of life and takes her place among the creative forces of Nature. In Jupiter's demand

of Winter that Venus be well treated, in the conscious
preference for an Autumn, time of harvest and plenty,
Ronsard accentuates the continuity of life in Nature. Indeed,
nowhere in these hymns is Nature "maratre," as in the poet's
most famous ode. The individual flower and the single
human being that "maratre" Nature destroys are forgotten
in this wider context of the work of philosophy and poet,
imparting eternal knowledge and beauty in harmony with
the inexhaustible regeneration of Mother Nature.

In addition, even if the seasons' love is passion gratified
with suddenness, Ronsard is careful to give ample discussion concerning their motivation. In the "Hymne de l'Esté'
Nature, though married to Time, seeks the attentions of
the Sun. Time is old and, grown impotent, can no longer
satisfy her. Nature's argument is centered around the concept of the gods' divinity:

> La foy de mariage est pour les hommes faite,
> Grossiers, mal-advisés, & de race imperfaite,
> Assujectis aux loix: & non pas pour les dieux,
> Qui pleins de liberté habitent dans les cieux.
>
> . . .
>
> Un magnanime cueur volontiers ne s'excuse,
> Et quand il est aymé, d'aymer il ne refuse.
>
> (*12*, 37, vv. 53–56; 39, vv. 93–94)

But the freedom of the great, the immortal, and the noble is
a mere aspect, the least important, of the seasons' comportment. In the same hymn Ronsard exposes in full the morality of his characters when Ceres entreats Summer to lie
with her:

> Je ne viens pas icy, tant pour me secourir
> Du mal de trop aymer dont tu me fais mourir,
> Que pour garder ce Monde, & luy donner puissance,
> Vertu, force, & pouvoir, lequel n'est qu'en enfance,
> Debile, sans effect, et sans maturité

Par faute de sentir nostre divinité.
Depuis que le Printemps, cette garse virille,
Ayme la Terre en vain, la Terre est inutile,
Qui ne porte que fleurs, & l'humeur qui l'espoinct,
Languist toujours en sceve, et ne se meurist point:
Dequoy servent les fleurs, si les fruicts ne meurissent?
Dequoy servent les bleds, si les grains ne jaunissent?
Toute chose a sa fin, & tend à quelque but,
Le destin l'a voulu, lors que ce Monde fut
En ordre comme il est: telle est la convenance
De Nature & de Dieu, par fatalle ordonnance:
Et pour-ce, s'il te plaist pour espouse m'avoir,
Pleine de ta vertu, je feray mon devoir,
De meurir les amours de la Terre infeconde,
Et de rendre perfait l'imperfait de ce Monde.

　　　　　　　　　　　　　　(*12*, 44, vv. 187–206)

The lines are of capital importance. Here is an echo of the
Nature–Time relationship. The sterile love of Spring and
Earth has disrupted the "natural" course of events. But
Ceres does more than speak up for the forces of love and
creation; she adds to her speech what Nature omits: they
are all subject to the will of Destiny. For if "Toute chose a
sa fin," it is nonetheless evident that Ceres is attempting to
define her role in the scheme of things. And significantly
enough, Ronsard has her analyze her actions as being not
the whim of a lovesick female, but the instinct to fulfill the
plans of destiny.

Despite the apparent sensual nature of these characters, it
is a sense of destiny which proves to be their basic motivation. Ronsard is careful to place physical desire below
Ceres' dedication to duty, and the eloquence of these
speeches effectively counterbalances the sensual preoccupation with which the union occurs. Neither coquettish nor
wanton, the allegorical figures are conscious of their rank

and of the obligations it places on them. If they claim freedom of will, the context makes clear that this freedom is
above all only the right to do what has been ordained. And
here, too, the allegories parallel Ronsard's definition of the
poet. The true poet, like the seasons or their partners, must
be subordinate to the calling of the Muses:

Ces jeunes aprentis deloyaux à leur maistre,
Ne peuvent du Laurier l'excellence cognoistre:
Mais ces gentils esprits, des Muses le bonheur
Cognoissent bien la plante, & luy font grand honneur.

(*12*, 69, vv. 27–30)

With these observations on the moral link between the
poet and the seasons, the circle of correspondence between
introduction and poem is complete. From the theme of
work Ronsard has progressed to a particular orientation of
his characters within the context of the allegory. Their
"work" is fundamentally sensual; they represent the seasons through fertility and production, not in the traditional
agrarian poses. Ronsard then proceeds to define the moral
attitude of the characters toward their act, and each step—
work, gift of the self, dedication—takes up some major
aspect of Ronsard's initial portrait of the poet. The
allegories are but another level, an analogous one, to the activities of the introduction. The analogy between philosophy and poetry, poet and philosopher, carries over into the
poems, in which philosophy and poetry are now represented by the four seasons and their companions. By enact-
ing the story of nature, they reveal the truths of philosophy; by creating, through that divine intervention which
suddenly prepares them for their acts, they repeat the
image of the poet, the inspired artisan who devotes his life
to the creative occupation for which he has been intended.
The hymns are not only an exposition of nature as work
and an apologia of sensuality when it is a basic creative

drive, they are a definition of the poet himself and of the relationship which exists between him and nature.

How original is this multi-leveled allegory? The notes of Laumonier's critical edition would indicate that here, as elsewhere, Ronsard's production is a patchwork of borrowings from identifiable sources. Close investigation of these "sources" shows, however, that all the essential elements of the hymns come from the poet's own imagination. The vast majority of Ronsard's borrowings, for example, prove to be simple classical clichés. They may be mere details, like Aurora's rising from Tithonus' bed, Summer's wearing a crown of wheat, Aeolus' dwelling in a cave. Sometimes they provide a description: Autumn's nurse weaves like the Fates in Catullus' *Epithalamium for Peleus* and Sleep is invoked to end Winter's contention with the gods much as the same personification is used in the *Iliad*. But none of these elements is basic to a formulation of the cycles. Unlike the thematic variety of the *Nouvelle Continuation* or the retreat in *Amours II* to a happy future which would both have been impossible without the poet's sources, the point of departure in the seasonal hymns is a personal one. Moreover, in dealing with material more closely related to his story, Ronsard displays the very opposite of slavish imitation, as he reworks his sources to maintain in even the smallest details a continuity between the material borrowed and the content of the allegories.

The integration of diverse borrowings into this world of concentrated attention on creativity is particularly noticeable in Ronsard's treatment of his main sources: Ovid and Folengo. Ronsard, like Ovid, speaks of the Hours as servants of the Sun, but while Ovid uses them as equerries, in Ronsard they attend his chamber and appear at the moment when Sun and Nature will lie together to beget the seasons. The description of the Sun's chariot, borrowed by Phaeton,

also was used by Ronsard, but the chariot here is a gift of
love, a present offered by Nature. In addition Ronsard notes
that the chariot had originally been a wedding present from
Vulcan, and by relating the object to the marriage of Nature and Time, he makes its eventual passage to the Sun a
formal symbol of Nature's abandonment of Time. When
Ronsard notes that Jupiter "detrancha le Printemps, & sa
saison entiere/ En trois pars divisa . . ." (*12*, 31, vv.
68–69), Laumonier suggests the source is again Ovid:
"Juppiter antiqui contraxit tempora veris/ perque hiemes
aestusque et inaequales autumnos." [4] But in Ovid the action
is pure allegorical notation to explain the division of the
year into seasons. In the "Hymne du Printemps" Jupiter is
given a specific motive: he is jealous of Spring's attraction
to Nature, a situation which underlines the consciousness in
Ronsard's characters of the force of passion. Finally, there
is the passage describing Earth's care to appear beautiful
before Spring. The passage is borrowed from Folengo,
where the couple is Spring and Cupid. In the source, however, Spring acts as a mere coquette to keep her husband
from wandering: "Elle porte tousjours sur soy du musc, de
la civette et autres parfums et odeurs par lesquelles le bastard
de Venus est alleché; et, en telles voluptez, ce paillard
s'afoiblit moins." [5] Ronsard gives the Earth quite different
reasons for her efforts. She beautifies herself,

> Pour retenir long temps cet amoureux flambeau,
> Qui luy donne la vie, & de qui la lumiere
> Par sa vertu la fait de toutes choses Mere.
>
> (*12*, 33, vv. 118–20)

It is hardly necessary to dwell at length on the fundamental
bond between this adaptation and the entire sense of the

4. Ovid., *Metamorphoses*, I. 116–17.
5. T. Folengo, *Histoire Maccaronique de Merlin Coccaie*, ed. G. Bru-
net (Paris, 1859), p. 245.

hymns as I have defined it. The character recognizes in the attractiveness that leads to physical union her only raison d'être, which is inseparable from creation, her quality of Mother.

Yet this final example of adaptation of material is only more eloquent than others in proving an independence of intent as well as a manipulation of sources which justifies this analysis of the hymns. Repeatedly Ronsard refashions a borrowed element to bring it directly into the realm of passion and creativity, the proper domain of Ronsard's seasonal characters. Even in these significant moments of borrowing, however, the poet cannot be said to have been profoundly influenced by the texts he imitated. If he chooses to use them, it is because they can be adapted to the pre-established theme of Ronsard's allegory. Like the classical clichés, these borrowings from other works have a totally secondary function. The hymns and their meaning are his.

We have already seen in general in what ways the allegorical characters share traits with Ronsard's conception of the poet. We may now understand the way in which they share traits with Ronsard himself. After *Amours I*, the *Continuations* had moved gradually to a crisis embodied in the tone of "A son Livre." The revolt was an emotional affair, however, as is evidenced by the temper of Ronsard's attack on Petrarch. It was also an outburst of little consequence regarding Ronsard's problems with the sonnet cycles, as can be seen from his subsequent use of Theocritus. In 1563, he portrayed a series of allegorical characters, likened indirectly to the poet, destined, even through infidelity, to enact their appointed role. Noble, devoted, existing only to create, all the seasons save Winter join Nature in a situation that transcends their previous alliances and obliges them to fulfill their destiny.

As if by a miracle, they are prepared inwardly, each struck by a sudden liking for the pre-arranged partner. There is no refusal possible.

With a moment's reflection, it is not difficult to see how this situation becomes a firm and far-reaching answer to Ronsard's infidelity to Cassandre. The painstaking depiction of the moral position of Nature and Ceres, like the exposition of the two introductory passages (passages which would appear purely gratuitous were one to treat the hymns as mere parables of natural phenomena), reveal a conscious development of the allegory by means of the addition of an entirely new element that can find its justification only in the poet's personal involvement with his work. The uncoupled seasons, Nature languishing beside Time, all reproduce the state Ronsard deplored in the fable of Petrarch's long fidelity to Laura, and the allegory, which encompasses the entirety of nature's creation, now makes clear the sterility of the situation. Accomplishment, action, and creation, factors inseparable from the reversal of this sterility and the coupling of the characters, now furnish Ronsard with a new theme and a forceful, positive excuse for leaving Cassandre.

Such an apologia of love through creation and dedication to the Muses is not entirely new. Even in "A son Livre," Ronsard had equated Petrarch's faithfulness with a denial of nature and poetry:

> Il estoit esveillé d'un trop gentil esprit
> Pour estre sot trente ans, abusant sa jeunesse,
> Et sa Muse . . .   (7, 317, vv. 46–48)

But he did not insist upon this point. The seasonal hymns are so significant because Ronsard creates a complete system of thought in which the relationship between nature, love, and poetry is made clear and unequivocal. With the story of the seasons as a guide, the poet will abandon all unfertile love. It is contrary to nature ("abusant sa jeunesse"), and, ultimately, it is contrary to the demands of poetry ("sa Muse"). In reconstructing Petrarch's love for Laura, Ronsard had made love precede the poetry: "Non, il en jouissoit, puis l'a faitte admirable" (7, 317, vs. 52). Here, however, fulfillment in love and poetry is presented as a single moment; if he is to remain faithful to his youth and Muse, the poet must move from love to love, like Time's restless wife. Thus, in the hymns, woman, desire, work, and poetry come together in an allegorical synthesis of striking originality. Like Nature, who never hesitates between perfection with Summer and a moral sense of duty to Time, Ronsard defends his pleasure without a qualm. Unlike Petrarch, who must always return anew to the problem of justifying his earthly love, Ronsard cannot see the utility of years of moral conflict and seems disturbed only by the means of formulating his apologia.

In its final form, this apologia creates a fraternity of self, poet, and woman to enrich continually the poet's inspiration, and never again in the portrait of personal love will Ronsard revert to the form of imitation we have seen in the period between 1555 and 1560. Imitation gradually becomes more and more subservient to the poet's own ideas, and he no longer surrenders his talent to the dictates of other styles. The spider is found fascinating because its work seems indefatigable, Nature is glorified because of her eternal powers of creativity, and the seasons are heroic because, recognizing the correspondence between joy and duty, they bring both into harmony. So, too, in love Ronsard must be true to his youth and his Muse because they alone are the secrets of his poetic prowess. That shudder of accession common to the characters in the hymns is an emotion which Ronsard recognizes as crucial both to man and poet.

A Test Case

No further proof concerning the relevance of these hymns to the world of love poetry may be needed than Ronsard's own application of their content to a love adventure also published in 1563.[6] The story relates Ronsard's meeting with a certain Genèvre. The identity of this woman, like that of Sinope, has resisted all biographers and biographical analysis.[7] The reader knows only what Ronsard tells him. While bathing he saw her dancing on the shore. He left the river and danced with her. He plunged back into the water after a simple kiss on the hand, thinking never to see her again. His nascent emotions ravaged his sleep that night, but the next morning he vowed to resist the lady's charms. When Ronsard saw her again, love seized him irrevocably. He confessed his passion. She answered that her only love was dead; and her desire entombed with him. When Ronsard returned five days later, she asked him his name and if he had experienced such emotion before. He spoke of his fame as the great poet Ronsard, of Marie and Cassandre. When asked the same question, she tells the story of her ill-starred love, and the first elegy ends with an exhortation by Ronsard to forget the past and turn her attentions toward him. The second elegy is a long lament occasioned by her absence which robs the poet of sleep and fills him with constant longing. He finds comfort in the juniper ("genevre"), compares his state to the tree, and concludes with a few verses to Genèvre, calling attention to these myriad signs of his fervent love. If the sequence with the tree is omitted, there

6. The hymns were published in the first book of the *Trois Livres du Recueil des Nouvelles Poésies;* the first two Genèvre elegies, in the third book.

7. "Genèvre, sa maîtresse de la Ville, n'a pas encore été identifiée et ne le sera probablement jamais" (Laumonier, *12*, xi).

is little in the second elegy which does not recall Ronsard's previous use of standard Petrarchistic themes and his evident attachment to a number of them. The first elegy, however, is more personal. In addition to the meeting and the dance, there is an indication that Genèvre was known to others, especially Belleau:

> Car si tost que Vesper, la brunette courriere
> De la Lune, eut poussé dans les eaux la lumiere,
> Prenant aveques moy pour compaignon Belleau,
> Comme le soir passé je retournay sur l'eau.
> Ce Belleau, qui si sied premiers sur Parnasse,
> Desja sentoit le trait de ta gentille face:
> Ton oeil l'avoit blessé, & me celoit ton nom,
> Car Amour ne veut point avoir de compagnon.
>
> (*12*, 260, vv. 63–70)

When the elegies were republished in 1567, Ronsard suppressed these verses and never reinstated them in the text. The reason can only be a matter of speculation. One definite statement can be made about the suppression, however. The later texts were as a consequence all the more literary, deprived of one of the few indications of biographical underpinnings in the adventure. Even the swimming scene, like the laments of the second elegy, can be interpreted as a literary device, providing, as it does, a fine occasion for use of the Petrarchistic clichés of *innamoramento:*

> Puis d'un agile bond je resautay dans l'eau,
> Pensant qu'elle esteindroit mon premier feu nouveau.
> Il advint autrement, car au milieu des ondes
> Je me senty lié de tes deux tresses blondes,
> Et le feu de tes yeux qui les eaux penetra
> Maugré la froide humeur dedans mon coeur entra.
>
> (*12*, 257, vv. 17–22)

It would be difficult to believe that the Genèvre episode was purely fictional, nevertheless, and this reflection on the real yet literary nature of certain elements in these elegies is in no way intended to suggest such a conclusion. It does, however, prepare us for an aspect of the elegies which provides substantial material to indicate a literary approach by Ronsard to this love story: the continuity of themes, situations, and attitudes between the seasonal hymns and the elegies to Genèvre.

Whether the swimming scene is a biographical fact or not, the nexus of the first elegy and the springboard for all its significant remarks related to love is a direct duplication of the triangular loves of certain characters in the hymns. Ronsard, Genèvre, and her departed lover re-enact the Time-Nature-Sun relationship with only a slight change in poses for each. As the woman insists upon her allegiance to her former lover, the man is obliged to adopt Nature's attitude:

> Madame, si l'on peut juger par le visage
> L'affection cachée au dedans du courage,
> Certes je puis juger en voyant ta beauté,
> Que ton coeur n'est en rien taché de cruauté.
> Aussi Dieu ne fait point une femme si belle,
> Pour estre contre Amour de nature rebelle.
>   (*12*, 260, vv. 79–84)

A more curious change occurs in the presentation of the third member of the triangle. Time was merely described as sterile and impotent. Through the memories of Genèvre, however, the unfertile member of this second group participates directly in the circle of candidness and accession to nature. After his death she may preserve an eternal love for him, he told her, or:

> Si ta jeunesse encore fresche et tendre
> Veut apres mon trespas nouveau serviteur prendre,
> Au moins je te supply de vouloir bien choisir,
> Et jamais en un sot ne mettre ton desir,

A fin qu'un jeune fat à mon bien ne succede,
Ains un amy gaillard en mon lieu te possede.

(12, 269, vv. 275–80)

The choice of words—"if your yet fresh and tender youth," as well as the insistence on a worthy partner—contains the essence of Nature's speech to the Sun, and facilitates the final moral argument of the first elegy:

Tu es encore jeune en la fleur de tes ans,
Use donq de l'amour & de ses dons plaisans,
Et ne seufre qu'en vain l'Avril de ta jeunesse
Au milieu de son cours se ride de vieillesse.

.   .   .

Quand celuy qui soubs terre est durement couché
Entendra nos amours, il n'en sera fasché:
Car, s'il faisoit au monde encor sa demeurance,
Il me feroit peut estre honneur & reverence.

(12, 276, vv. 465–68, 477–80)

This transformation of the third party is perhaps best viewed as a part of Ronsard's overall attempt in the elegies to transcend a simple story of seduction and give to the situation of Genèvre a general moral connotation. Under the influence of the seasonal hymns, Ronsard could not resist inserting within the Genèvre story a definite moral philosophy and accentuating throughout the episode the ideas basic to his newly formed attitudes on love. The accent on youth and love and conformity to nature has already been noted. Just as significant is the fact that all the participants in the love triangle recognize the problem of "le naturel" and the imperative to conform to nature. The lover castigates the woman's attitude:

Ce n'est le naturel d'une dame bien née
De vivre contre Amour fierement obstinée:
Aux Lyons, aux Serpens, qui sont plains de venin,

> Convient la cruauté, non au coeur feminin,
> Lequel plus est benin, & tant plus, ce me semble,
> Aux Dieux qui sont benins de nature ressemble.
>
> (*12*, 262, vv. 107–12)

The departed partner foresees the demands of a "jeunesse encore fresche et tendre," and even the woman is made to say, though paraphrasing the poet:

> Il n'y a que les marbres,
> Les pilliers, les cailloux, les roches & les arbres,
> Privés de sentiment, qui se puissent garder
> D'aymer, quand un bel oeil les daigne regarder.
>
> (*12*, 264, vv. 163–66)

In such a context, it is easy to understand why the poet would be unabashed in explaining his philosophy of love:

> Ores j'ayme la noire, ores j'ayme la blonde,
> Et sans amour certaine en mon cueur esprouver,
> Je cherche ma fortune où je la puis trouver.
>
> (*12*, 264, vv. 152–54)

Even more interesting is the general interplay between this independent attitude and the very definite Petrarchistic context of the elegies. Although Ronsard introduces the theme of the demands of youth and one's "naturel," the elegies never attempt to recreate the rustic intimacy of "Mignongne, levés-vous," and the freedom of the elegies derives rather from a careful manipulation of the love story within the Petrarchistic context. The woman is addressed as "Madame." In the course of the relationship, the decisive moments are still those in which he sees the woman, who by her beauty can undo all the poet's rationalizing against love. The *innamoramento* is complete with the clichés of heat, cold, and net-like tresses. Yet, while the poet has been "caught," unlike the meeting of poet and lady in *Amours I*, the *innamoramento* here does not necessarily suffice to create the love affair. There is a choice to be made. Despite the power of the woman, the poet searches more deeply, more objectively, when attempting to understand the character of Genèvre. He looks into her heart to seek the quality of her sensibility. Is she cruel, is she sympathetic, he asks himself. Like the aggressive partners of the seasonal hymns, the poet does not offer his sentiments to someone who is unworthy, and least of all to a woman who does not show an inclination to share his love. In keeping with the hymns' philosophy, love is now offered to a genuine partner. The lover, no less than the third member of the triangle, requires this, and when Ronsard insists upon his qualifications as a worthy successor, he is incorporating yet another aspect of the seasonal hymns into the love story.

At the same time, as the programmatic ideas and the concept of choice in particular reappear throughout the narration, it is clear that the Petrarchistic conceits, though present, do not succeed in defining the position of the woman or the poet. Through the element of choice and merit in love, which is reinforced by the dialectic undertaken between lady and lover concerning "le naturel," Ronsard imposes his own definition of love and loving which finally rejects the very fundamentals of the Petrarchistic tradition: fidelity in the man ("Ores j'ayme . . .")—a foreshadowing of the outcome of the affair—and insensitivity in the woman. The lexical borrowings from the Italian tradition can be easily recognized, but they are pale in value and importance beside the elaboration of the love story, which has its own characters and its own philosophy.

Finally, independence and richness are each attested to in a last but no less significant parallel with the seasonal hymns: the lack of source material. For the hymns Ronsard may have consulted Ovid and Folengo, but Laumonier gives no suggestion of the existence of even such distant

possibilities for the Genèvre elegies of 1563. His edition is
not without indications of source material, but they are
comparable to the literary frills or commonplaces of the
hymns. Even more than the seasonal allegories, the passionate yet programmatic story of Genèvre seems to spring
from a single source: the poet himself. Proponents of an
approach based on biographical data may insist on the historical truth of the events and the obvious lack of necessity
to invent what reality presented. But no writer of the period was likely to describe exterior events without allusions
and borrowed metaphors; Ronsard's own odes to the royal
family attest to that. The relative purity of these two
elegies, especially of the first, in regards to imitation is,
therefore, all the more startling. It stands with the seasonal
hymns as the first monument to Ronsard's maturity in handling the love theme.

In the domain of style also the poet has turned against
certain tendencies of his period of crisis. The Genèvre
elegies succeed admirably in replacing the love story in the
present after the pastoral episode of *Amours II.* The unmistakable Petrarchistic character of the peripheral material
in the elegies attests to the restricted use of Ronsard's "stille
bas" and the very evident belief—a belief which, was at the
heart of Petrarch's presence in the *Deffense et Illustration*
—that the Italian tradition was the finest expression of an
elevated, poetically serious account of love.

Nevertheless, the critic is forced to note that, despite
these facts, the problem of genre remained unsolved. Since
1556 Ronsard has introduced all his major innovations in
long poems such as the elegy, where the poet could not be
hindered by the sonnet's conciseness. The lover's lament,
the lady's narrative, the story's final turning flourish in the
facile extension of rhymed couplets. It is all the more significant, therefore, that Ronsard was to experiment again
with the sonnet form at the same moment or shortly after

he composed the third and final elegy for Genèvre. Though the third elegy was not published until 1571, it must have been in Ronsard's mind before this date, so that the time of its germination corresponds to a period which spans the years between the writing of the seasonal hymns and a return to the sonnet. When he did complete the story, time had taken him away from the original events, and as Desonay observes:

> Il suffit de relire les deux textes pour voir que l'*Elegie* . . . doit avoir été composée à distance de l'événement. Déjà le lointain du souvenir estompe les contours, brouille les dates . . . . Tout se passe comme si Ronsard retiré dans son prieuré de Saint-Cosme . . . aurait voulu, retournant vers ses plus belles amours, donner le 'doux fruit . . . d'un si aigre tourment'." [8]

This distance in time and thought proved of priceless value to Ronsard, for much more interesting than the distance that "blurs the outlines" of the story is the presence in the third elegy of a revelation which Genèvre makes to Ronsard and which Ronsard makes to himself. Because this revelation contains a spectacular and definitive conclusion about the love emotion, the final elegy suggests that between 1569 and 1571 it was not possible for Ronsard to reopen his efforts with the love sonnet and to continue the Genèvre episode without these two activities influencing each other. The influence of the final elegy to Genèvre upon the sonnets of 1569 will be discussed later. Of more immediate interest is its definition of the love emotion in terms, at last, of direct literary import.

The Elégie, "Le Temps se passe & se passant, Madame," continues the lover's state of mental disarray which dominated the second elegy. He again doubts the wisdom of

8. Desonay, *Ronsard, poète de l'amour*, 2, 226.

love, but is checked in his reasoning by a new glimpse of
his lady, "Et tellement me laissa la raison," he admits, "Que
tout muet je r'entre en la maison" (*15*, 333, vv. 167–68).
Then Love plants a juniper in his breast and announces that
he has also planted a rose tree in the heart of Genèvre.

> Ainsi tous deux n'estions que mesme chose.
> Vostre ame estoit dedans la mienne enclose,
> La mienne estoit en la vostre, & nos corps
> Par sympathie & semblables accords
> N'estoient plus qu'un: si bien que vous, Madame,
> Et moy n'estions qu'un seul corps & qu'un'ame.
> $\qquad\qquad$ (*15*, 335, vv. 233–38)

The idea is hardly original with Ronsard or new in the
Genèvre elegy. In *Amours I* he had once written:

> En toy je suis, & tu es dedans moy,
> En moy tu vis, & je vis dedans toy:
> Ainsi noz toutz ne font qu'un petit monde.
> $\qquad\qquad$ (sonnet 72, vv. 9–11)

> S'il vit, je vy, s'il meurt, je ne suis riens:
> [The "il" being "le tison de ⌈s⌉a vie"]
> Car tant son ame à la mienne est unie,
> Que ses destins seront suyvis des miens.
> $\qquad\qquad$ (sonnet 161, vv. 12–14)

But again the philosophy of the seasonal hymns continues
to transform the old clichés. The "petit monde" of
Cassandre and Ronsard grows out of the interplay of light
—his star, her eyes—in keeping with a favorite Petrarchistic bond between lady and lover, while the Genèvre elegy
places the bond in the heart, not the eyes. This new union
of lovers is one of soul and body, in contrast to the bond
of soul alone, with which Ronsard was content in 1552.
From this complete union, communal feelings give way to

communal desires and their satisfaction. Then "nous rom-
pismes le cours," the narrator relates, "Sans y penser, de
l'amitié premiere . . ." (*15*, 337, vv. 288–289) Such frankness persists even to the final line of the elegy: " 'Rien n'est
si sot qu'une vieille amité' " (*15*, 338, vs. 316).

At the same time, this sympathy between Ronsard and
Genèvre proves to be the beginning of the last step in Ronsard's analysis of the affair with Genèvre. Only now does
the poet make his great discovery: the poet discovers love!

> Lors vous trouvant aussi douce & traitable
> Qu'auparavant vous n'estiez accostable,
> L'aspre fureur qui mes os penetra
> S'esvanouit, & Amour y entra:
> La difference est grande & merveilleuse
> D'entre l'amour & la rage amoureuse.
> Adonc la vraye & simple affection
> Loin de fureur, de rage & passion
> Nourrit mon coeur, passant de veine en veine,
> Qui ne fut point ny frivole ny vaine:
> Car vous, ayant de mon amour pitié,
> Me contraignez de pareille amitié.
>   (*15*, 335, vv. 217–28)

The lines suggest a startled awakening, as if, working so
many years with "la rage amoureuse," Ronsard had been
blinded to the real emotion of love, as if, writing these
elegies, he could suddenly see himself with enough clarity
to define his passion.

The nature of this discovery comes essentially from the
nature of the investigation which preceded it. Just as Ronsard's handling of sources beginning with the hymns reveals a far greater maturity than is present in 1552 or 1556,
the entire procedure of investigation which encompasses
the hymns and the elegies to Genèvre points to a similar
advancement in vision. As Ceres and Nature reveal to their

future partners the place of their love in the greater system of natural creation, so Ronsard has just defined his recognition of the relationship between love and its expression.

This is not the first time Ronsard has praised the use of a simple style in love poetry. There are these verses of "A son Livre":

> Les amours ne se souspirent pas
> D'un vers hautement grave, ains d'un beau stille bas,
> Populaire & plaisant . . .
>
> (7, 324, vv. 173–75)

One might be tempted to remark that Marie, too, was a sympathetic partner and that "la vraye et simple affection" is but a second manifestation of the style Ronsard defined in "A son Livre." But such equating of terms would be most unjust. The "stille bas" can be said to have three essential aspects. It was meant to be clear, where *Amours I* had been obscure: "Thiard, chacun disoit à mon commencement/ Que j'estoi trop obscur au simple populaire" (7, 115, vv. 1–2). It was the expression of love for a girl not of noble birth, whose world was not the court but the realm of nature, and Ronsard felt that neither the girl nor her world could be sung in the style he used for Cassandre:

> Marie, tout ainsi que vous m'avés tourné
> Mon sens, & ma raison, par vôtre voix subtile,
> Ainsi m'avés tourné mon grave premier stile,
> Qui pour chanter si bas n'estoit point destiné.
>
> (7, 188, vv. 1–4)

In execution, it became the mode of diminutives, roses, and May. These elements are no more characteristic of the Genèvre elegies than of the kind of sympathy which exists between Ronsard and Genèvre. Marie loved simply, ingenuously, in keeping with her setting. While there was pleasure in Ronsard's love for Marie, it was not a pleasure shared by equals. More than a little vanity and levity pierce through as the aristocrat tells of his peasant adventures. (The bantering of his aubade ("levés-vous" or "je vous punirai du peché de paresse") gives the poem no tinge of pathos, no regret at waking at the end of the night of bliss. The tone has much more the gallant and vaguely frivolous resonance Ronsard) rejects in the Genèvre elegy. Here the sympathy of emotion embraces a sympathy of being as Ronsard defined it in the first elegy through a general insistence on the necessity to choose one's partner carefully. Genèvre needs no "stille bas" to communicate her being and her sentiments. Now that the poet has been brought to understand and portray the quality of emotion that the traditions have so long eclipsed, he can work behind the embellishment of roses, diminutives, and aubades. (He no longer needs the pretext or the reality of a simple love) like Marie's to assure his poetry a psychological and literary force.

The expressions serve admirably to distinguish themselves. The "stille bas" permitted Ronsard to surround the Petrarchistic portrait of love with a new stylistic embroidery, while the "vraye et simple affection" defines a new emotion. There had been new emotions in the past, of course. "Mignongne" and Sinope prove that all is not Platonic before Genèvre. But the poems addressed to these women do not represent Ronsard's only attempt to write in a "stille bas." It was used in the most Petrarchistic settings, such as "É que me sert, Paschal . . . ," or "Le vintiéme d'Avril . . . ," and there is no reason to equate the sensual intimacy of the aubade with the "stille bas." The phrase designates above all a form of expression, not a new vision of the love experience. The place of "mignongne" in Ronsard's poetry of 1555–56 is an isolated one. The signs of sensuality in the Sinope poems seem more promising and more prophetic, and yet the new cycle of 1560 shows no new vein. The poet prefers to exploit the themes of memory and pastoral bliss suggested by Theocritus.

As a result, it is very difficult to say that there is a sustained new emotion in the "stille bas" or in the rare verse of sensuality of the period. Ronsard assembles, mixes, and reassembles the most diverse styles without seeming to abide by any, and without considering at length any of them in terms of himself, his personality, and his talent. The sonnet to Tyard quoted above continues: "Aujourd'hui, chacun dit que je suis au contraire,/ Et que je me dements parlant trop bassement" (7, 115, vv. 3–4). There is a certain petulance here as well as frustration in having failed to silence his critics. This petulance reveals the poet-novice who has been perhaps too aware of public sentiment and too eager to please to contemplate his situation more astutely. This liminal sonnet documents with amazing frankness the poet's position. His first cycle of love sonnets did not meet with success, and the only path to success seemed that of a change in expression to the "stille bas." The "vraye et simple affection," however, is less a change than a reevaluation. It is not a sounding of public taste but a reassessment of his subject in accordance with the self. Finally, it *is* a new emotion because it is a commitment, not a concession. For this reason the point of departure for conceiving the love story can no longer be the same.

A comparison between the theme of union in *Amours I* and the elegies exemplifies this fact; *Sonnets pour Hélène* is to prove it conclusively. The poet waited until 1578 to publish this new cycle, yet already one might foresee the implications of the "vraye et simple affection": love as nourishment, love enveloping the body, and so forth. And such will be the growing content of Ronsard's late sonnets, beginning with those of 1569. While the third elegy postdates the publication of these poems, it is still our finest point of transition from the philosophical preoccupations of the early sixties to the rebirth of lyric energy. The circle of investigation begun in 1563 closes with the "vraye et simple affection," which, at the crucial moment of Ronsard's return to the sonnet form, becomes the touchstone for his new lyric renaissance.

A RETURN TO THE SONNET

Between 1569 and 1578 Ronsard devoted himself to the sonnet form with an intensity equalled only in the years 1552–56. It is during this time that he produced the sonnets of the *Septième Livre des Poèmes, Sonnets et Madrigals pour Astrée, Sonnets sur la Mort de Marie, Amours Diverses* (in part), and *Sonnets pour Hélène*. Despite this rather impressive list of titles and the wide span of years, however, the number of sonnets Ronsard wrote in the later years is smaller than the production of his first attack on the sonnet. These discrepancies are a first indication that Ronsard's approach has changed to become more painstaking and more studied. The way in which Ronsard published these poems also suggests a modification in attitude. Of this new group of sonnets only a very few poems can be dated. The sonnets published in 1569 in the *Septième Livre des Poèmes* are certainly among his earliest efforts in this later group of sonnets. The poems of *Sur la Mort de Marie*, the vast majority at least,[9] date from the death of Marie de Clèves in 1574. But the others—*Sonnets pour Hélène, Sonnets et Madrigals pour Astrée, Amours Diverses*—all unpublished before 1578, must be assumed the result of a continuous process of creation beginning early in the seventies and proceeding into the time prior to the general edition of 1578. There is a total absence of

9. It seems that some verses were interpolated to make a link between the sonnets to Marie de Clèves and statements made of Marie. See Laumonier, *17,* 136, n. 2.

"loves" and "continued loves," of previous publication and subsequent re-editing with new titles and added genres; that is, of all the intermediate stages through which the cycles of 1555–60 passed. When Ronsard at last prepared for publication the poems he had written over a long span of years, he planned, separated, and grouped his poems with care. Ronsard's change in attitude can be observed within the context of the individual poems as well, notably in the poet's choice of themes. It is not possible to over-emphasize this fact, as no aspect of Ronsard's new methods with the sonnets and the sonnet cycle proves so fruitful as his reassessment of, and reduction in, the range of themes suitable for his love verse.

This phenomenon appears both in individual poems composed of themes used in earlier poems, as well as in individual sonnets of the 1569 group, which show a pronounced preference for thematic elements of the seasonal hymns, even when the poems have recognizable sources. Thus, before turning the sonnets of 1569 and the question of imitation during this period, I should like to examine two singular examples of the new truncated scale of themes: "L'absence, ny l'obly . . ." and "Comme on voit sur la branche. . . ." Of exceptional value in themselves, both poems have been repeatedly examined outside the context of Ronsard's development, whereas like "Mignonne, allon voir" and "Quand vous serez bien vieille . . . ," they are no less important as milestones in the preparation of *Sonnets pour Hélène*.

In 1569, Ronsard published one of his most moving praises to Cassandre, "L'absence, ny l'obly. . . ." Laumonier lists no sources for the poem's forty-six lines. Yet the poem immediately calls to mind a number of themes Ronsard has capitalized upon in the past in the Genèvre elegies, Sinope cycle, and *Amours II*. The opening verses, for example:

> L'absence, ny l'obly, ny la course du jour
> N'ont effacé le nom, les graces, ny l'amour
> Qu'au coeur je m'imprimé des ma jeunesse tendre,
>
> *(15, 191, vv. 1–3)*

resemble closely the opening lines used only two years before in an "Elégie" to Mary Stuart:

> Bien que le trait de vostre belle face
> Peinte en mon coeur par le temps ne s'efface,
> Et que tousjours je le porte imprimé
> Comme un tableau vivement animé . . .
>
> *(14, 152, vv. 1–4)*

In like manner the singular compliment of continued fire and charms:

> Et si l'age, qui rompt & murs & forteresses,
> En coulant a perdu un peu de noz jeunesses,
> Cassandre, c'est tout un! Car je n'ay pas esgard
> A ce qui est present, mais au premier regard,
> Au trait qui me navra de ta grace enfantine
> Qu'encores tout sanglant je sens en la poitrine.
>
> *(15, 192, vv. 23–28)*

takes up the theme not only of the Sinope poem (I) indicated by Laumonier,[10] but of a poem written to Marie:

> Car je n'ay pas égard à cela que tu es,
> Mais à ce que tu fus, tant les amoureus traits
> Te graverent dans moy, voire de telle sorte
> Que telle que tu fus telle au coeur je te porte.
>
> *(10, 218, vv. 91–94)* [11]

---

10. See pp. 80–81.

11. There appears in this recapitulation of themes an obvious element of embarrassment for any critic who attempts to hold firm to an exclusively biographical approach to Ronsard's love works. Each time Ronsard reworks this theme he is apparently addressing a different woman. Thus, while there is no direct evidence to prove his loves were

It is not difficult to understand why Ronsard remained so long attached to this theme. Ever since the *Sonets amoureux*, Ronsard had been repeatedly tempted by themes which displaced the temporal context from the present time to some desired, pastoral world. Both the world inspired by Theocritus and this theme of memory participate in the portrayal of undisturbed happiness. The first tells how perfect their love was in the pastoral paradise; the second returns the poem to the happiest moment of their relationship. Memory makes relive what was perfect in the past; it disguises the romantic differences by

merely literary adventures, devoid of any biographical reality, there is no lack of evidence to show that his increasing number of adventures was accompanied by a predilection for a decreasing number of possible poses. He now returned regularly to those already used. No matter how much his eye wandered, the pen remained steady and grew increasingly so. As with the whole question of a new love portrait, it is probable that the Genèvre elegies played a decisive role. In these poems Ronsard had already formulated with modern intuition his thoughts on the function of memory:

> J'ay certes esprouvé par meinte experience
> Que l'amour se renforce & s'augmente en l'absence,
> Ou soit qu'en ravassant le plaisant souvenir
> Ainsi que d'un apast la puisse entretenir,
> Ou soit que les portraits des liesses passées
> S'impriment dans l'esprit, en l'ame ramassées,
> Soit que l'ame ait regret au bien qu'elle a perdu,
> Soit que le vuide corps plus plain se soit rendu,
> Soit que la volupté soit trop tost perissable,
> Soit que le souvenir d'elle soit plus durable. (*12*, 291, vv. 149–58)

And by the period of the return to the sonnet this fascination with the poetic value of the memory theme has so taken hold that in the edition of 1578 the original Genèvre verses,

> Ainsi le cours des ans ta beauté ne fanisse
> Ains maitresse du temps contre l'age fleurisse . . .

had become

> Souvent le souvenir de la chose passée,
> Quand on le renouvelle, est doux à la pensée. (*12*, 256–57)

effacing the reality of unrequited love. It even permits the poet to sing of love and passion in the face of change and time-ravaged women, for all that is essential is in the mind's eye, not the beholder's.

Whatever the biographical background and the supposed context of the poet's inspiration, the force of "L'absence, ny l'obly . . ." lies in the strength of its themes; the poem begins with a categorical statement, and this sureness never leaves the poet. Just as, thematically, nothing disturbs his pleasure and nothing challenges his excitement, no series of empty enumerations and piecemeal borrowings betrays uncertainty and experimentation. At no point does the poem lag or collapse for want of material, for around these happy notes of remembrance Ronsard has gathered peripheral, yet related themes, also already tried and guaranteed to fill the Petrarchistic void.

> Et si j'estois un Roy qui toute chose ordonne
> Je mettrois en la place une haute Colonne
> Pour remerque d'amour: où tous ceux qui viendroient
> En baisant le pilier de nous se souviendroient,
>
> (*15*, 192, vv. 31–34)

returns us to the temple of "Elégie à Marie" and the projection into eternity. More salient yet are the echos of the seasonal hymns: the full recognition of the mistress-Muse figure,

> Cassandre qui me fut plus chere que mes yeux,
> Que mon sang, que ma vie, & qui seule en tous lieux
> Pour sujet eternel ma Muse avoit choisie,
> A fin de te chanter par longue Poësie,
>
> (*15*, 191, vv. 5–8)

or the *innamoramento* which is a clear physical attack,

> Car le trait qui sortit de ton regard si beau,
> Ne fut l'un de ces traits qui dechirent la peau:

> Mais ce fut un de ceux dont la pointe cruëlle
> Perce coeur & poumons & veines & mouëlle.
>
> $$(15, 191, vv. 9-12)$$

Of course, not all these themes might be adapted to the sonnet, nor does the range presented in "L'absence, ny l'obly . . ." exhaust the possibilities inherent in the ideas of the seasonal hymns and Genèvre elegies. Yet in the "Colonne" and the themes of eternal love there is the announcement of the "Stances de la Fontaine d'Hélène," and while the poet could not go on describing his love story indefinitely in the present through this return in time to a past moment, the technique of accentuating positive aspects of the love affair to the conscious exclusion of an unhappy reality will prove an integral part of the structure of Ronsard's final love cycle. Finally, the range of themes and their grouping to create "L'absence, ny l'obly . . ." exemplify Ronsard's accrued poetic sense and the increasing importance of words, phrases, and attitudes which the poet knows he can manipulate with sureness.

The relationship of Ronsard's exquisite "Comme on voit sur la branche . . ." to the other poems of *Sur la Mort de Marie* is no less an example of this poetic sense. No other poem in the group can approach the perfection of this sonnet; yet key phrases, words, images, and rhythms appearing in "Comme on voit sur la branche . . ." reappear throughout the cycle. We unfortunately have no indications as to the order of composition of these pieces; it is impossible to say whether the remarkable success of "Comme on voit sur la branche . . ." was the result of intensive work preceding its composition or whether Ronsard, struck by the force of certain aspects of this sonnet, sought to reuse them in others of the poems. The distinction is not all-important, however, as either possibility indicates the poet's awareness of the value of these elements, and it is undeniable that the repetition exists.

Like the theme of memory, the basic comparison of Marie's death to the withering of a flower, springs repeatedly into the poet's mind:

Tu as seul laissé ton Ronsard
Dans le ciel trop tost retournée,
Perdant beauté, grace, & couleur,
Tout ainsi qu'une belle fleur
Que ne vit qu'une matinée. ("Stances")

La Mort a moissonné mon bien en sa verdeur. (II)

Du monde elle partit aux mois de son printemps. ("Elégie")

The rhythm of the sonnet's last line, "Afin que vif et mort ton corps ne soit que roses," is also reproduced in the elegy: "Afin que vous soyez ma flamme morte et vive." Finally, the image of the Fates, "la Parque t'a tuée" occurs three times:

La Parque maintenant ceste guerre a desfaite. (IV)

Et la Parque, d'avoir un si beau fil trenché . . . ("Elégie")

Quand l'une Soeurs aura le fil coupé . . . ("Elégie")

As with the theme of death as withering, Ronsard's reuse of the theme is never quite the same; there is the starkness of the expression "la Parque t'a tuée," the Petrarchistic overtones of "ceste guerre a desfaite," the compliment-regret of the elegy's "beau fil." With this variety the poet succeeds in conveying through a basic image the nuances of sentiment the context demands.

Such efforts in varying a given theme were not new to Ronsard. *Amours I* is already a game of constant experimentation resulting from the meager possibilities of the Petrarchistic tradition. What is different at this time is the selection of material to be reworked—not everything, but the striking images, the richest ones, the most lyric rhythms, the themes with which the poet felt a personal involvement and which gradually break down the love story into positive and negative moments complete in themselves. This development is essential for appreciating the sonnets of 1569 although a return to the sonnet form was not tantamount to a conquest of it. Just as Ronsard repeatedly varied his moral views and his style in the *Continuations,* so in 1569, the sonnet becomes a thematic soundingboard. Ronsard toys with the old clichés but at the same time essays those themes more in harmony with the views on love expressed in the seasonal hymns. As with the *Continuations,* the reader encounters once again on the threshold of change a respect for the past, for what was tried, for what was accepted: further evidence that Ronsard was not by nature an innovator. On the other hand, the Ronsard of the *Continuations* is a poet vacillating among various possibilities all of which suddenly seem valid. From 1563 to 1569 to 1578 a noticeable progression takes place as Ronsard moves from the purest Petrarchism, reminiscent of the poems of 1552, to a cultivation of those emotions which will dominate *Sonnets pour Hélène.*

Not a single woman's name appears in the sonnets of 1569—an important indication of the poet's attitude—for no pretense is made about the source of inspiration. It arises in the poet, in the craftsman. All but three of the sonnets appear in two groups: the first of thirteen sonnets, the second of five. The production, then, is small in keeping with Ronsard's more restrained attitude toward the sonnet form. Thematically, the production is divided between the most banal and the most promising devices. At this late moment, for example, Ronsard is still content to belabor the images of Argus:

> Un autre Argus à deux yeux redoutable,
> En corps humain non feint, non inventé

> Espie, aguete, & garde la beauté,
> Par qui je suis en doute miserable.
>
> (*15*, 201, vv. 5–8)

the jealous Sun:

> Jaloux Soleil contre Amour envieux,
> Soleil masqué d'une face blesmie,
> Qui par trois jours as retenu m'amie
> Seule au logis par un temps pluvieux.
>
> (*15*, 199, vv. 1–4)

and other mythological trappings so prevalent in *Amours I*. To combat Argus, whom he addresses, he asks, "A mon secours vienne un autre Mercure,/ Non pour ta mort, mais bien pour t'endormir" (*15*, 201, vv. 13–14). In castigating "Jaloux Soleil," he alludes to the Sun's many loves as mere fable and evokes an old legend to denigrate one entrusted with so great a task: "Ah! tu n'es digne au Ciel d'estre un flambeau,/ Mais un qui meine en terre les boeufz paistre" (*15*, 200, vv. 13–14). As the last two quotations reproduce the final verses of the poems, it is not difficult to appreciate with the poet's continued use of mythology his continued interest in ending sonnets with a "pointe." This device, like the themes and vocabulary that prepare it, summarizes eloquently the link between these two poems, the 1569 sonnets in general, and the past trends of Ronsard's love poetry. Certain images remain; there is no attempt at times to hide that the love sonnet of the period can be a kind of joke and an instrument of social amusement.

Beside the trite and the lighter verse there appears in greater proportion the serious expression of a serious love poet. In philosophy, in emotion, in attitude, he is easily recognizable as the poet of the hymns and the lover of Genèvre. While it had not been unusual, for example, to write a poem on the occasion of the lady's illness, the poem's content usually consisted of a plea for her quick recovery, as in sonnet 161 of *Amours I:*

> Quelle langueur ce beau front deshonore?
> Quel voile obscure embrunit ce flambeau?
> Quelle palleur despoupre ce sein beau,
> Qui per à per combat avec l'Aurore?
> Dieu medecin, si en toy vit encore
> L'antique feu du Thessale arbrisseau,
> Las, pren pitié de ce teint damoyseau,
> Et son lis palle en oeilletz recolore.
>
> (vv. 1–8)

In 1555 Ronsard had already broken with the mythology of Apollo the healer. Sonnet 44 of the *Continuation*, "Si vous pensés que Mai, & sa belle verdure," makes the cure similar to the presentation Ronsard will use in 1569: a linking of her illness and the lover's anguish:

Il faut donque premier me garir la pointure
Que voz yeus dans mon coeur me font par leur rigueur,
Et tout soudain apres vous reprendrés vigueur,
Quand vous l'aurés gary du tourment qu'il endure.

(vv. 5–8)

But in 1555 Ronsard is still playing with terms and preparing "pointes." He makes of love a game of illness and cure in which, only by "curing the lover's illness" can the lady return to health.

In "Non, ce n'est pas l'abondance d'humeurs," from the 1569 sonnets, Ronsard abandons word games for the expression of the serious new themes:

> Non, ce n'est pas l'abondance d'humeurs,
> Qui te rend morne & malade & blesmie,
> C'est le peché de n'estre bonne amie,
> Et la rigueur par laquelle je meurs.
>
> (*15*, 203, vv. 1–4)

The choice of terms—"peché," "bonne amie"—underlines the new leitmotivs: the insistence on loving as natural, its opposite as a sin against nature, and the serious invocation to the lady to be a true partner in love. Twice in these works of 1569 Ronsard curses the lady's pride and insists on the necessity of fulfillment:

> Depuis trois ans pour voz yeux je soupire,
> Mais mes soupirs, ma Foy, ma Loyauté
> N'ont, las je meurs! de vostre coeur osté
> Ce doux orgueil auteur de mon martire.
> Et ce-pendant vous ne connoissez pas
> Que ce beau mois & vostre age se passe,
> Come une fleur qui languist contrebas,
> Et que le temps passé ne se ramasse:
> Tandis qu'avez la jeunesse & la grace,
> Et le temps propre aux amoureux combaz,
> De tous plaisirs ne soyez jamais lasse,
> Et sans aimer n'atendez le trespas.
>
> $\qquad\qquad$ (*15*, 233, vv. 5–16)

Le Temps s'enfuit, cependant ce beau jour,
Nous doibt aprendre à demener l'Amour,
Et le pigeon qui sa femelle baize.
Baisez moi doncq & faison tout ainsi
Que les oyseaux sans nous donner soucy:
Apres la mort on ne voit rien qui plaise.

$\qquad\qquad\qquad$ (*15*, 195, vv. 9–14)

Thus does the hymns' philosophy revitalize one of Ronsard's most successful themes to pave the way for the famous "Quand vous serez bien vieille" of *Sonnets pour Hélène*. Such revitalization is yet another essential consequence in the selection of new themes as Ronsard is drawn farther and farther away from the impersonal devices and games of the past toward ideas with which a personal identification has been established.

The two poems just quoted, for example, contain quite familiar sentiments. There is not only desire but tragic insistence on how fateful hesitation can be. To appreciate the influence of the hymns on the quality of emotion expressed here, we need only cast a backward glance at sonnet 35 from the *Continuation des Amours:*

> Je vous envoye un bouquet de ma main
> Que j'ai ourdy de ces fleurs epanies:
> Qui ne les eust à ce vespre cuillies,
> Flaques à terre elles cherroient demain.
> Cela vous soit un exemple certain
> Que voz beautés, bien qu'elles soient fleuries,
> En peu de tems cherront toutes flétries,
> Et periront, comme ces fleurs, soudain.
> Le tems s'en va, le tems s'en va, ma Dame:
> Las! le tems non, mais nous nous en allons,
> Et tost serons estendus sous la lame:
> Et des amours desquelles nous parlons,
> Quand serons morts n'en sera plus nouvelle;
> Pour-ce aimés moi, ce pendant qu'estes belle.

Here Ronsard wants to transmit essentially the same idea just quoted from the 1569 sonnets, but in the *Continuation*, the idea is introduced and developed through the tacit simile: you and your beauties are like the flowers of my bouquet. The sense of the simile does not appear until the very last line. As a result, the poem strikes mainly through its didactic character (the exposition of the simile best exemplified by the tone of line 5: "Cela vous soit un exemple certain . . ."). In the works of 1569 the structure is reversed. The accent falls first upon the poet's own sentiments, not his philosophy:

> Que maudit soit le mirouër qui vous mire,
> Et vous fait estre ainsy fiere en beauté,

Ainsy enfler le coeur de cruauté,
Me refuzant le bien que je desire.
                            (*15*, 232–3, vv. 1–4)

Ce jour de May qui a la teste peinte,
D'une gaillarde & gentille verdeur,
Ne doibt passer sans que ma vive ardeur
Par vostre grace un peu ne soit estainte.
                            (*15*, 195, vv. 1–4)

The ravages of time are evoked to sustain his arguments, but true to the vision of the seasonal hymns, Ronsard does not hesitate to expound his desire first, independent of the simile.

Throughout the sonnets of 1569 Ronsard returns to this note of personal, insistent emotion to formulate in his choice of themes the last of the essential ties between the years of 1560–70 and the flowering of *Sonnets pour Hélène*. In general, the vocabulary of the sonnets offers little that is new; "fire," "death," and "care" remain the dominant clichés. But as elsewhere there is a movement toward the key phrases. In the context of the poet's reaction to the *innamoramento*, for example, the poet passes from a general portrait of the meeting,

Voz yeux au coeur m'ont jetté telle braize,
Qu'un feu treschaut s'est depuis ensuivy,
Et des le jour qu'en dansant je vous vy,
Je meurs pour vous, & si en suis bien aize,
                            (*15*, 194, vv. 5–8)

to an accent upon the actual physical shock:

De veine en veine, & d'artere en artere,
De nerfz en nerfz le salut me passa
Que l'autre jour Madame prononça,
Me promenant tout triste & solitaire.
                            (*15*, 229, vv. 1–4)

Reminiscences of the seasonal hymns are everywhere. Love is a necessity; love is a physical force. When in one of the sonnets of this group Ronsard writes,

> Non pas du nés mais du coeur je te sens,
> Et de l'esprit que ton odeur surmonte,
> Et tellement de veine en veine monte,
> Que ta senteur embasme tous mes sens,
>   (*15*, 202, sonnet XI, vv. 5–8)

or in another,

> De vostre Amour tout le coeur me bouillonne,
> Devant mes yeux sans cesse je vous voy,
> Je vous entends absente, je vous oy,
> Et mon penser d'autre Amour ne raisonne.
> J'ay voz beautés, voz graces voz yeux
> Gravez en moy, les places & les lieux
> Où je vous vy danser, parler & rire,
>   (*15*, 202, sonnet X, vv. 5–11)

it is evident that the love experience has left behind static poses and portrayals of composite beauty. The poetry has a new force, a new sureness, because the seasonal hymns have helped to define its subject. The words flow smoothly because Ronsard has thought out the progression and association of emotion. Above all, the poetry vibrates because, in contrast to the Petrarchistic poses, the poet and lady have been profoundly humanized. The lover has come alive ("tout le coeur me bouillonne"), the woman appears human ("où je vous vy danser, parler & rire"). Instead of choosing the disembodied eye of the lady as the means by which the lover is captured, Ronsard relates that she has ensnared him with her essence, a far more successful image as it permits the poet to use again the theme of physical reaction ("de veine en veine monte") without the dissonant

strains of death, mourning, and grief found in *Amours I*
and the poems to Sinope.

Once armed with these new themes which he has now
rather successfully adapted to the sonnet form, Ronsard has
accomplished the initial steps for a return to the sonnet
cycle. The sonnets of 1569 are not all devoid of the old devices. The Petrarchistic vocabulary abounds, but the significance of these sonnets lies elsewhere, beside or beneath
this vocabularly: in the seeds of *Sonnets pour Hélène.*

At the very moment Ronsard reveals an accrued personal
and poetic sensitivity in selecting the themes of his love
story, he reveals in his choice of sources a similar percep-
tion and maturity. This statement can be made even in
view of Ronsard's continued use of Petrarchistic devices
because their place in his poetry has changed so significantly. In the sonnets of 1569, for example, in spite of
Ronsard's avowed break with Petrarch's authority, the Petrarchistic elements remain but only as background material and poetic style much as they had in the Genèvre
elegies. Ronsard published in the same year a surprising
sonnet to a Madame de la Chastre, admitting:

> Heureuses mille foix, rimes si bien escrites,
> Que j'ay cent & cent fois en cent sortes redites,
> Les premiers passetemps de ma douce jeunesse.
> Perles & diamans, les flames, les glaçons,
> Ces motz mignards, ces rais, sont les jeunes chansons
> Qu'à vingt ans je chantois pour fleschir ma Maitresse.
>
> (*15*, 151, vv. 9–14)

This boastful embracing of the Petrarchistic clichés appears quite out of harmony with Ronsard's recent evolution away from the Italian mode of love poetry. It warns
the critic, however, against losing sight of the importance
of this vocabulary as the lyric vehicle of the day. Piéri has

wisely remarked about the Pléiade's attitude toward the Petrarchistic traits: "Les disciples les plus fervents du maître ont l'air parfois de s'en défendre et presque de les condamner. C'est une attitude passagère qu'ils prennent pour faire croire à la franchise de leurs accents." [12] He is eminently correct in drawing attention to the transitory quality of their remarks. Petrarchism was irreplaceable, and protest accompanied by a faithful return to the conceits became for Ronsard the pattern of a struggle to tame, not supplant a foreign and treacherous tradition.

The sonnets of 1569, like the seasonal hymns and the elegies to Genèvre, show a decided paucity of identifiable sources.[13] And, to continue the parallel between these sonnets and the poems of 1563, even when the source is identified, close scrutiny shows that Ronsard insists more and more on bending the model to accommodate his personal

12. M. Piéri, *Pétrarque et Ronsard* (Marseille, 1896), p. 62.

13. Besides Petrarch, only the *Greek Anthology* appears a possible single source, and Ronsard's technique in borrowing from it varies little from that he used in imitating Petrarch. The attribution of "Pren cette rose aimable comme toy" to erotic poems 143 and 144 of the *Anthology* is a fine example of the great distance which remains between Ronsard's poems and their "sources." As James Hutton has admitted concerning Ronsard's poem, "This is evidently a variation on the theme he had just borrowed from the Greek epigram, of which, however, there remains little but the phrase *'sers de rose aux roses, fleur aux fleurs'* " (*The Greek Anthology in France* [Ithaca, N.Y., 1946], p. 363). The other poem referred to by Hutton, "Douce beauté, meurdrière de ma vie," is, with "J'avois l'esprit tout morne & tout pesant," one of the two clear cases of imitation. The important element in common, of course, is Ronsard's imitation of a theme in keeping with his new ideas. "Douce beauté . . ." exhorts the woman to love: "Aprens à vivre . . . / Par le plaisir faut tromper le trespas." And the gift of the apple, which allows Paulus Silentarius to make the obvious comparison, "instead of breasts my feeble hands clasp apples" (*The Greek Anthology,* ed. and trans. Shane Leslie [New York, 1929], p. 74), prompts Ronsard to make this sweeping statement: "l'Amour n'est qu'un beau jeu de pommes," a definition whose physical implications escaped no one. (See Belleau's commentary, Laumonier, *15, 197.*)

vision. The sonnets "Heureux le jour, l'an, le mois & la place" and "Je suis larron pour vous aymer Madame" both have their source in Petrarch, but the original Italian poems only point up Ronsard's evolution, not servility to his sources. The happy meeting, the transformation to ice, the loss of spirit which lodges in the woman—all of which comprise the beginning of "Heureux le jour . . ."—could not be more traditional. But as the poem moves to its "pointe," the narrator draws together these clichés to present in the first tercet their effect—a very physical effect:

> Aucunefois quand vous tournez un peu
> Vos yeux sur moy, je sense un petit feu,
> Qui me r'anime & reschaufe les veines.
>
> (*15*, 200, vv. 9–11)

In "Je suis larron pour vous aymer Madame" the resemblances between Ronsard and Petrarch are patent:

Je suis larron . . .	mi fai divenir ladro . . .[14]
Un seul regard . . .	Cosí dal suo bel volto
Me paist trois jours . . .	L'involo or uno or un altro sguardo; E di ciò inseme mi nutrico et ardo.[15]

But behind the resemblance lie extensive differences in temperament and vision. The Petrarch poem, a canzone, "Ben mi credea . . . ," relates the story of a lover's despair at separation from his lady. Grown aware that the lady's presence is essential to his life, he has become a thief, robbing his lady's glances:

> Or, poi che da madonna i' non impetro
> L'usata aita, a che condutto m'hai,
> Tu 'l vedi, Amor, che tal arte m'insegni.

14. Petrarch, *Rime*, p. 295.
15. Ibid., p. 297.

Non so s'i' me ne sdegni;
Ché'n questa età mi fai divenir ladro
Del bel lume leggiadro
Senza 'l qual non vivrei in tanti affanni.[16]

What strikes in the Petrarchan verse is the preoccupation with the moral sense of "ladro" and the act of stealing, which, like most of Petrarch's attitudes, was subsequently transformed into Petrarchistic clichés of compliment. The compliment—the lover's total dependence on his lady—is for Petrarch, however, inextricable from the ethical question posed by the poet's reaction to his state and even posed by the state itself. "You see, Love," he says to the god, "you teach me such an art! I know not if I should abhor myself." And he reveals his crime. "Had I only adopted in my early years this style, now forced on me," he sighs, "for youthful error is less shameful." Thus, the poet gathers around the theme of theft a proliferation of ideas—shame, necessity, divine imposition—which combine to place the compliment on an unexpected plane where desire fuses not only with necessity but also with revulsion. He insists that the beginning of their acquaintance rested on a complete ignorance by both parties of the worth of the lady's glance: "Thus did I offend neither eyes nor person." But then came the realization that her glance was his source of life and "love thirst and helplessness excuse [his] acts." [17] Before committing the crime, he insists on a struggle for another solution, but to no avail, and the remaining stanzas emphasize his suffering and desire to die.

The Ronsard poem, while drawing its inspiration from the part of the canzone just analyzed in detail, strips away virtually every moral connotation. The very introduction, "Je suis larron pour vous aymer" ("I have become a thief

16. Ibid., p. 295.
17. Ibid., pp. 295-96.

for loving you") states bluntly and without qualm or excuse what Petrarch avows only with self-recrimination.
Ronsard avoids the problem because his concern is the portrait of his state in love:

> Je suis larron pour vous aymer Madame:
> Si je veux vivre il faut que j'aille embler
> De vos beaux yeux les regards, & troubler
> Par mon regard le votre qui me pasme.
> De voz beaux yeux seulement je m'afame,
> Tant double force ilz ont de me combler
> Le coeur de joye & mes jours redoubler,
> Ayant pour vie un seul trait de leur flame.
>   (*15*, 230, vv. 1–8)

Since Petrarch cannot divorce the act of loving from the
state of loving, his narrative must flash back and forth between the subjective sentiment (what her glance represents
to him) and the objective judgment (what his loving requires of him or creates in him). Ronsard's reader was
meant to feel the total rapture, even to the point of "crime"
—an attitude which explains the change of order. The idea
of necessity which ends Ronsard's sonnet, "Larron forcé
de chose defenduë,/ Non par plaisir mais par necessité,"
appears early in the canzone, linked with the word "ver-
gogna" and the apostrophe to Love. Ronsard prefers to
heighten the compliment in his closing tercet. What for Petrarch has been created by Love's treachery and is an occasion for moral indignation, Ronsard proudly offers as a
parting shot of adulation: this exquisite act of theft, justifi-
able for its pleasure, is prompted by an even more profound impetus, necessity. Through the "pointe," the accumulation of poses ("me pasme," "m'afame," "combler/
Le coeur de joye"), an entirely new emotion is created.
Leaving behind the moral disquietude, the wish for pain
and death, Ronsard infuses pleasure into a moment of emo-

tion so ambiguous for Petrarch ("Non so s'i' me ne sdegni").

This comparison raises an important question of vision, especially pertinent at this turning point in Ronsard's handling of the sonnet. Can Ronsard be accused of insensitivity and crass Epicurean interests? Can we not expect growing complexity in the poet's sentiments at the threshold of perfection? Yet Ronsard consistently eschews the moral traps and perplexities which Petrarch saw in all aspects of love. The answer, and Ronsard's justification, lie, I think, in the problem our poet faced: how to transform the Petrarchistic tradition into a successful personal vision. As "Ben mi credea" proves, there can be no doubt that Petrarchan love suffering is inseparable from moral bewilderment. To reenter the world of moral complexity was to adopt anew the tradition which Ronsard had once embraced and sought, since *Amours I,* to refashion. By beginning "Je suis larron . . . ," the poet refuses to open the discussion to all that will destroy his pleasure.

Of course, the entire question of the poets' different attitudes toward love could be reduced to a difference in personality. Petrarch clearly possesses the more religious, the more indecisive character, while in the main Ronsard's attitudes portray a man endowed with an exceptionally strong will. But this opposition of personalities oversimplifies the problem. For example, to remain for a moment within the context of personality, we might note that it is traditional in literary criticism to speak of Petrarch as "the first modern man," a phrase which immediately suggests a definite relationship between Petrarch's personality and the age in which he lived and which he helped to create. Ever since the writings of Burckhardt, it is also traditional to associate such independent will as Ronsard exhibits with the dominant spirit of the Renaissance. Thus, defining each poet's personality only returns the problem to a larger question of the historical context in which the poets were writing.

However, if it is impossible to determine with precision the cause and effect relationship between the nature of the Renaissance and the men of the Renaissance, there can be no doubt that the tradition of love poetry inherited by Ronsard from earlier Petrarchists had passed beyond that stage in the Renaissance when nascent feelings of independence were still in conflict with medieval religiosity, a stage which Petrarch exemplifies. Ronsard's tradition was in essence a literary, not a moral phenomenon. The Petrarchistic lover's laments and struggles with love arise because the lady is cruel, not because he himself cannot accept or justify in a moral context the emotion which binds him to his cruel mistress. Naturally, Ronsard was free to return to the moral question, but he did not. Instead he gave further proof that he belonged to a later, more literary stage in the development of Renaissance lyric poetry by exhibiting a personal reaction to the love experience based firmly on the question of creation and the tenet that to preserve one's creativity all fidelity was owed to Muse and youth. At the same time, precisely within this literary context Ronsard found fertile ground for contemplating those problems of self-justification which apparently troubled him. Thus, to accentuate the element of youth at the expense of Ronsard's equal emphasis on his Muse, as if Ronsard conceived of love in purely "carpe diem" terms, is to ignore the profounder connotations with which Ronsard surrounded his analysis of love. Unlike Petrarch, Ronsard finds conflict in refusing love, not in acceding to it. Unlike Petrarch, too, Ronsard was not affected by the idea of a dichotomy between allegiance to God and loyalty to love, for the theory of divine inspiration made the poetic demon and love's inspiration merely gradations of the same experience.

We have no better example of this cleavage of views between the two poets in the period before *Sonnets pour*

Hélène than Ronsard's treatment of Petrarchan verse in *Sur la Mort de Marie*. The poems of 1569 can only point ahead; *Sur la Mort de Marie*, however, supplies ample evidence of Ronsard's mature and individualistic use of Petrarch's poetry. That he should think of the Italian's "In Morte" poems at the moment of Marie de Clèves' death was quite natural. Yet the manipulation of the Petrarchan material bears the mark of its author. The sonnet "Deux puissans ennemis," is imitated from "Due gran nemiche," which Petrarch chose to end with the thought, "if these two enemies are now parted,"

> Forse averrà che 'l bel nome gentile
> Consecrerò con questa stanca penna.[18]

This conclusion is weak, banal, and only incidentally related to the preceding ideas introduced in the sonnet. Ronsard rejected it completely. In its place he sought a long, ringing phrase, the same aesthetic effort that can be found in "Afin que vif et mort ton corps ne soit que roses." He declines to introduce any new element into the poem but works and reworks the key words of the poems to Marie, "sépulchre," "Mort," "amour," and, of course "cendre." Here is the result:

> Amour d'autre lien ne sçauroit me reprendre,
> Ma flame est un sepulchre, & mon coeur une cendre,
> Et par la mort je suis de la mort amoureux.
>
> (IV, vv. 12–14)

Elsewhere Ronsard's efforts can be observed in his choice of theme. Petrarch's Laura in death is at first regretted and mourned by a man whom she has left behind and who would join her. This death underlines the fragility of human life and things earthly; it leaves the lover adrift with no one to guide him. All this Ronsard borrowed from

18. Ibid., p. 410.

Petrarch: it was the natural territory of the poet, how *he* felt, how she appeared to *him*, how her death affected *his* life. But for Petrarch, the love story did not end there:

> Lei non trov'io, ma suoi santi vestigi
> Tutti rivolti a la superna strada
> Veggio, lunge da' laghi averni e stigi.[19]

Petrarch never loses sight of these traces and maintains a sentimental attachment that permits contact beyond death,

> Sol un riposo trovo in molti affanni;
> Che, quando torni, ti conosco e 'ntendo
> A l'andar, a la voce, al volto, a' panni.[20]

This is more than the consolation of a comforting image, for Petrarch is not insensitive to the function of Laura, even in death. "Né trovo in questa vita altro soccorso," [21] he says of her appearance to him. The world holds no equal sight or pleasure; he is aware of her alone; and through this awareness, Laura may make her influence felt:

> L'acque parlan d'amore e l'ôra e i rami
> E gli augelletti e i pesci e i fiori e l'erba
> Tutti insieme pregando ch'i' sempre ami.
> Ma tu, ben nata che dal ciel mi chiami,
> Per la memoria di tua morte acerba
> Preghi ch'i' sprezzi 'l mondo e i suoi dolci ami.[22]

We would seek in vain such pronouncements in Ronsard. Marie is solidly ensconced in Heaven. But she exerts no force save through the regret occasioned by her death. Once, according to the elegy, she did uplift him, "Vous m'ostastes du coeur tout vulgaire penser,/ Et l'esprit jusqu'au ciel vous me fistes hausser" (vv. 75–79). But then

19. Ibid., p. 421.
20. Ibid., p. 395.
21. Ibid., p. 395.
22. Ibid., p. 393.

she was alive! The poet willingly ascribes to the living woman powers he shows no interest in ascribing to her after death. The juxtaposition of certain sonnets to Marie and their sources in Petrarch shows that the poet meant consciously to prevent her having any further influence on him. Ronsard imitated openly Petrarch's plaintive themes in the quatrains of sonnets CCXXIII, CCLXXV, CCLXXX, or CCCVI, for example, but stopped short when, in the tercets, the Italian moved from earth to heaven and to a Laura-Beartrice. The women Ronsard loved and offered to make the Lauras of France are without exception Lauras "In Vita." The lifeless woman has no function in Ronsard's poetic universe. The moment of excitement presented by the seasonal hymns or Genèvre elegies is here-and-now. The outcome of the poet's passion for Genèvre underscores, as does his whole frame of mind after "A son Livre," the very opposite of any eternal quality in love. Ronsard's formulation again and again insists upon the intense but ephemeral, upon the reality that love is the product of inclination and factors which fate can destroy in a moment, only to restore with another partner.

Thus Ronsard set the stage for another love story, his final sonnet cycle. The vision is there, the choice of the suitable partner, the unabashed emotion, transmitted in forceful verse. The sonnets of 1569 show that Ronsard was fully conscious of the significance of the seasonal hymns; *Sur la Mort de Marie* proves that still later Ronsard refused to compromise even when finding inspiration in Petrarch. Naturally all of *Sonnets pour Hélène* is not contained in the sonnets of 1569 or the other sonnets published in 1578. In singing of Hélène de Surgères, Ronsard would for the first time identify his inspiration within the sonnet cycle in unmistakable terms, and her reality had to be dealt with. Moreover, the philosophy of the hymns did not form a story, and Ronsard would be obliged to formulate some means to interlock the general themes of love in structure. Much still awaits us in *Sonnets pour Hélène*. If we have witnessed, beginning with the time of the seasonal hymns, the gradual creation of a new vision, it is only now that we see its fullest application.

3. The Conquest of the Sonnet Cycle

RONSARD, PROPERTIUS, AND TRIUMPH OVER STRUCTURE

WHEN Ronsard wrote *Sonnets pour Hélène*, he was an old man, and especially so according to the age in which he lived. As early as 1560, he had begun to parallel his physical decline and a decline in poetic inspiration:

> Monseigneur, je n'ay plus cette ardeur de jeunesse
> Qui me faisoit chanter des armes & d'amour:
> J'ay le sang refroidy, le jour suyvant le jour
> En derrobant mes ans les donne à la vieillesse.
> Plus Phoebus ne me plaist, ny Venus la deesse,
> Et la Grecque fureur qui bouillonnoit autour
> De mon cueur, qui estoit son fidelle sejour
> Comme un vin escumé sa puissance rabaisse.
>
> *(10, 336, vv. 1–8)*

Yet when he found himself viciously attacked by the Protestants, his *Response* (1563), voiced the outrage of a man for whom poetry was his mainstay, despite his lessening production. In the same year Ronsard confessed to Aluyot in an essay with the eclogue form, "Je ne puis qu'en chantant ma douleur contenter,/ Mon confort seulement ne vient que de chanter" (*12*, 107, vv. 279–80.) Still later (1569), ill and tired, Ronsard confided to Bäif:

> J'auray toujours un Baïf dans le coeur,
> Ayantz passé souz Dorat noz jeunesses,
> Tous deux amis des neuf belles Déesses
> Qui t'ont planté les Lauriers sur le front,
> Qui vont dansant sur Parnasse, & qui ont

> Soucy de moy, quand la fiebvre me ronge,
> Me consolant, soit que je veille ou songe,
> Par Poësie, & ne veux autre bien,
> Car ayant tout, sans elle je n'ay rien.
>
> (*15*, 59–60, vv. 258–66)

The crucial relationship between life and poetry could not be more clear. With the arrival of Desportes at the court, however, Ronsard found his vogue gravely threatened.

On the surface, the important exterior elements surrounding the writing of *Sonnets pour Hélène* do not seem more complex than those associated with his other significant publications. *Amours I* and the *Odes* were necessary to make his name; the *Discours* and the *Response*, to defend his integrity; the *Franciade*, to crown an honored head with laurel. In the case of *Sonnets pour Hélène*, Ronsard was forced to rival Desportes and meet a need to preserve this laurel. Champion even claims that Desportes had sung Hélène de Surgères upon returning from Poland and that it was he who gave Ronsard the idea of writing a cycle for her. But Champion's interpretation falls short of presenting, as do the biographical elements just mentioned, a complete picture of the genesis of *Sonnets pour Hélène*. The mere impetus of rivalry and old age would make these poems pot-boilers, work forced upon the poet by outside needs. When we examine the whole tableau of the years before the publication of this final cycle, and the poetic, not biographical problems he struggled with in it, then we see the cycle in a light much closer, I think, to the truth of the matter and to an appreciation of Ronsard's assumed and personal position vis-à-vis *Sonnets pour Hélène*.

In this total picture, there is Ronsard's return to the sonnet form in 1569, some time before Desportes became a serious rival. There is the accrued poetic sense, the new themes and the new vision which Ronsard has developed since 1563. There is Ronsard's particular reluctance to publish his new cycle before 1578, though we know that he began the poems to Hélène much sooner. There is the singular orientation which the question of age and faith in poetry gives to the last cycle above and beyond the element of rivalry. It is very likely that the mastery of technique involved in *Sonnets pour Hélène* would not have been so intense without the problem of Desportes which bore directly upon his view of himself as well as the world's esteem and his right to fame. But without a consideration of the new themes, the new vision, there is no appreciating in detail the poetic achievement that *Sonnets pour Hélène* represents and the enormous distance between its Sonnets and those of his earlier cycles.

In subject, style, and structure, the genesis of *Sonnets pour Hélène* is equally complex, for rivalry and a new poetic sense may explain why Ronsard could have been particularly interested in discovering a new lady, but not why he finally chose Hélène de Surgères or created a sonnet cycle so different from his others. There is, in fact, every reason to be astounded by his choice of subject. In a chapter entitled "Hélène de Surgères" Desonay has collected the known evidence concerning this woman. She was, in rapid summary, "une jeune 'Pallas' sans beauté, sans fortune malgrè sa naissance. . . ."[1] That she was noble, of the court, and gifted intellectually spoke in her favor. The elegies to Genèvre show renewed preference for the prototype of Cassandre, not Marie. On the other hand, Hélène's lack of beauty (which in truth appears to have been spoken of more often as blatant ugliness) would make her seem from the outset an undesirable candidate for the homages of the love cycle, and the use of her intelligence had carried "Pallas" into dangerous territory—Platonism,

1. Desonay, *Ronsard, poète de l'amour, 3,* 207.

the very antithesis of Ronsard's philosophy in the seasonal hymns.

Theories are not lacking to explain Ronsard's commitment to Hélène de Surgères despite these obstacles. Binet suddenly remembered only in time for the third edition of his *Vie de Ronsard* that all was done at the command of the queen, but the tardiness of this recollection makes its content rather suspect. More recently Desonay has proposed that Ronsard was "infiniment sensible à l'efficace poétique de ce prénom 'fatal'; ce qu'il veut, par ce constant rappel de l'héroïne homérique, c'est servir sa propre gloire d' 'Homère de la France.' " [2] Impressive textual evidence in *Sonnets pour Hélène* substantiates Desonay's theory: Ronsard was indeed impressed by the poetic possibilities of Hélène's name. Mere love of her name could not solve, however, the gamut of difficulties Ronsard had to face. While the rapprochement Hélène de Surgères–Helen of Troy certainly did provide Ronsard with a positive vehicle for expression, it did not solve, for example, the evident difficulties which arose from a choice of a "Pallas" for a love partner. Hélène de Surgères was publicly known to prefer a philosophy of love incompatible with Ronsard's. A frank portrait such as the elegies to Genèvre would have been scandalous.

Finally, how was the story of so imcompatible a pair to be handled structurally? The cycle could not end with her surrender, and Ronsard had every reason to reject the Petrarchistic monotony of *Amours I*, where lover and lady were forever separated. Moreover, given that among these new problems posed by Hélène de Surgères many are old questions which Ronsard had faced since *Amours I* (presentation of the woman, definition of the lover's attitude, the inspired narration of the love story in the present) the

2. Ibid., p. 231.

decision to create a sonnet cycle for Hélène de Surgères must have represented much more than a biographical legerdemain; it was in every sense a profound poetic challenge.

By the same token, the cycle's genesis must have been a difficult, yet extremely satisfying experience to Ronsard. When completed, the cycle of 1578 brought together under a single title all the cherished themes we have seen develop since 1563: the praise of inspiration, the praise of what is "naturel" (with which Hélène's Platonic ideas furnished a perfect contrast), the physical assault of love. All this he accomplished, moreover, within a portrait of Hélène de Surgères, her poetic name and her intellectualizing.

Basic to *Sonnets pour Hélène,* whether in the poet's vision of the affair, the cycle's structure, or the description of the woman, is the idea of Hélène's duality—Hélène, source of beauty and suffering. On the surface, there is nothing new in such a duality. All Petrarchistic women, Cassandre, Francine, even Marie, share such an effect upon their lovers. And, in fact, *Sonnets pour Hélène* does suggest a return to the Petrarchistic love cycle. The sonnet is by far the dominant form; the dominant tone is neither the light and bantering style of Marullus nor the pastoral bliss of Theocritus, but rather the joy–lament of an inspired but not reciprocated love. Certain sonnets actually reproduce the typical compliment–hyperbole of *Amours I.* In sonnet I/23,[3] for example, Ronsard returns to the theme of madness inspired by the woman in her lover. He seeks to excuse by this madness even the act of touching her hand, but not before he has sufficiently humbled himself before her. "If you will remove from sight your rare gifts," the poet says,

3. The Roman numeral indicates the book in which the sonnet is placed in 1578; the number, its position within that book.

"Je ne vous seray plus d'une importune presse/Fascheux comme je suis" (vv. 5–6). Sonnet II/14 is even more excessive:

> Si de voz douz regards je ne vais me repaistre
> A toute heure, & tousjours en tous lieux vous chercher,
> Helas! pardonnez moy: j'ay peur de vous fascher,
> Comme un serviteur craint de fascher à son maistre.
>
> (vv. 1–4)

And as if the simile of the servant were not sufficient, the poet terminates with a commonplace of the Petrarchistic tradition: "Aimer ce qui fait mal, & revoir ce qu'on craint,/ Est le gage certain d'un service fidele" (vv. 13–14). The poet could not be more faithful in his use of Petrarchistic material, nor more explicit concerning the tradition in which he placed his final love cycle. Nothing in the general style and presentation of *Sonnets pour Hélène* betrays the poet's original commitment to become the Petrarch of France (which is perhaps more applicable to Ronsard's intent in *Sonnets pour Hélène* than "Homer of France"). Nevertheless, we have observed in Ronsard's use of the Petrarchistic style since 1563 the gradual but sustained development of an independent vision which employs, yet is not dominated by, the Petrarchistic material. *Sonnets pour Hélène* is not an exception to this development, despite the sonnets I have just quoted. The Petrarchistic elements mark the mode with which Ronsard wished to be compared and his final challenge to Petrarch and the genre he had progressively abandoned in the late fifties. But the essential vision, structure, tone, and imitation in this last cycle— those elements which contributed to the formulation and development of Hélène's portrait—are not Petrarchistic.

Naturally, the Petrarchistic setting of desired and unconsummated love was a perfect vehicle for a love story which was not and could not be a passionate adventure. Desonay quotes an anecdote from the *Perroniana* to prove conclusively that there could have been no love between Ronsard and Hélène de Surgères.[4] But in truth the question need never be raised. Without relying on the pastoral myth or resorting to an aubade, without involving the woman in any compromising pose or returning completely to the lament–compliment of *Amours I*, Ronsard found a source of inspiration in Hélène de Surgères. Through an essential and definitive rapprochement, he transformed the duality of the Petrarchistic lady to embrace the tenets of the seasonal hymns. Instead of admiring the woman in a purely complimentary context, regretting (again in a complimentary way) her fierce cruelty, Ronsard delved beneath the portrait of a woman who inspired yet rebuffed him and created between the woman's philosophy and her "naturel" an opposition which made the Petrarchistic tradition a stepping stone to the familiar themes of 1563. If Hélène's Platonic leanings were a constant impediment to their possible happiness,

> Vous aimez l'intellect, & moins je vous en prise:
> Vous volez, comme Icare, en l'air d'un beau malheur:
> Vous aimez les tableaux qui n'ont point de couleur.
> Aimer l'esprit, Madame, est aimer la sottise.
>
> (I/42, vv. 5–8)

the poet also perceived in the woman a "bonne nature," which we are led to believe, would have brought her love into harmony with the poet's feelings had it not been for her corruption by society:

4. "Une nouvelle édition des *Oeuvres* de Ronsard—peut-être celle de 1597—allait voir le jour; rencontrant Du Perron chez le cardinal de Retz, Hélène de Surgères l'aurait prié de faire précéder cette édition d'une 'epistre, . . . pour monstrer qu'il ne l'aymoit pas d'amour impudique'; et voici l'insolente réponse de Du Perron: 'Je luy dis: au lieu de cest Epistre, il y fault seulement mettre vostre portraict.' " Ibid., p. 219.

> Ny ta simplicité, ny ta bonne nature,
> Ny mesme ta vertu ne t'ont peu garentir,
> Que la Cour ta nourrice, escole de mentir,
> N'ait degravé tes moeurs d'une fausse imposture.
>   (II/48, vv. 1–4)

Although Ronsard makes quite clear that their affair was far from consummated, he persists in presenting Hélène as endowed with a "bonne nature" and capable of turning a promise of happiness into reality.

No poem defines better than sonnet I/3 the particular duality of his final love:

> Nom, malheur des Troyens, sujet de mon souci,
> Ma sage Penelope, & mon Helene aussi,
> Qui d'un soin amoureux tout le coeur m'envelope:
> Nom, qui m'a jusqu'au ciel de la terre enlevé,
> Qui eust jamais pensé que j'eusse retrouvé
> En une mesme Helene une autre Penelope? (vv. 9–14)

Again the Italian tradition leaves its mark. The Petrarchistic lady, too, was a composite of virtues, but she and her effect were also a composite of conflicting adjectives or expressions, "doulce inhumaine," "doulce mort," and "aigre doulceur." [5] In *Sonnets pour Hélène* Ronsard prefers to make of Hélène two different women (Penelope and Helen), a contrast in techniques that is reminiscent of a technical and philosophical phenomenon we have already witnessed in Ronsard: the schism of the single Petrarchistic theme of joy–lament into the themes of joy through inspiration and regret or condemnation before all impediments to love. In Penelope Ronsard finds virtue, the woman's "bonne nature"; in Helen, beauty but also "Nom, malheur des Troyens," that source of unhappiness which in the case of Hélène de Surgères is the woman's adherence to

---

5. Sonnet 113, vs. 5; sonnet 59, vs. 8; and sonnet 104, vs. 13 of *Amours I.*

Platonic love. Thus, without in the least violating the rank
or the position of Hélène de Surgères, Ronsard defined
the woman in such a way as to permit as well that expression of pleasure drawn from virtue, beauty, and the mere
joy of loving which he had begun to perfect in the sonnets
of 1569.

In the same poem (I/3), Ronsard defines the woman as
his life's breath, quite in keeping with the philosophy of the
seasonal hymns:

> Ma douce Helene, non, mais bien ma douce haleine,
> Qui froide rafraischis la chaleur de mon coeur,
> Je prens de ta vertu cognoissance & vigueur. (vv. 1–3)

The pun has its facile side, but Ronsard does not lose sight
of a more profound interpretation and reinforces the statement whenever possible: "Helene est tout mon coeur, mon
sang & mes propos," (I/43, vs. 3). As should be expected,
his life's breath ("coeur," "sang") is also his poetic breath
("propos"), and once, when Hélène seems ready to abandon her admirer, the poet begs:

> Ne verse point de l'eau sur ma bouillante flame,
> Il faut par ta douceur mes Muses enhardir:
> Ne souffre de mon sang le bouillon refroidir,
> Et tousjours de tes yeux aiguillonne moy l'ame.
> (I/53, vv. 5–8) [6]

Most often, however, Ronsard insists upon the life's breath,
the sweet transfusion of nourishment from the lady to the
lover. Taking up the physical description of sonnet III
(1569), "De veine en veine, & d'artere en artere," [7] he fash-
ions the beautiful "De voz yeux, le mirouer du Ciel," one
of the emotional high points of the cycle. This nourishment,
he says,

6. See also II/46, vv. 7–8.
7. See pp. 146–47.

Je la sens distiller goutte à goutte en mon coeur,
Pure, saincte, parfaite, angelique liqueur,
Qui m'eschaufe le sang d'une chaleur extrême.

                    (I/21, vv. 9–11)

The mirror and the eye are familiar Petrarchistic clichés,
but the emotion is not. The jargon—"ulcere," "furie,"
and so on—disappears entirely before a new vocabulary.
This vocabulary is particularly forceful because it combines rather skillfully the mild terms,

De voz yeux . . .

. . .

D'où pleut une douceur, . . .

. . .

. . . une douce pasture,
Une joye, un plaisir . . .

which describe the quality of the emanation, with the violence of such words as "exchaufe" and "extrême" which
the poet also uses but now with the intention of rendering
palpable a deep shudder that goes far beyond the Petrarchistic ocular attack. The poet draws the reader into his
experience by reproducing it in slow motion, first by the
expression "goutte à goutte," then with the savored slow-
ness of the following line which repeats in its lilt the de-
scent of the drops.[8] In keeping with the hymns, the shudder of accession is indistinguishable from the life substance
and nourishes all of him like the fulfillment of the seasons
through coupling.

Naturally, there is no refusal of such an emotion. When
the lady seeks the quiet of Montmartre where she will be
able to defy "les traicts & les flames d'Amour," the poet re-
plies:

---

8. For a variant of this technique, see I/49.

Sur les cloistres sacrez la flame on voit passer:
Amour dans les deserts comme aux villes s'engendre.
Contre un Dieu si puissant, qui les Dieux peut forcer,
Jeusnes ny oraisons ne se peuvent defendre.

I/28, vv. 11–14)

Finally, as in the hymns, harmony or disharmony with nature appears in the cycle as a function of love. Beside the exultation such poems as "De voz yeux . . . ," there is the sadness in knowing that the nightingale, the rose—the pleasures of nature—are, without love, osprey's singing and thistles. The clinging vine and springtime are changed into "une dure playe" (I/27), and from Penelope to Helen and back the thematic pendulum swings as Ronsard plays now on his joys, now on his frustrations.

The image of the pendulum shows in a most precise manner how the duality of the woman is also the source of the cycle's structure. In detail, the themes may take on variant forms of the Penelope–Helen dichotomy but the latter remains, nonetheless, the crux of the structure of *Sonnets pour Hélène* (1578).[9] As long as the Penelope image dominates, the cycle progresses and overlooks the short-comings of Helen, "Nom, malheur." But once the desire to remain faithful despite the lover's difficulties is passed, the duality becomes untenable, and the *Sonnets pour Hélène* comes to an end. The cycle is much like a poem in itself as the themes branch and proliferate about the central dichotomy. This structure contrasts with those of the earlier cycles: the monotony in *Amours I* produced by an infinite repetition of the same themes or the discontinuity of the *Continuations* which stems from the juxtaposition of an excessive variety of moral poses.

9. For the reasons behind my reference to this edition, see the Appendix.

The first few sonnets of each book of *Sonnets pour Hélène* introduce the dominant themes. In I/1, independence and sureness in the poet's choice of mistress:

> J'ay par election,
> Et non à la volee aimé vostre jeunesse:
> Aussi je prins en gré toute ma passion.
> Je suis de ma fortune autheur . . .
>   (vv. 9–12)

The assurance is based on positive pleasure: "Vous seule me plaisez" (vs. 9), another theme strongly reminiscent of the seasonal hymns and the story of Genèvre, in which the lover chooses his or her partner for similar reasons of independence and recognition of merit and virtue. No wonder then that in *Sonnets pour Hélène* Ronsard's initial assurance of deep personal inspiration, not fancy, opens the way to a prolonged equation between love and emotional fulfillment, love and poetry, love and virtue. In I/2, we are immediately meant to feel the emotional impact of the woman:

> Quand à longs traits je boy l'amoureuse estincelle
> Qui sort de tes beaux yeux, les miens sont esblouys:
> D'esprit ny de raison, troublé, je ne jouys,
> Et comme yvre d'amour tout le corps me chancelle.
>   (vv. 1–4)

His very rational choice indicates also that there is no little detachment in his love. Again in I/1: "La vertu m'a conduit en telle affection:/ Si la vertu me trompe, adieu belle Maistresse" (vv. 13–14). The word "adieu" is significantly pronounced in the very first sonnet, and conditions for its use are clarified. A subtle announcement of the final turning of Ronsard's cycle, the verses contribute as well to the essential exposition of his double perspective. Admission of pleasure and admonition of separation follow in rapid order within the introductory sonnet to warn the reader as well as the lady (an unthinkable gesture in *Amours I*) that the entire experience is contingent upon certain conditions, with the end, if not in sight, at least defined. As a result, if I/2 upholds the positive themes of I/1, I/3 "Ma douce Hélène, non mais bien ma douce haleine," where the dual image of Penelope–Helen appears, is no less announced and prepared by the liminal sonnet and reinforced by the intervening poem.

As if to sustain at so early a stage a sure equilibrium between the "Nom de malheur" and "sage Penelope," Ronsard inserts in I/3 a recognition of the all-important "vertu" on which hangs their relationship: "Je prens de ta vertu cognoissance & vigueur." The next sonnet is devoted exclusively to a Platonic equation of Penelope and "vertu." "Endowed with all that is holy, honorable, and virtuous, she was clothed," he says, "in that which leads to the love 'du vray bien' and forces one to flee its opposite." But having arrived at this pinnacle of praise, the poet must slowly descend to the reality that his love is not reciprocated. Sonnet I/5 effects this movement by turning from the present to the future: "Naisse de noz amours une nouvelle plante,/ Qui retienne noz noms pour eternelle foy" (vv. 5–6). The wish evokes immediately Hélène's resistance, and the poem ends in lament:

> O desir fantastiq, duquel je me deçoy,
> Mon souhait n'adviendra, puis qu'en vivant je voy
> Que mon amour me trompe, & qu'il n'a point de frere.
>
> (vv. 12–14)

The movement of emotion here has great importance for an understanding of the complicated relationship between time and emotion in *Sonnets pour Hélène*. As in all Petrarchistic poetry, the present is ambivalent, but instead of the traditional joy-lament ambivalence, it encompasses

pleasure and detachment, a detachment which even suggests total abandonment of the woman, though this has remained so far a threat more than a reality. In *Sonnets pour
Hélène* the future, rather than the present, provides disappointment and lament. The poet can be happy in the present: the mere presence of the woman is necessary as
inspiration. Moreover, the question of her changing to
become a true partner is rarely of immediate concern when
the poet is blinded by her presence as in sonnet II/44:

> Mon ame mille fois m'a predit mon dommage:
> Mais la sotte qu'elle est, apres l'avoir predit
> Maintenant s'en repent, maintenant s'en desdit,
> En voyant la Maistresse, elle aime davantage.
>
> (vv. 1–4)

But projection into the future excludes this presence. The
poet travels ahead over the period of the woman's becoming and sees in all clarity the impossibility of his ideal.
Through this future awakening lament passes into the present, "Dedans les flots d'Amour je n'ai point de support"
(I/6, vs. 1). Naturally, once the entire pattern has been ex-
posed, full repetition is no longer necessary in presenting
any one of the elements. Nevertheless, the fullness of the
exposition at the beginning of Book One would seem to indicate that Ronsard was desirous of defining at the outset
the respective time values and their emotional equivalents
before entering upon their branching and development.

Aside from recurrently referring to the moral virtues of
his lady and her power over him, Ronsard extends her influence to poetry and to the poetic breath. Love is also a
command to sing of Hélène. "Je la garde pour toy le sujet
de ta plume," are Love's words to the captured poet (I/7).
Elsewhere, taking up the flower device, but in the present,
Ronsard incorporates into the story the outward symbols
of his love, the gifts that pass between them (I/26, I/31,

I/54), and blesses the objects associated with her (I/38). Sometimes they themselves seem symbols to him, as when he likens his first resistance to her to the Giants' revolt against the gods (I/22), or when, in the final sonnet of Book One, Ronsard compares himself to a mirror "qui tousjours represente/Tout cela qu'on luy monstre, & qu'on fait devant luy" (vv. 13-14).

Hélène's resistance is presented in three main forms: awareness and lament (I/5 and I/6), philosophical attack, or, more interesting, personal attack. Though not numerous (I count five examples in the first book, I/9, I/11, I/16, I/25, I/44), the sonnets which attack the woman provide the finest portrait of the poet and his lady as a real couple in contrast to the bard who sings of his Penelope and his Helen. These scenes are not very flattering to the woman. He charges her with perfidy (I/11, I/44), egotism (I/16), feigned emotion (I/25), though with a good deal of indulgence. The sour portrait seems to represent at best, another aspect of the story, at worst, a menace to complete praise. As Ronsard proceeds with his story, however, the tone of indulgence is gradually transformed into something more serious and more final. At the same time, the proportion of poems celebrating their relationship grows smaller among the other themes until, together, these devices make separation seem imminent and indeed, unavoidable.

We have seen above how Ronsard introduces the major themes of the cycle within the first six sonnets, progressing through the predominantly positive attitude of the first four to the negative attitudes of sonnets 5 and 6. This proportion is highly representative of the overall relation between praise and lament in Book One. If we read on through the song "Quand je devise assis aupres de vous" into the sonnets following, we see that Ronsard does not leave I/5 and I/6 uncountered. Sonnet I/7 recounts love's command to sing of Hélène; sonnet I/8 continues the theme of poetry by announcing "Un superbe trophee" which the poet will give to his heart "D'avoir contre [s]es yeux si long temps combatu." The song, sonnets I/9 and I/10, all return to the atmosphere of inspiration. This alternance is maintained throughout nearly all Book One, where such sonnets as I/21–25 provide some of the most positive songs of pleasure in love. The motiv of joy is not without less happy thoughts, but, at the same time, it is never overshadowed or seriously undermined.

Still, there is decided movement. The book does not end exactly as it began. Although it runs to fifty-seven sonnets, the central motiv disappears with I/50. The dominant attitude of the final pages is more neutral and less exalted. Sonnet I/54 tells of a gift of flowers and ends on a sad note: "Voyez combien ma vie est pleine de trespas,/Quand tout mon reconfort ne depend que du songe" (vv. 13–14). Sonnet I/55 is an unimpassioned blason filled with classical allusions. I/57 closes the book on the poet's equivocal remark that he writes as she acts, and only a change in her attitude can produce a more pleasing voice. He has reason to suggest that a possible contrast in attitude might be desirable since in I/56 he has called for vengeance against her indifference. "Not death but old age he wishes to attack her," he says in the sharpest poem so far addressed to Hélène. The traditional blason, the undistinguished gift verse, the sharp outburst, and the warning of the final sonnet form together a significant modulation in the tonality of the first book. The story will go on but not as it started. The poet and his lady have passed a definite stage in their relationship.

Book Two ostensibly maintains the story formulated by Book One. The initial sonnets introduce the same themes: II/1 recalls I/1 with its justification of the poet's love and the conscious embracing of love; II/2 returns to the theme of love–inspiration and the woman, "Je vous fais un present

·de ceste Sempervive"; II/3 calls attention to her ample
beauty; II/4 and 5 pick up the lover's lament; and II/6, the
theme of inspiration again: "Tu es seule mon coeur, mon
sang, & ma Deesse." But while the variety in attitudes has
changed little, there is an important shift in the proportion
and distribution of themes. The positive poems still predominate, but they are decidedly less positive than before.
If, in II/1, the poet justifies his love, it is through a general-
ity: "volontiers le tison/Cache un germe de feu sous une
cendre grise." There is no mention of the woman's irresistible charms. So, too, in II/2 the accent falls away from the
woman in the second quatrain,

> Afin que d'âge en âge à noz neveux arrive,
> Que toute dans mon sang vostre figure estoit,
> Et que rien sinon vous mon coeur ne souhaitoit,
> Je vous fais un present de ceste Sempervive,

to the poet:

> Elle vit longuement en sa jeune verdeur.
> Long temps apres la mort je vous feray revivre,
> Tant peut le docte soin d'un gentil serviteur,
> Qui veut, en vous servant, toutes vertus ensuivre,
> Vous vivrez (croyez moy) comme Laure en grandeur,
> Au moins tant que vivront les plumes & le livre.

In Book Two there is no more returning to what was once
the central theme of inspiration. At the expense of this
theme Ronsard devotes more space to the love–immortality
theme (correspondence between Homer's subject and his)
which with the sonnets and "Stances de la Fontaine d'Hélène," makes the reader much more aware of the poet *qua*
poet in Book Two than in Book One. And without the
omnipresent antidote of inspiration, the lover's bitterness
grows until, after insistent displeasure, he closes the cycle.
The end of *Sonnets pour Hélène* is no less complex a

grouping of moods and poses. Because this complexity goes beyond the problem of a lover's hurt feelings but encompasses the poet's final and finest words on love, death, and poetry, it is only fitting to devote an independent section to the conclusion of this cycle. The gradual schism of narrator into lover and poet here reaches new heights, opening the entire cycle to a new and eloquent function.

In his book entitled *The Aesthetics of the Renaissance Love Sonnet* (Geneva, 1962), Laurence Harvey has used the poems of Louise Labé to define the general orientation of the love sonnet. First, regarding the love experience: "Briefly it is the doomed aspiration toward ideal happiness in the here and now. All transcendental preoccupations are absent and perfection is sought, though not achieved, solely in the earthly area of human activity." [10] Regarding the beloved: "There has been so much preoccupation with the beloved as a real-life person that his universal value as a symbol of the unobtainable dream has often been obscured." [11] Finally, regarding structure: "To be sure, the narrator is more lucid in some poems than in others, but she is always restricted to the self-contained unity of the individual sonnet. . . .[12] If the individual sonnet captures and freezes the fleeting instant, the series represents the negation of crystallization and triumph of flux." [13]

Of the three norms, it is the first, the clash between ideal and reality which seems most immediately applicable to *Sonnets pour Hélène*. The temporal pattern is slightly altered since "the here and now" does not lack ideal happiness. The problem as Ronsard conceived it arises out of a clash between the *moments* of inspiration and the desired

10. Harvey, *Aesthetics*, p. 77.
11. Ibid., p. 77.
12. Ibid., p. 78.
13. Ibid., p. 84.

duration of these moments into the future, between the virtue the woman *is* and the Platonist she *remains*. Of course the joys of "the here and now" in *Hélène* do not include physical gratification, but they are nonetheless presented by Ronsard as supreme emotions. This fact provides our first insight into the complexity of *Sonnets pour Hélène*, for if the Labé pattern were true in Ronsard's case, the cycle would end with the rejection of further suffering and frustration (II/47) where the poet suggests that his ideal is indeed a "doomed aspiration." Yet in fact there are more sonnets and the "Stances" to come. The "Stances" with its fountain, nymphs, and wishes for uninterrupted peace seems to portray some bucolic ideal which has collapsed. But no such thing. The fountain is meant to perpetuate the memory of their love, not to provide them with a place of retreat inspiring "folastres jeux":

> Advienne apres mille ans qu'un Pastoureau desgoise
> Mes amours, & qu'il conte aux Nymphes d'icy pres,
> Qu'un Vandomois mourut pour une Saintongeoise,
> Et qu'encor son esprit erre entre ces forests.
>
> (vv. 77–80)

The ideal world appears much earlier, in Book One, under the title "Chanson." After earthly loves, their shades will descend to Elysium to lead an enchanted life:

> Tantost nous danserons par les fleurs des rivages
> Sous les accords divers,
> Tantost lassez du bal, irons sous les ombrages
> Des Lauriers tousjours verds.
>
> (vv. 25–28)

The cycle's extension beyond the sonnet of "doomed aspiration," the variance in portraits between the "Chanson" and the "Stances" suggest that Ronsard somehow shifted ideals before completing *Sonnets pour Hélène*. The ideal of "Chanson" is that of Louise Labé and all Petrarchistic sufferers inclined to physical gratification. Its appearance in Book One could be expected, as an appreciation of its content has shown that there the lover-lady relationship is still not seriously threatened. When in Book Two the tension breaks, Ronsard transcends the dichotomy of reality and ideal love and extracts from the experience another ideal which carries the cycle beyond the equation of Love and Death which ends the final sonnet. That second ideal is immortality.

One reason, perhaps the principal one, behind Ronsard's movement of ideas within *Sonnets pour Hélène* is his evident conceptual break with the woman as "symbol of the unattainable dream." Since the time of the seasonal hymns and Genèvre, when the "dream" is no longer treated as such but as allegorical or historical truths, the woman has been woman. "La Venus Cyprienne est des Grecs la mensonge,/ La chaste Saintongeoise est une verité" (I/12, vv. 3–4), says Ronsard of Hélène de Surgères. Transcendental qualities and not so transcendental feelings are seen in her, but not through her, as was so true of "Quand au premier. . . ." We have definitely passed the moment when Ronsard moves from the quality to the woman. Ronsard's sonnets to the "beauty" of Hélène may be a fabrication, but there is one definite and definable sentiment attributed to Hélène which explains immediate allegiance to the woman who refused him Elysium as a community of lovers: inspiration.

> Ah, belle liberté, qui me servois d'escorte,
> Quand le pied me portoit où libre je voulois!
> Ah, que je te regrette!   (II/46, vv. 1–3)

he moans, only to admit that he was so born,

> Que sans aimer je suis & du plomb & du bois:
> Quand je suis amoureux, j'ay l'esprit & la vois,

L'invention meilleure, & la Muse plus forte.
(vv. 6–8)

The theme has even reversed the usual Petrarchistic order
of sentiments. Traditionally, the poet loves and turns to poetry to sing his lady's beauty and his own suffering. Ronsard, like the characterization of Nature in the seasonal
hymns, is clearly more conscious of the need for fulfillment
and as a result falls in love. Given this beginning, love is a
gamble. In the case of Genèvre he wins, with Hélène, he
loses, though only in a relative sense, since the poet is never
without inspiration. The change in attitude that dominates
the two stories can be seen in the fact that *Sonnets pour
Hélène* and the Genèvre elegies are full of exhortation
while *Amours I* is full of lament. The cycle of 1552 is written to an abstraction. There is really no one to entreat, nor
is there really anything to beg for. Compliment is the poet's
primary end, and lament, its willing handmaiden.

With the demise of the "symbol of the unattainable
dream" the fiction of the deluded narrator disappeared. I
quote again a revealing passage from *Hélène*,

Mon ame mille fois m'a predit mon dommage:
Mais la sotte qu'elle est . . .

. . .

En voyant ma Maistresse, elle aime davantage,
(II/44, vv. 1, 2, 4)

where Ronsard makes the unequivocal statement that the
cycle continues despite a knowledge of disaster, not
through ignorance of it. The complimentary assurance that
the sight of the lady undoes his premonitions maintains an
excellent rational balance between the two states of clair-
voyance and blindness, but there is no denying both exist
and are recognized from the very beginning—in the "adieu"
and conditions of I/1. The poet's detachment within mo-

ments of rapture even possesses a definite sylistic trait in
Sonnets pour Hélène: the insertion within a very subjective context of pithy generalities which serve to transform
a personal event into a situation representative of the
normal course of love.[14] On his suffering: "Dieu nous
vend cherement les choses qui sont belles,/ Puisqu'il faut
tant de fois mourir pour les avoir" (II/17, vv. 13–14). On
her imperious attitude: "A tout homme mortel la misere est
commune:/Tel eschappe souvent, qu'on pense bien
tenir," (I/8, vv. 3–4). The intrusion of these universal facts
within what is normally a deep, unflinching commitment to
an individual experience could only come from a poet
whose optic had widened to include a judgment as well as a
narration of the personal event. Sometimes (II/17), the
comment universalizes the personal; elsewhere (I/8), it opposes to the literary tradition the greater wisdom of life.
Here the detachment shows itself in full force, and in one

14. In his analysis of the Sinope episode, Desonay has suggested that a
similar technique among the *Sonets amoureux* announces *Sonnets pour
Hélène:* "Dans les *Sonets amoureux* à Sinope, Ronsard est plus proche
de nous parce qu'il s'est dégagé, dirait-on, d'une aventure qui nous
touche désormais presque autant que lui. D'où ces 'maximes' de sagesse
érotique qui lui montent aux lèvres" (Desonay, *Ronsard*, 2, 165–66).
He cites seven examples of such maxims and concludes: "Proportion-
nellement, ce n'est guère; mais ce qu'il convenait peut-être de noter,
c'est, à partir de 1559, ce sens de l'humain qui aboutira quelque jour
aux *Sonnets pour Hélène*. L'expérience individuelle débouche, à mesure
que se creusent les rides du visage, sur la méditation universelle" (Ibid.,
p. 166). For Desonay, then, there is little or no difference between the
origins of the maxims in the *Sonets amoureux* and in *Sonnets pour
Hélène*. Certainly in both works the value of detachment cannot be
refused these maxims by their very content. Yet it is worth recognizing
that, while in the *Sonets amoureux* this attitude is but one of many,
in *Sonnets pour Hélène*, like each recurrent element, it participates
directly in the presentation and structure of the cycle. Ronsard may
well have given more time in his later years to "la méditation universelle." But *Sonnets pour Hélène* proves he also gave greater consideration to the meditation of his themes and their interrelation.

case at least it succeeds in effecting a total reversal of the tradition.

Weber has remarked of II/23 where the poet enjoys in dream what reality refuses, "En 1552, le songe était déjà pour lui une compensation de l'absence, mais le réveil en était encore cruel, maintenant il s'abandonne à l'illusion sans réserve, mais non sans quelque amertume." [15] The expression "sans réserve" stems no doubt from the sonnet's last line: "S'abuser en amour n'est pas mauvaise chose." Instead of Weber's "amertume," however, I would choose "detachment," if not "humor." For, while the poem does in fact recreate the dream sonnet without lament, the poet takes yet another step and in turn reflects upon the experience, thus inverting the normal sequence of emotions. Not only is the lament suppressed, the poet expresses satisfaction from his dream.[16] The contemporary reader could hardly have been insensitive to this turning of the tables on the traditional dream sonnet, and if he read on, he fell straightaway upon "Quand vous serez bien vieille . . ." The term "detachment" is almost mild to describe Ronsard's attitude in this sonnet. The reader must have begun to wonder if, indeed, this was a true love cycle.

According to Harvey's conclusions on structure, the reader is always more lucid than the narrator and foresees the catastrophe which is hidden from the narrator. In *Sonnets pour Hélène* not only does the narrator generally share the reader's detachment and perceptions, he is more lucid than the reader, for he envisages as well as the catastrophe the double ending of dashed love and triumphant immortality.

The disquieting poses of humor and pride in II/23 and

15. H. Weber, *La Création poétique en France au XVIe siècle* (Paris, 1956), p. 366.
16. For contrast, see *Amours I*, sonnet 30.

II/24 ("Quand vous serez bien vieille . . .") are in fact
only franker expressions of the tendency toward greater
preoccupation with the poet *qua* poet we observed in the
opening sonnets of Book Two. This tendency sees its culmination in the "Stances de la Fontaine d'Hélène." Surrounding the "Stances" Ronsard placed at least one sonnet
devoted to each of the dominant attitudes of the cycle's
final movement: recrimination against the woman's cruelty,
II/45, II/48, II/49; regret at the failure of their love, II/53,
II/54; justification of the choice of Hélène, II/46; promise
of immortality, II/49. As sonnets II/50 and II/51 are directly related to the "Stances" and the justification of II/46
is the poet's need for inspiration, it is not hard to see that
poetry shares an equal place with love in the closing moments of the cycle. Through the "Stances," these themes
are brought together and poetry is given its implicit victory
over love and death.

Of the three speakers in the "Stances" the first and second
only are developed. The third intervenes to bring their discussion to a close. At the beginning they are suffering
lovers à la Petrarch. The water's flow suggests to the first
speaker the desire to rid himself of his "soucy" as the water
runs into the grass; to the second how Love's arrows
flowed into his veins. No respite from their condition
appears, for, instead of drowning the love fire, the water is
itself fire (vv. 9–12). The birds, the winds are invoked to
carry their lament to the ladies (vv. 17–24). From this invocation, which is maintained through the repetitive struc-
turing of renewed apostrophes, the "Stances" pass from
suggesting the site's perfection to recalling past lamentation
before the Dryads and Echo. Then follows a long series of
hortatory quatrains, each of which calls for the continu-
ance of some element of the site, and the poem terminates
with the hope that future generations will eternally remem-

ber Ronsard and Hélène. The insistence on lament, coupled with the opening portraits, assures a continuity
between the stanzas and the gathering storm without. If the
speakers do not go so far as the cycle's narrator to de-
nounce their loves and break with them, it is because all
that matters in the realm of this poetic site is that they once
loved and that this pose, enshrined in a fountain of flowering verse, will remain. The woman's comportment is a subject of indifference, just as it is in "Quand vous serez bien
vieille. . . ." In both poems, where the lover has failed,
the poet secures his immortality. Ronsard brings his cycle
to a close insisting that "l'Amour & la Mort n'est qu'une
mesme chose" (II/54, vs. 14), but not until he has de-
posited the memory of both in a "lieu sacrè" ("Stances,"
vs. 28) where the love lament is the music of poetry, and
the threat of death the vision of immortality "a thousand
years hence" ("Stances," vs. 77).

In the preceding pages we have seen Ronsard progress
from the initial difficulty posed by a choice of Hélène de
Surgères to be his final love to the creation of a sonnet
cycle which transcends each one of his problems, whether
Hélène's rank, the cycle's structure, or the singular nature of Hélène's philosophy. In an analysis of the content
of *Sonnets pour Hélène*, the very intimate relation between the solution of these difficulties and the new love
vision of the seasonal hymns has also been emphasized in
order to show how profoundly different is the conception
of this last cycle from the other cycles Ronsard composed
before 1563. This does not mean, however, that *Sonnets
pour Hélène* is without precedent or source. On the contrary, the resemblance between the structure of *Sonnets
pour Hélène* and the *Elegies* of Propertius is quite striking,
and it is not at all impossible that Ronsard drew his inspira-

tion for the general presentation of this cycle to Hélène de Surgères from the Latin works.[17]

A linking of the *Elegies* and *Sonnets pour Hélène* was established long ago, but it has always been based on a few textual borrowings by Ronsard. Of those who have studied the question (there are two critical editions of *Sonnets pour Hélène*—J. Lavaud, Paris, 1947 and P. Laumonier, Paris, 1959—and a comparative study by Professor Hallowell [18]) none present the same list of imitations, and the lone point of agreement is that the elegiac themes of the "Stances" recall Propertius. Hallowell's cases of direct borrowing from Propertius, in particular, cover a wide area of minor possibilities. Certain notations of influence are most likely legitimate, for example, sonnet I/27, "Mon plaisir en ce mois c'est de voir le Coloms/S'emboucher bec à bec de baisers doux & longs" and elegy II.15.27–28,[19] "Be doves thine example: they are yoked together in love, male and female made one by passion." [20] Hallowell also lists as a source for the same verses, elegy I.9.5–6: [21] "Not Chaonia's doves could better divine than I what youths each maiden shall enslave." [22] The juxtaposition of texts speaks for itself. Past criticism, then, has sensed the influence of Propertius on Ronsard, but by restricting its examination to the repetition of diverse words and devices, it has discovered very little evidence to prove that an intimate literary affinity exists between Ronsard's sonnets and

17. I am indebted to Eleanor Winsor Leach for her valuable remarks concerning Propertius.

18. R. Hallowell, *Ronsard and the Conventional Roman Elegy* (Urbana, 1954).

19. All references to Propertius are from the Loeb Classical Library edition, ed. H. E. Butler (Cambridge, Mass., 1962).

20. "Exemplo vinctae tibi sint in amore columbae,/ masculus et totum femina coniugium."

21. Hallowell, p. 139.

22. "Non me Chaoniae vincant in amore columbae/ dicere, quos iuvenes quaeque puella domet."

the elegies of Propertius. At the same time there can be no doubt that Ronsard read Propertius, and if we look through Propertius' text in search of attitudes, not words, a far greater affinity can be found than Ronsard's editors have indicated.

When Ronsard writes in sonnet I/1 of his choice of Hélène and of his conscious embracing of his situation, "Je suis de ma fortune autheur . . . ," he is echoing a very similar confession by Propertius: "Whilst thou singest, Ponticus, of Cadmean Thebes, and the bitter warfare of fraternal strife, . . . I, as is my wont, still pursue my love" (I.7.1,2,5).[23] Ronsard's portrait of himself as impatient at having too long nurtured Love, "Il ne faut plus nourrir cest Enfant qui me ronge" (II/52, vs. 9), recalls Propertius' question of Love: "What delight hast thou to dwell in this withered heart of mine?" (II.12.17).[24] Propertius warns Cynthia that there is no escape from love, "nulla est fuga" (II.30.1), just as Ronsard reminds Hélène in sonnet I/28 that it will do no good for her to withdraw to a convent to flee Love's arrows. Such similarity in attitude, moreover, is not without a direct relation to Ronsard's general conception of *Sonnets pour Hélène*. The conscious choice of subject and the theme of inescapable love, coupled with the poet's growing exasperation, retrace quite precisely the dual perspective around which Ronsard constructed his cycle.

There are striking parallels between the poets' situation, as well. At a glance, there seems to be no comparison possible between Hélène de Surgères, *fille d'honneur* of Catherine de Médicis, and Propertius' Cynthia, poetess,

23. Dvm tibi Cadmeae dicunter, Pontice, Thebae,
armaque fraternae tristia militae,

. . .

nos, ut consuemus, nostros agitamus amores.

24. "Quid tibi iucundum est siccis habitare medullis?"

but of singular morals. Ronsard, however, does not seem to
have been particularly ill-disposed to Cynthia because of
her private life. In a revealing sonnet of the *Continuation
des Amours* he defends her and calls her "honneste":

> Pourtant si ta maitresse est un petit putain,
> Tu ne dois pour cela te courrousser contre elle,
>
> . . .
>
> Tu me diras qu'honneste & gentille est t'amie,
> Et je te respondrai qu'honneste fut Cynthie,
> L'amie de Properce en vers ingenieus,
> Et si ne laissa pas de faire amour diverse.
>
> (sonnet 62, vv. 1–2, 9–12)

Whatever may have been the precise reason for Ronsard's
attribution of this adjective to Cynthia, it is his own secret.
We might note, however, that Ronsard is only expressing
an attitude he could well have formed from reading
Propertius, who himself possessed an ambivalent attitude
toward his love. Like Hélène, Cynthia was a "docta
puella" (I.7.11), and though fickle and unfaithful, she appeared to Propertius as capable of understanding his
crusade against her *luxuria*. His faith in her was all the
more firm as he believed in the goodness of her nature
which he saw corrupted by Roman society: [25] "But here
the race of brides is faithless; here doth no woman show
Evadne's faith or Penelope's loyalty. Happy the young
country-folk that dwelt in peace of old, whose wealth was
in harvest and orchard" (III.13.23–26).[26] To tame and
guide his Cynthia, Propertius resorts to examples such as
"Evadne's faith" just mentioned. But most frequent

25. Cynthia is once described as scorning "fickle-hearted maids" and
therefore disliking the *Iliad* because of Helen (II.1.50).
26. Hoc genus infidum nuptarum, hic nulla puella
        nec fida Euadne nec pia Penelope.
    felix agrestum quondam pacata iuventus,
    divitiae quorum messis et arbor erant!

among the examples to be followed or shunned are those of Penelope and Helen of Troy. Penelope appears at least three times (II.6.24, II.9.3ff, II.13.24) evoked as the image of fidelity, once (II.6) preceded by its contrary, Helen of Troy—the inciter of jealousy and ruin. "Where thou art, peace hath for me no pleasure," Propertius says to Cynthia to conclude III, 8, but not without reference again to Helen, in whose arms Paris "waged a mightier war" (vs. 32).[27] But above all Helen was beauty, tempting and tragic. When Propertius wants to offer Cynthia a supreme compliment, he does not hesitate to associate the beauty of Cynthia with that of the adulteress (II.3.32), even though, as other references show, Propertius by no means totally approves of Helen. A beauty like Helen, Cynthia excites the same devastating passions while the poet helplessly tries to reform her and calls on the model of Penelope.

With very few changes, this situation duplicates the nexus of Ronsard's relationship to Hélène, although not *luxuria* and fickleness but Hélène's Platonic philosophy destroys their possible happiness.[28] We find the same role

27. Ille Helenae in gremio maxima bella gerit.

. . .

. . . . . in te pax mihi nulla placet.

28. It is not without interest to note, however, that if the criticism of luxury is absent from *Hélène*, in *Astrée*, also first published in 1578, there appear three poems duplicating Propertius' attack against luxury and excessive ornaments:

> Dequoy te sert mainte Agathe gravee,
> Maint beau Ruby, maint riche Diamant?
> Ta beauté seule est ton seul ornement. (Madrigal II)

> Si tu m'en crois, fuy l'or ambicieux:
> Ne porte au chef une coiffure telle.
> Le simple habit, ma dame, te sied mieux. (Madrigal III)

> La femme laide est belle d'artifice,
> La femme belle est belle sans du fard. (Sonnet V)

These works, written in decasyllabic verse, may well have been written for the *Hélène* cycle, but on arranging the final form of his cycles in

of lover–reformer adopted by the poet who attacks the
lady's failing: "Vous aimez l'intellect, & moins je vous en
prise:/Aimer l'esprit, Madame, est aimer la sottise . . ."
(I/42, vv. 5, 8). Moreover, no less than Propertius, Ronsard
declares society to be the real villain:

> Ny ta simplicité, ny ta bonne nature,
> Ny mesme ta vertu ne t'ont peu garentir,
> Que la Cour ta nourrice, escole de mentir,
> N'ait degravé tes moeurs d'une fausse imposture.
>   (II/48, vv. 1–4)

Finally, there is the portrait of the woman's double personality: "Nom, malheur des Troyens, sujet de mon
souci,/ Ma sage Penelope, & mon Helene aussi," (I/3,
vv. 9–10). Thus do Propertius' favorite examples reappear
in *Sonnets pour Hélène*. Whether examples or aspects of
the woman, the names have the same function. For Ronsard,
too, jealousy, perfidy, and destruction, as well as irresistible
beauty, turn about Helen's name and Penelope symbolizes
that virtue each lover sensed and believed existed beneath
society's corruption.

Just as the poets' general attitudes reveal a resemblance
detailed in their portraits of the lady, so is there resemblance even in the structure of the two love stories. This
aspect of the relationship between Ronsard and Propertius
is diametrically opposed to the situation assumed in the Petrarchan canzoniere. Petrarch never loses sight of the
woman's perfection, which in the "In Morte" section becomes for the poet a palpable force leading to the divine.
At the same time Petrarch never succeeds in forgetting his
own imperfection, to wit, his succumbing to an earthly

1578, Ronsard refused entry into *Sonnets pour Hélène* to all decasyllabic
poems (save one, II/16, later supressed, but kept in 1578 because Helen
of Troy was its subject). It is not improbable that only then were these
three poems placed in *Astrée*.

love. In the world of Propertius, on the other hand, imperfection lies with the woman. The poet is ensnared despite her failings, but the lack of harmony remains sharp and permanent save through a change in the woman. The story, therefore, is never free from the threat of collapse. Just as Ronsard pronounces the word "adieu" in the first sonnet of *Sonnets pour Hélène*, Propertius, in analyzing the situation in his liminal elegy, writes that his mistress' heart must change or he must be weaned from love: "Or else do ye, my friends, that would recall me all too late from the downward slope, seek all the remedies for a heart diseased. Bravely will I bear the cruel cautery and the knife, if only I may win liberty to speak the words mine anger prompts" (I.1.25–28).[29] Like Ronsard, Propertius plays with the possibility of completion or rupture as the drama develops.

It is probably more than coincidence that *Sonnets pour Hélène* and the *Elegies* are divided into books. Both poets interrupt their story to take stock, so to speak, of the progress of their love. In the final elegy of Book One addressed to Cynthia (elegy 19), we find Propertius worried, not by death, but "that [she] [may] spurn [his] tomb." "Wherefore, while yet may be," he concludes, "let us love and be merry together."[30] Yet, while their love thus seems in jeopardy, Book Two begins with unqualified praise: " 'Tis not Calliope nor Apollo that singeth these things; 'tis my mistress' self that makes my wit."[31] A glance at the

29. Aut vos, qui sero lapsum revocatis, amici,
quaerite non sani pectoris auxilia.
fortiter et ferrum saevos patiemur et ignes,
sit modo libertas quae velit ira loqui.
30. Quam vereor, ne te contempto, Cynthia, busto
abstrahat ei! . . .

. . .

quare, dum licet, inter nos laetemur amantes.
31. Non haec Calliope, non haec mihi cantat Apollo,/ ingenium nobis ipsa puella facit.

corresponding poems in *Hélène* shows the same division. I/57 also indicates that the past has not brought the couple total harmony. "S'il vous plaist, ostez moy tout argument d'ennuy," he asks, stating that the future, as in Propertius, depends on a change in the woman, "Et lors j'auray la voix plus gaillarde & plaisante." But sonnet II/1 is categorically in favor of love: "De mon gré je me noye & ne brusle moymesme." Within each book there is the same vacillation from adoration to complaint. The compliment of II.7.19, "Thou only pleasest me; let me in like manner, Cynthia, be thy only pleasure." [32] Propertius follows immediately in II.8.12 by "Yet never did she soften her iron heart nor say, 'I love thee,' " [33] a pattern reproduced a number of times in *Hélène*. Amid the soft note of pleasure the attacks are maintained. Cynthia is repreatedly described in unflattering terms: "infelix" (II.3); "periuria" (I.8); "perfida" (II.9); "impia" (II.9, II.17). And whereas in elegy 20 of Book Two Propertius assures Cynthia of his love, he closes: "Herein forever am I justified: alone of lovers I neither rashly begin nor rashly end my love," [34] This objectivity becomes structure when the poet's pleasure from love cannot erase his realization of the immutability of the woman's position. Thus, in Book Three, Propertius writes, "Enough for me the hard warfare I wage with my mistress" (III.5.2), [35] and sounds the note which in III.24 ends the affair: "Now at last my senses return to me, aweary of the wild sea-tides; my wounds have closed, my flesh is healed." [36]

32. Tu mihi sola places: placeam tibi, Cynthia, solus.

33. Illa tamen numquam ferrea dixit, "Amo."

34. Hoc mihi perpetuo ius est, quod solus amator/ nec cito desisto nec temere incipio.

35. Sat mihi cum domina proelia dura mea.

36. Nunc demum vasto fessi resipiscimus aestu,/ vulneraque ad sanum nunc coiere mea.

The moral views behind this structure would not have shocked Ronsard. Propertius' position of avid but not un-bounded fidelity comes very close to Ronsard's own lesson in the elegies to Genèvre or Nature's speech to the Sun. Nor was Ronsard likely to be unsympathetic to the im-mediate framework in which Propertius abandoned Cyn-thia. If the rupture with Cynthia is effected at the end of the third book, the *Elegies* continue, nonetheless. Pro-pertius' poetic horizons expand, and the subject of love is replaced by historical and patriotic material. Again, faithful to what by his own definition is a deliberative personality, Propertius has prepared this shift in interest as carefully as he has prepared the close of the love story. The first elegy of the third book praises poetry and its force: how else would Helen and the Trojan war be known except for Homer! The second elegy insists upon the immortality he has acquired for Cynthia and himself. Significant and prophetic also are the third and fourth elegies, which Propertius devotes to celebrating the Emperor's victories and which precede immediately the elegy that sounds the knell of his love: "Enough for me the hard warfare I wage with my mistress." The detailed analysis of Ronsard's final poems to Hélène has already shown a parallel shift in in-terest. And even if Ronsard in his movement toward the theme of immortality and the apotheosis of poetry does not go so far as Propertius, the evolution in thought from love to poetry is evident in both poets.

Can we conclude from such similarities and parallelisms that Ronsard consciously imitated Propertius in creating *Sonnets pour Hélène?* Did Ronsard, after having read Propertius some years before, recall unconsciously the story of Cynthia, which he seems to have known so well? In view of the lack of any protracted textual resemblances between the two poets, these questions much necessarily

remain unanswered.[37] The parallels are in no way deval-
ued by this fact, however, and deserve to be contemplated
in their own right. First of all, they prove without a doubt
that the critic need not be overly deceived by the Petrarchistic exterior of *Sonnets pour Hélène*. The cycle's
development possesses little in common with Petrarch's
canzoniere or the numerous Petrarchistic cycles of compliment and lament. Ronsard, since the seasonal hymns, has
securely abandoned such a vision. *Sonnets pour Hélène* is
in every sense as personal and detached as *Amours I* was
impersonal and complimentary. Such an imperious tone—
which ends by rejecting the woman and portraying the
poet supreme in his sureness of immortality—Ronsard
shared, not with the Petrarchistic tradition, but with the
Latin tradition of Propertius. Ronsard was not meant for a
Petrarchistic love.

The comparison with Propertius shows also that for his
final cycle, Ronsard was keenly sensitive to certain problems of structure and presentation which had long been
ignored in favor of stylistic and thematic problems. The
choice of a structured story, built around some of his now
favorite, personalized themes, testifies to that accrued sense
of the poetic theme (how it can be varied, heightened by
juxtaposition with other themes, and intensified by its relation to other poems of the same theme) so prominent after
the seasonal hymns. Ronsard's assurance of immortality to
the woman he loved is not new in *Sonnets pour Hélène*.
The theme is also not the same throughout. Sonnet II/2 repeats the theme in its most traditional form: "Vous vivrez
(croyez moy) comme Laure en grandeur/Au moins tant

---

37. I think it important to recognize, however, that a few very close
textual borrowings from Propertius *do* exist in *Sonnets pour Hélène*.
For I/1, vs. 9, Ronsard could well have used Propertius, II.7.19; for vv.
43–46 of the "Chanson," II.13.33–36; for II/45, vv. 13–14, II.3.37–38.

que vivront les plumes & le livre" (vv. 13–14). When it next appears, in "Quand vous serez bien vieille," the theme has already moved from this gallant idea of an immortality given to the woman to an immortality acquired by the poet and indicative of a possible difference in destinies. Finally, in sonnet II/37, Ronsard says tersely:

> Si pour sujet fertil Homere t'a choisie,
> Je puis, suivant son train qui va sans compagnon,
> Te chantant, m'honorer, & non pas toy, sinon
> Qu'il te plaise estimer ma rude Poësie. (vv. 5–8)

The poet is appreciably less and less gallant, more and more taken with the thought of his own glory. The end of the cycle is near. Yet there is no biographical reason why Ronsard had to bring his cycle for Hélène de Surgères to a climax of disgust. His cycle would have been far more representative of the sonnets of his century had he maintained a long and faithful, if chaste, admiration of his "Pallas." He chose to do otherwise, and whether it was on his own, or in imitation of Propertius the conclusion must be the same— that in every respect, even the resemblances to Propertius, *Sonnets pour Hélène* represents Ronsard's coming of age in the sonnet cycle. He no longer pursues the monotony of *Amours I;* he no longer appreciates the hyperbolic pose of suffering eternal humility before the lady.

The preceding study of the cycle *Sonnets pour Hélène* as a whole has brought to the fore certain traits, notably richness, complexity, and independence which dominate Ronsard's technique. Through Harvey's summary of Petrarchistic aesthetics we have seen Ronsard outdistancing, reversing, refashioning the tradition that held him slave in 1552. Such revision naturally led to complexity: commitment-detachment, discouragement-pride, defeat-victory. But through this complexity Ronsard achieved that richness in content and vanity of poses that his earlier sonnets had failed to attain. The division into books, each with a particular tone and proportion in theme, transforms *Amours I*'s monotony into movement. The joy of inspiration and "ravissement," the indignation and lament at lost youth or unsympathetic philosophies oppose to the emptiness of *Amours I* a full, robust scale of emotion.

As we turn now to an examination of the cycle's individual poems, we will do well to keep these remarks in mind.

Ronsard and Triumph over Form

As we have recently noticed in reference to Ronsard's use of the theme of immortality in *Sonnets pour Hélène*, the particular vision and structure designed for the cycle could affect the individual sonnets as well. The richness, complexity, and independence so evident in Ronsard's choice and arrangement of his themes within the cycle are no less perceptible in the sonnets themselves. To heighten an appreciation of Ronsard's success in the individual poems of *Sonnets pour Hélène*, I have selected for analysis a series of themes which are rather constant throughout Ronsard's diverse love cycles and which were examined earlier in a discussion of *Amours I*. Here the contrasts in Ronsard's evolution are the sharpest; the change in focus, the most profound; the lesson of the seasonal hymns, the most concrete.

In contrast to the portrait of *Amours I:*

> Quand au premier la Dame que j'adore
> Vint embellir le sejour de noz cieulx,
> Le filz de Rhée appella tous les Dieux,
> Pour faire encor d'elle une aultre Pandore.
> Lors Apollin richement la decore,
> Or, de ses raiz luy façonnant les yeulx,
> Or, luy donnant son chant melodieux,
> Or, son oracle & ses beaulx vers encore.

Mars luy donna sa fiere cruaulté,
Venus son ris, Dione sa beaulté,
Peithon sa voix, Ceres son abondance.
L'Aube ses doigtz & ses crins deliez,
Amour son arc, Thetis donna ses piedz,
Cleion sa gloyre, & Pallas sa prudence. (sonnet 32)

there is this description in *Sonnets pour Hélène:*

J'errois en mon jardin, quand au bout d'une allee
Je vy contre l'Hyver boutonner un Soucy.
Ceste herbe & mon amour fleurissent tout ainsi:
La neige est sur ma teste, & la sienne est gelee.
O bien-heureuse amour en mon ame escoulee
Par celle qui n'a point de parangon icy,
Qui m'a de ses rayons tout l'esprit esclarcy,
Qui devroit des François Minerve estre appellee:
En prudence Minerve, une Grace en beauté
Junon en gravité, Diane en chasteté,
Qui sert aux mesmes Dieux, comme aux hommes, d'exemple.
Si tu fusses venue au temps que la Vertu
S'honoroit des humains, tes vertuz eussent eu
Voeuz, encens & autels, sacrifices & temple.   (II/38)

The sonnet to Hélène is as complex as its Cassandre counterpart is simple, as emotionally rich as Cassandre's portrait is arid. Its structure alone suffices to point out this complexity. Whereas in the sonnet of 1552 the poem ceases to develop its theme after the first quatrain, "J'errois en mon jardin . . ." enriches its central theme at each structural turning, quatrains and tercets. The initial verb "errois" establishes for the entire poem a movement which is sinuous though tightly constructed. Each part contributes a new element to the poet's praise of Hélène but nuances this praise so as to transform what could have been another arid compliment into a narrative of great density.

The first scene—the poet wandering in his garden—is a typical Petrarchan pose, but Ronsard immediately assimilates it to himself. As the early blooming flower braves the winter's cold, so the poet, by his love, braves age's winter symbolized by the snow upon his head. In addition, the garden setting is more than gratuitous. Providing the general atmosphere of solitude wherein the poet may contemplate his love, it justifies his coming upon the flower. This meeting in turn provokes a comparison which permits the mention of "amour," the key word and sentiment to link the quatrains. The manner in which the effect of the atmosphere and the symbolism of the flower concentrate the poet's thought on love and from it on his lady, shows, from the very first quatrain, how far Ronsard has come since *Amours I*. The frigid simplicity of "j'adore" in the sonnet to his early love cannot compare with this sympathetic portrait continually varied by the careful distribution of terms pertaining to the central subject of love—his love has bloomed though he is old, it has flowed into his soul, it is blessed. As a result, when we arrive at "Qui devroit des François Minerve estre appellee," we are already well aware of the poet's sentiments. By his expression we are prepared to accept the image of the woman-goddess with all her attributes. The force of his emotion excuses the exaggeration, "celle qui n'a point de parangon icy"; more important, it replaces the cliché of *Amours I*, "embellir," with a personal voice that immediately takes precedence over the literary device. The rather brusque way in which Ronsard rushes to the enumeration of Cassandre's attributes only serves to underline the poet's intention to write a complimentary poem about gods and gifts. In *Hélène* the literary device flows out of the poet's emotional portrait of himself. The device subtly emerges from a fusion of self and form, as the poet, musing about the woman's effect, concludes that she is worthy of being called Minerva.

In the first tercet the enumeration technique reappears but now it follows naturally from the poet's observation that for her perfection she should be likened to a goddess. It is also significant that the echo of the enumeration in "Quand au premier . . ." (vv. 5–14) is restricted here to two verses only. Compliment is no longer the raison d'être of the poem. Although still presented in the form of a correspondence between gods and their attributes, the compliment is incidental to the poet's musing and to his gathering of symbols to translate his feelings, in short, to his lyric expression.

In the sonnet from *Amours I*, the artificiality of the entire description attracts attention by the very nature of the compliment. The woman as she is "described" hardly comes to life nor does she seem an existing object. With each added gift, she grows more incredible, more unreal, and more fictitious. In the sonnet to Hélène, the love object has already been created before the device of god-attribute correspondence is introduced. The poet has already convinced us admirably that he is in love. Then, as he penetrates more deeply into his soliloquy, he centers the reader's attention upon one trait, the lady's ability to "esclarcir tout l'esprit," [38] whence the justification for the

38. Verse 7 presents a fine example of the return to, yet outdistancing of, the Petrarchistic tradition in *Sonnets pour Hélène*. The woman is characterized by a quality, implicit, of course, in the Petrarchistic tradition but presented previously only in an exterior, physiological way. The change of expression from "oeil" to "rayons" corresponds to the entire reorientation of the poem, which draws its inspiration from an interiorization of the love emotion. In *Amours I* the poet thought of his lady in terms of certain abstract clichés, "beaulté," "gloyre," "prudence" but the accent is equally, if not more heavily placed on the physical traits possessed by the woman, "yeulx," "doigts," "crins," "arc," "piedz." This is all absent in the poem to Hélène. Only the "rayons" remain, that indefinable quality which the woman emanates (rather than possessing physically) and which the poet receives interiorly (not on the surface of the retina).

Minerva appellation, which forms the bridge between the quatrains and the first tercet.

Cassandre was merely the composite of her gifts. Hélène, become like Minerva, remains throughout the sonnet the individual woman who has struck the poet, for she is only in her wisdom (like) Minerva. When the poet ends his first tercet with "Qui sert aux mesmes Dieux, comme aux hommes, d'exemple," this ultimate praise is also the ultimate unification of the woman and the very opposite of the presentation in *Amours I*. In 1552 the point of departure for a description of the woman was the many attributes of the gods; now the movement is from the woman to the gods. She is one, and from her emanate the qualities to be associated with the respective deities. The supreme model, she is also the supreme goddess. Thus, the image of the last tercet, "Voeuz, encens & autels, sacrifices & temple," succeeds to perfection in uniting the past elements of the poem. Finding its essence in the virtue of the woman, the poet's love imagines her *the* goddess and finds a common mode of expression in the attitude of worship. There is adoration, but not that of the "j'adore" of *Amours I*—a distinction that is only representative of the many differences in expression, conception, and emotion between the two sonnets.

The rapid reference to love has grown into a prolonged evocation, complete with setting and symbol. The woman grows not with words but with the growing consciousness of the lover. She is made beautiful not by a verb but by the evident depths of the poet's emotion, which in the last tercet retains its force even in a time shift to an imagined past. For what are the poet and the poem if not the present's equivalent of those "Voeuz, encens & autels, sacrifices & temple!" From *Amours I* to *Sonnets pour Hélène* the poet continues to write of his love and his lady and to compliment her. What has changed is the poet's understanding of the elements that communicate his intent. From an exterior vision of himself and his love dictated by a foreign tradition, he proceeds through the seasonal hymns to an interior, personal vision of love; from a sterile simplicity of expression, he passes to an exceptional complexity: the garden, the flower, the Minerva image, the temple scene—each is woven into Ronsard's new comprehension of the love emotion.

The difference in beloved is accompanied by a change in emotion. A scene of good-by furnished our initial definition of the Petrarchistic sentiment:

> Ciel, air, & vents, plains & montz descouvers,
> Tertres fourchuz, & forestz verdoyantes,
> Rivages tortz, & sources ondoyantes,
> Taillis razez, & vous bocages verds,
> Antres moussus à demy front ouvers,
> Prez, boutons, fleurs, & herbes rousoyantes,
> Coustaux vineux et plages blondoyantes,
> Gastine, Loyr, & vous mes tristes vers:
> Puis qu'au partir, rongé de soing & d'ire,
> A ce bel oeil, l'Adieu je n'ay sceu dire,
> Qui pres & loing me detient en esmoy:
> Je vous supply, Ciel, air, ventz, montz, & plaines,
> Tailliz, forestz, rivages & fontaines,
> Antres, prez, fleurs, dictes le luy pour moy.
> (sonnet 57)

A similar scene can be our initiation into the emotional sphere of *Sonnets pour Hélène:*

> D'un solitaire pas je ne marche on nul lieu,
> Qu'Amour bon artisan ne m'imprime l' image
> Au profond du penser de ton gentil visage,
> Et des mots gracieux de ton dernier Adieu.
> Plus fermes qu'un rocher, engravez au milieu

De mon coeur je les porte: & s'il n'y a rivage,
Fleur, antre ny rocher, ny forest ny bocage,
A qui je ne les conte, à Nymphe, ny à Dieu.
D'une si rare & douce ambrosine viande
Mon esperance vit, qui n'a voulu depuis
Se paistre d'autre apast, tant elle en est friande.
Ce jour de mille jours m'effaça les ennuis:
Car tant opiniastre en ce plaisir je suis,
Que mon ame pour vivre autre bien ne demande.

                                                (I/40)

A superficial glance at the atmosphere of the sonnet to
Hélène would seem to indicate a return to the scene of
1552 in all its aspects. The poet walks in nature; he is alone,
wandering, and expressing his sentiments aloud to certain
objects of nature: "rivage/Fleur, antre. . . ." But there
the resemblance really ceases. Now, as in "J'errois en mon
jardin . . . ," the natural setting serves a double purpose.
It not only fosters the contemplation which leads the poet
to his reflections, but actively represents them, as does the
flower blooming in the snow. Through Love's work all nature reflects the poet's beloved and her last good-by. The
image, a familiar one in Petrarchistic poetry, symbolizes the
sympathetic nexus between poet and nature that dominates
"Ciel, air, & vents. . . ." At the same time Ronsard
marks his later voice by making explicit in the second
quatrain that this poem is about independence from nature,
not dependence upon it. His bond is superficial and secondary to the true image of the lady which he carries in
himself. Gone is the Cassandre pose of entrusting to nature
the interior thoughts; in the poem to Hélène, the poet is
the firmer custodian of their love. Such interiorization is
masterfully rendered by the sonnet's structure where the
woman's parting, carried within the poet (second quatrain)
brings the notion of interior nourishment (first tercet).
Finally, there is recapitulation in the second tercet as the

entire experience of the parting ("Ce Jour") is summarized in a pleasure which may now be specifically defined: "Mon ame pour vivre autre bien ne demande." Through this independence and interiorization, Ronsard gives the key to his change in tone since 1552. Self-assured, the poet feels the essence of their love within himself, in contrast to Cassandre's lover, who in every way is separated from his lady and calls upon nature to be his emissary. All the lexical excesses have disappeared; the normal adjectives, such as "bel," "doux," "cher," the poet now replaces with a striking variety, "gentil," "gracieux," "rare," and "friande"; each adjective in its context now shows the captivating quality of the woman herself or some aspect revealed on this day of separation.

In the "stille bas" experiment of 1556, Ronsard had taken up again the theme of the "adieu":

> Comment au departir l'adieu pourroy je dire,
> Duquel le souvenir tanseulement me pasme:
> Adieu donc chere vie, adieu donc ma chere ame,
> Adieu mon cher soucy, par qui seul je souspire.
> Adieu le bel object de mon plaisant martire,
> Adieu bel oeil divin qui m'englace & m'enflame,
> Adieu ma doulce glace, adieu ma doulce flame,
>
>   . . .
>
> Il est temps de partir, le jour en est venu:
> Mais avant que partir je vous supplie, en lieu
> De moy, prendre mon cueur, tenez je le vous laisse,
> Voy le là, baisez moy, maistresse, & puis adieu.
>
>   (7, 271–72)

The poet's description of the woman as "chere vie," "chere ame" suggests that Ronsard was already moving forward to the "douce ambrosine viande" of Hélène's sonnet; yet note once again that, nonetheless, the "stille bas" is in essence quite unlike the vision of *Sonnets pour Hélène*. For example, as with "Ciel, air, & vents . . . ," this poem of 1556 relies heavily on enumeration to communicate the force of the poet's emotion.

Just as revealing is the difference in conception between the two poems regarding the dramatic aspect of the farewell. In the poem from the *Nouvelle Continuation*, Ronsard chose the moment when the lover assessed the value of what was to be lost through the woman's parting. In 1578 the period represented occurs much later, when time has justified the poet's love: the couple has remained intact despite distance. The nervousness of the 1556 moment—a tension in the fleeting second before separation—and the cascade of "adieu's" has long passed. The lover has entered a stage where this love, even though separated from its object, fills him completely and satisfies his every need. By reducing the woman's qualities to the single element of "viande," the poet renders any other attribute superfluous and achieves far greater intensity than in either preceding poem of good-by. Because he realizes more of the value of love, he can replace the empty despair of *Amours I* with a fuller appreciation of their parting; because he recognizes firmly the role of love, he can abandon the enumeration of the *Nouvelle Continuation* and focus the poem on the true center of his vision: the woman as continuity of love and life. The tone, the vocabulary ("fermes," "opiniastre," "effaça"), translate the poet's state most clearly. There is no Petrarchistic lamentation but only the vision of total dedication to the love object which has reciprocated. Nothing structurally or ideologically stirs the poem from its manifold stability.

It may be questioned as to what degree the evolution presented here is distinguishable from a simple stylistic development. The preceding comparisons have revealed a decided stylistic movement, and there can be no doubt that the sonnets of 1578 are in the main more complex and more rich stylistically than their counterparts in *Amours I*. But, then, in the seasonal hymns and in the elegies to Genèvre, we have also seen Ronsard's vision of the love experience grow more refined, more intimate, and more mature. In the sense that Ronsard in 1552 avidly reproduced the Petrarchistic mode of love verse, instead of refashioning it, dozens of the *Amours I* poems show a complete correspondence between intention and execution. But insofar as Ronsard also sought to rival Petrarch's fame through the creation of a personal Petrarchistic cycle, the attempt of 1552 was not a success. The poet gives every sign indirectly, and even directly in "A son Livre," of recognizing this fact himself. For it was surely to obtain such a successful expression that Ronsard turned to other traditions after *Amours I*. But the lighter style of "chere vie," "chere ame," which in truth did not revolutionize the poet's vision, did not revolutionize his style either. The repetition of "adieu" marks the vestiges of 1552, which are equally evident in the use and meaning of the antithesis of fire and ice: "Adieu bel oeil divin qui m'englace & m'enflame,/ Adieu ma doulce glace, adieu ma doulce flame." When Ronsard used an aubade, moreover, whose portrait coincided more closely with his purpose, he passed quite outside the traditional sonnet world. Marullus, Theocritus, a pastoral world, and Petrarchistic portraits alternated as the poet tried to solidify his efforts, forging new styles for each pose. Only in 1563 did Ronsard secure a vision of love suitable for both his temperament and the sonnet cycle. A concomittant devaluation of the Petrarchistic mode led to a style that serves, but does not dominate the new philosophy.

To see how profoundly vision and style have each evolved, and yet evolved together, we need only note sonnet 18 of *Amours Diverses* (1578):

Genévres herissez, & vous Houx espineux,
L'un hoste des deserts, & l'autre d'un bocage:
Lhierre, le tapis d'un bel antre sauvage,

Sources qui bouillonnez d'un surgeon sablonneux,
Pigeons qui vous baisez d'un baiser savoureux,
Tourtres qui lamentez d'un eternel vefvage,
Rossignols ramagers, qui d'un plaisant langage
Nuict & jour rechantez voz versets amoureux:
Vous à la gorge rouge estrangere Arondelle,
Si vous voyez aller ma Nymphe en ce Printemps
Pour cueillir des bouquets par ceste herbe nouvelle,
Dites luy, pour-neant que sa grace j'attens,
Et que pour ne souffrir le mal que j'ay pour elle
J'ay mieux aimé mourir que languir si long temps.

Read rapidly, this poem is nearly the equivalent of "Ciel,
air, & vents. . . ." And yet the two sonnets have striking
differences. Structurally, the later poem reveals its superiority by avoiding the unfortunate repetition of the enumer-
ated objects of nature throughout most of the sonnet. It is
cut naturally after the quatrains and once the introductory
apostrophe is terminated, the poem does not deviate from
its purpose nor introduce but what is pertinent. The objects in the early sonnet are often undescribed, "Ciel, air, &
vents . . . ," while others receive a vague adjective,
"montz descouvers,/ Tertres fourchuz, & forestz verdoyan-
tes. . . ." The number of objects in the poem to Hélène
is radically reduced, and to each element is devoted gener-
ous description. The poet forces his reader to consider
them carefully. And when the poem is completed, the full
reason for their selection is revealed. The choice of the
juniper and the holly has its immediate explanation in the
qualifying verse, "L'un hoste des deserts, & l'autre d'un
bocage." As the poem continues, it is more difficult to seize
the particular sense of each object until one realizes that the
poet is addressing only those objects which are to give a
message to his beloved. This is their function and the reason

for their selection: the ivy on which she may walk ("tapis"), the spring from which she may drink, the birds she may listen to or watch, the ones most likely to be abroad in this season. Moreover, when choosing the birds (pigeon, turtle dove, and nightingale), Ronsard differentiates among them. The pigeons will present to her the vision of a "savory kiss"; the turtle dove, the sound of a love's lament; the nightingale, the songs of love. As a result, their general function is made to correspond to the particular nature of the message the poet would have them transmit. The kiss will remind her of the lover's desire ("sa grace j'attens"), while the turtle dove echoes his torment ("le mal que j'ay pour elle") and the nightingales simulate the poet's many songs to her.

By means of unity, complexity, density, the sonnet reflects all the stylistic features of the poems of 1578, but all their conceptual ones as well. If its *Amours I* counterpart is composed of indifferent objects placed indifferently within the poem, it is because the poet's vision of the love adventure at that time is comprised of a few clichés and poses for which only indifferent words can be used to round out the composition. Style is part of the vision in that Ronsard feels bound to recognize and reproduce the Petrarchistic clichés, but style is also quasi-independent in that the poverty of the vision cannot direct at each moment the choice of words. Consequently, we find the style serving as compensation for what the love story cannot provide rather than as an exploitation of the poet's emotion. In the poem of 1578, Ronsard has mastered the plot; he knows precisely the pose to adopt and the elements to depict it. Nothing is superfluous because his vision has succeeded in coupling judiciously the roles and the symbols. The poem was perhaps placed in *Amours Diverses* because of the lack of freshness in the final "pointe." But this does not negate the overall control the poet displays in adding another chapter to his love story. Here, as in *Sonnets pour Hélène,* each element introduced, foregoing the unfortunate stylistic independence of *Amours I,* serves the vision and maintains the richness of the story.

Despite this evidence of great originality and creative power, *Sonnets pour Hélène* is not without its sources, or so it would seem. Laumonier's critical edition points accusingly at the many Petrarchan echoes, and studies by Hutton and Vianey offer careful catalogues of Ronsard's debt to the *Greek Anthology* and the quattrocento Petrarchists, respectively.[39] Of course, as in the case of the seasonal hymns, most references in the critical edition are to a line, or characteristic turn of phrase which at most proves that the Petrarchistic idiom remained the basic stylistic idiom of the period. Very rarely indeed do we find a sustained reference to Petrarch. One exception is Ronsard's use of "Stiamo, Amor" in sonnet II/3. This revealing statement of Ronsard's individuality within the context of imitation deserves to be studied in detail.

> Stiamo, Amor, a veder la gloria nostra,
> Cose sopra natura, altere e nove:
> Vedi ben quanta in lei dolcezza piove;
> Vedi lume che 'l cielo in terra mostra.
> Vedi quant'arte dora e'mperla e'nostra
> L'abito eletto e mai non visto altrove,
> Che dolcemente i piedi e gli occhi move
> Per questa di bei colli ombrosa chiostra.
> L'erbetta verde e i fior di color mille
> Sparsi sotto quel' elce antiqua e negra
> Pregan pur che 'l bel piè li prema o tócchi:

39. Hutton, *Greek Anthology in France,* pp. 350–74 and J. Vianey, *Le Pétrarquisme en France au XVIᵉ siècle* (Montpellier, 1909), pp. 256–62.

E 'l ciel di vaghe e lucide faville
S'accende in torno, e 'n vista si rallegra
D'esser fatto seren da sí belli occhi.[40]

When Ronsard first used the Petrarch sonnet he extracted a single line, vs. 5, which became in *Amours I*, "Le seul Avril de son jeune printemps/ Endore, emperle, enfrange nostre temps" (sonnet 88, vv. 9–10). The early sonnet shows no other relationship to "Stiamo, Amor." The poem to Hélène, on the other hand, follows it through from beginning to end:

Amour, qui as ton regne en ce monde si ample,
Voy ta gloire & la mienne errer en ce jardin:
Voy comme son bel oeil, mon bel astre divin,
Reluist comme une lampe ardente dans un Temple:
Voy son corps, des beautez le portrait & l'exemple,
Qui ressemble une Aurore au plus beau d'un matin:
Voy son esprit, seigneur du Sort & du Destin,
Qui passe la Nature, en qui Dieu se contemple.
Regarde la marcher toute pensive à soy,
T'emprisonner de fleurs, & triompher de toy,
Pressant dessous ses pas les herbes bienheureuses.
Voy sortir un Printemps des rayons de ses yeux:
Et voy comme à l'envy ses flames amoureuses
Embellissent la terre, & serenent les Cieux.

(sonnet II/3)

The difference in approach from 1552 is best explained by a phenomenon already observed indirectly in an analysis of Propertius and *Sonnets pour Hélène*. The mature artist has also acquired a mature attitude in dealing with sources. Where Ronsard once sought conceits for piecemeal insertion in moments of dragging inspiration, he now looks beyond the level of vocabulary to the more central issues of

---

40. Petrarch, *Rime*, pp. 277–78.

structure, tone, and even vision. Ronsard does not lose sight of the poetic value of the Italian's conceits in "Stiamo, Amor," but sees them above all within a masterful framework that arranges their presentation and will come back to them to treat them his way. The repetition of the imperative "see," so simple but so effective in ordering the sonnet's material, is the only element Ronsard transcribes verbatim, and this is because it is essential. In setting and content Ronsard adapts Petrarch to express his own vision of the lady.

The Petrarchan sonnet has been justly praised for its communication of the ethereal quality of Laura, who is defined from the second verse as "Cose sopra natura, altere e nove." Grass and flowers beg to be pressed or touched by her foot (vv. 9–11). The sky is illuminated with sparks, and her eyes bring cheer for having made it serene (vv. 12–14). For Petrarch the relationship between woman and world can be translated only through her powers and her effect. We know that she is about and moving as the poet speaks, but the setting is vague ("Per questa di bei colli ombrosa chiostra"), and she herself is vaguely described. A force, supernatural but human, inhabiting the earth but not really a part of it: this is Petrarch's Laura. Quite different from Petrarch is Ronsard's second verse, "Voy ta gloire & la mienne errer en ce jardin." The setting is made precise, earthly, not ethereal, a procedure applied also to the description of the woman in the lines following. While Petrarch calls attention to "dolcezza" (vs. 3) and "lume" (vs. 4)—nouns without articles that define less an attribute than the woman herself—Ronsard lists "son bel oeil" and "son corps" (a word totally absent from Petrarch's poem). He paints a rapid portrait, "Regarde la marcher toute pensive à soy," which concludes his description.

When we have passed through this description it is not difficult to understand why Ronsard's second verse and his choice of vocabulary are so different from their counterparts in Petrarch. To the ethereal optic of Petrarch, Ronsard opposes the portrait of a beloved who grows increasingly present *as a woman*. Thus, we have rapidly reached the point at which "imitation" can no longer describe the relationship between the two poems. Hélène is not like Laura; the resemblance between diverse words and their functions in the two sonnets merely obscures a gradual drawing apart in philosophies as Ronsard rejects the mystic forces of good and beauty for what is unequivocally human. This does not mean that there is a necessary change in attributes. Ronsard makes no attempt to refuse love its power or its beauty, but he must describe them in the name of a different object. And when the conceits are retained, he treats them quite differently. When Laura walks, the flowers beg to be touched; earthly things move toward her, and in an attitude symbolic of Petrarch himself in love, seek to be oppressed by the weight of such a contact. When Hélène does the same, she, too, exhibits a form of power by triumphing over Love (vs. 9). But when Ronsard comes to the image of Laura and the flowers, he rejects entirely the Petrarchan image of the flower's humble adoration. She presses, naturally, "dessous ses pas les herbes bienheureuses." The adjective "bienheureuses" ("fortunate" because they were trod upon by Hélène) seems to suggest that perhaps a bit of Petrarch's attitude of adoration has been kept after all. But the attitude of humility is totally absent, and instead, within the use of "bienheureuses" we find the essence of Ronsard's vision: the pleasure of love expressed as the result of that physical contact so clearly reflected in the physical portrait of Hélène. The contrast of views persists to the very end of the sonnet, where Hélène, like Laura, "embellishes the earth and calms the skies" (vs. 14). While the Petrarchan image is a functional indication in the poem of Laura's affinity with the heavens, in Ronsard, because of the absence of the woman's ethereal dimensions, the conceit becomes a simple compliment to the power of her enrapturing glance. Finally, to a different love object belongs a change of expression. Petrarch, describing what he admits is "sopra natura," relates all without similes; she is not *like* the light "che 'l cielo in terra mostra" (vs. 4) she *is* this light. Hélène must be compared to these things. Her eye shines "comme un lampe ardente dans un Temple" (vs. 4); her body resembles "une Aurore au plus beau d'un matin" (vs. 6).

In view of so many fundamental distinctions between these two poems, in what way can we speak meaningfully here of imitation? If, as in the sonnet of *Amours I*, we point to the words Ronsard translated, and say that Ronsard took them from Petrarch, we find that we have learned little from an analysis of imitation. If, on the contrary, we are not prejudiced by the term to the point of ignoring the poem because it is unoriginal and instead seek to appreciate its uniqueness, then we welcome a case of imitation as "Stiamo, Amor" and the sonnet to Hélène. From an examination of "Stiamo, Amor" and Ronsard's imitation, we see nowhere slavish borrowing. There is first the poet as artisan who recognizes and retains the model's structural excellence, then as a pseudo-Petrarchistic lover, content to reuse the devices of Petrarch's poem, but in his own context. The more we move within the sameness of structure and conceit, the more the differences between Petrarch and Ronsard become apparent. The imitator emerges the borrower who defines his own love and erects within the Petrarchistic vocabulary a personal creation replete with new setting and a new style. The poems are similar in the inconsequential—if we speak of imitation as mere lexical borrowing—and different in the essential. The lexical similarities identify a tradition with which Ronsard wanted to associate himself, but at the moment of departure from

Petrarch's vision, we meet the poet Ronsard, individual and inimitative.

Far more devastating quantitatively than Laumonier's references to Petrarch are the studies of Vianey and Hutton. There is, however, an almost humorous disproportion between their forceful assertions and certain backtracking admissions about the exact amount of imitation, between the quantity of "identified sources" and the total content of the cycle. Vianey's statements tend to be sweeping: "Ce qui est indubitable, c'est que dans les *Sonnets pour Hélène* domine l'influence des quattrocentistes et en particulier celle de Tebaldeo, de maître préféré de Desportes." [41] Yet he is not a critic given to analyzing the texts he associates under the rubric of imitation. His work of 1909 has maintained an honored place in Ronsard studies and is quoted and unquestioned in its conclusions. Desonay, for example, while careful to refer to Vianey's admission ("Dans *Sonnets pour Hélène*, s'il y a beaucoup de réminiscences, il n'y a, je crois, aucun plagiat") [42] draws the obvious conclusion from Vianey's work: "Certes, un peu plus loin, le même Vianey s'interdit-il de prononcer le mot de 'plagiat': n'en subsiste pas moins l'impression très nette que les sources italiennes sont particulièrement nombreuses dans les *Sonets* [sic] *pour Helene*." [43] And he accepts this conclusion. The fact remains, however, that in the edition of 1578 of the 111 sonnets to Hélène a bare fifteen are singled out by Vianey as being in the vein of the quattrocenti: I/26, 31, 34, 35, 6, 17, 13; II/1, 15, 28, 4, 5, 8, 39, 29. Secondly, among these fifteen poems, of those which are said to bear a clear thematic relationship to the Italian poems—gifts, I/26, 31, II/39; letters, II/28, 29; the planting of a tree, II/8—it is evident that none figure among the great poems of the

---

41. Vianey, p. 257.
42. Ibid., p. 261.
43. Desonay, 3, 265.

cycle. They are the peripheral pieces at the most and, as Vianey suggests, the product of a current fashion. For the remaining sonnets, Vianey used criteria of style and sentiment in identifying the sources. He gives no Italian texts to compare with Ronsard, but it is significant that none conflict with the love story and on the contrary contribute directly to it. For example, in I/6 the Petrarchan image of the port unattained in no way counters the Helen–Penelope portrait, as Ronsard sees but cannot benefit fully from the virtue of Hélène. However one examines Vianey's listings, the sweeping statements lose their force. Thus, the quattrocenti sources, if they are sources at all, are hardly numerous; the poems they inspired are inconsequential or cleverly worked into the general thematic fabric.

Of fifteen borrowings noted by Hutton from the *Greek Anthology*, only seven appear in *Sonnets pour Hélène* in 1578: I/44, 54, 24, 34, 56; II/15, 41. Two, I/34 and II/15, are already cited by Vianey in his list. This overlapping not only reduces the absolute list of borrowings but shows the subjectivism of Vianey's source hunting and a definite lack of rigor in technique. James Hutton has been more circumspect in tracing Ronsard's debt to the *Greek Anthology*. Texts are identified and sometimes compared, so that beneath the claim of imitation Hutton sees the thin veneer of penetration and, as in the case of "Stiamo, Amor," the large measure of personal effort. Of I/24 and its source he writes, "*De vostre belle, vive* merely alludes to the theme [of the epigram]." [44] Elsewhere the resemblances cannot be denied, but then neither can the quantitative relationship between the poem and its source. From this epigram, "Callignotos a juré à Ionis que jamais il ne mettrait audessus d'elle ni un ami ni une amie. Il l'a juré; mais on dit bien vrai: les serments d'amour n'entrent pas dans l'oreille des Immortels. Maintenant, c'est pour un garçon qu'il brûle;

44. Hutton, p. 368.

quant à la malheureuse fille, elle ne compte plus,"[45] Ronsard fashioned this sonnet:

> Dessus l'autel d'Amour planté sur vostre table
> Vous me fistes serment & je le fis aussi,
> Que d'un coeur mutuel à s'aimer endurcy
> Nostre amitié promise iroit inviolable.
> Je vous juray ma foy, vous feistes le semblable.
> Mais vostre cruauté, qui des Dieux n'a soucy,
> Me promettoit de bouche, & me trompoit ainsi:
> Ce-pendant vostre esprit demeuroit immuable.
> O jurement fardé sous l'espece d'un Bien!
> O perjurable autel! ta Deité n'est rien.
> O parole d'amour non jamais asseuree!
> J'ay pratiqué par vous le Proverbe des vieux:
> Jamais des amoureux la parole juree
> N'entra (pour les punir) aux oreilles des Dieux.
>
> (I/44)

The point of contact is but a line in the Greek, but a tercet in the sonnet. Around each the poets fashioned what the device suggested to them. Moreover, like certain of the Vianey examples, the sonnet reproduces an episode completely in keeping with the basic portrait of the cycle. The easy conversion no doubt explains Ronsard's interest in the epigram.

The other examples hardly vary from this one. In the Hélène cycle not one of the identified epigrams is imitated throughout the sonnet. Although there is imitation, it is even proportionally slighter than in the case of the Italian quattrocenti, and when present, there is no evidence of wholesale transcription but rather of an eye quick to catch pregnant conceits for reworking. The time has perhaps come to admit once and for all that Vianey exaggerates in his chapter on the sources of *Sonnets pour Hélène*. The

45. *L'Anthologie grecque*, ed. Pierre Waltz (Paris, 1928), p. 23.

potent independence which transforms a majority of
the sonnets cannot be erased by these rare and inconsequential borrowings. Moreover, where textual confrontation is possible, it can only corroborate a definition of the
mature artist as a mature craftsman as well. *Sonnets pour
Hélène* is not imitative. Propertius and Petrarch may at
times explain the presence of certain details and movement
in the cycle, but they cannot begin to explain the consummate art of the cycle. The moment of conception may
not have found Ronsard alone, but there is nothing to
prove that the execution of these sonnets came from any
talent other than his own.

Conclusion: A Definition of Terms

THE traditional interpretation of Ronsard's development suggests a movement from Petrarchism to an immersion in the Graeco-Latin style, culminating in a final amalgam of Petrarchism and sensuality.[1] Although few, if any, students of Ronsard would refuse to admit that Petrarch is the model for *Amours I*, there is much to review regarding the subsequent trends. The degree to which classical and neoclassical themes appear in the *Continuations* or their re-edition in 1560 as *Amours II*, for example, must be qualified in several ways. These themes appear most frequently outside the sonnets, and the sonnets in which the poet presents a sensual portrait of his love such as "Mignongne, levés-vous" are very few. Throughout the cycles the material adapted from Marullus or Theocritus is continually impregnated with Petrarchistic traits. Beneath Ronsard's lighter style and often sensual overtones, the basic Petrarchistic attitudes of humility, compliment, hyperbole, and complaint persist.[2] If, in the case of Ronsard's adaptation of Theocritus, the vision was different, the adjuncts—*innamoramento*, sight of the woman, sorrow of separation—remain distinctively Petrarchistic. On the other hand, the Petrarchism of *Sonnets pour Hélène* is slight, as the stylistic resemblances to Petrarch have little influence over the conceptual problems of tone, structure, or vision.

In view of such a variety of contexts in which the Petrarchistic tradition appears in Ronsard's poetry, it is not

1. Cf. H. Weber, *La Création poétique en France au XVIᵉ siècle*, p. 259.
2. See p. 63.

surprising that this aspect of the poet's work is still so poorly defined. By suggesting a break with the Italian style after 1552, critics have perhaps consciously oversimplified Ronsard's development to avoid the perplexing nuances which the Petrarchistic tradition adds to each of the cycles following *Amours I*. At the same time, the problem appears disturbingly complex only because past criticism has not always distinguished between Petrarchism as style and Petrarchism as a vision of the love experience. If we recognize the Petrarchistic mode as basically a stylistic phenomenon, always potentially divisible from the narrative sequence of *innamoramento*, slavery, resistance, and lament, we can begin to appreciate the place of Petrarchism in Ronsard's work. It was, and remained through *Sonnets pour Hélène*, the accepted stylistic vehicle for elevated expression in love verse. It is true that Ronsard was tempted once to bastardize it with the roses and diminutives of the ode, confusing, as his public seems to have done, his problems of vision with those of style. In analyzing the textual evidence in the seasonal hymns and elegies to Genèvre, I have attempted to substantiate, however, the idea that the essential movement in Ronsard's love cycles occurs at the level of vision rather than style.

When Ronsard began *Amours I*, one might say a near-total harmony existed between vision and style. The lover, the lady were genuine Petrarchistic figures in a genuine Petrarchistic world. But Ronsard was not one to present abstract and composite beauties; he felt the tension between the exaggerated praises to virtue and the emotional urge to sing of love, not compliment. He sought a resolution during the middle years of the *Continuations* and the 1560 edition. Paradoxically, in terms of Ronsard's future poetry, the most important of these efforts are not the few complete rejections of Petrarchism ("Mignongne, levés-vous"), but the poems of Petrarchistic style imitated from Marullus and Theocritus. Not sensuality, but Petrarchistic style was to become the constant element in Ronsard's sonnet cycles. The portrait of the young Marie in the aubade, while really not repeated in many sonnets, has nevertheless appeared to several readers of Ronsard as his most satisfying description of the love adventure. But these critics, to whom Desonay has offered an elegant answer,[3] must in the last analysis argue outside the context of Ronsard's development. The experiments represented by "Mignongne, levés-vous" are truly failures to recast the sonnet. They go too far stylistically and break too radically with the elegance Ronsard inevitably associated with Petrarch and the sonnet cycle. The proof: *Sonnets pour Hélène*, where the purest vision of sensual longing and communal bliss, "Plus estroit que la Vigne . . ." is a song, not a sonnet. Secondly, while the songs imitated from Marullus, "Voyage de Tours," and "Elégie à Marie" do succeed in combining old poses with new developments, we may not forget in judging these middle years how much Ronsard's borrowings from Theocritus and the entire arrangement of the 1560 edition reveal an indecision and bewilderment attributable directly to the poet's own unsettled views on morals and poetry.[4] The success and sureness of "Mignongne, levés-vous" does not permeate the entire cycle. Once the conceptual patterns had been formulated in the seasonal hymns, however, the poet cautiously returned to the sonnet and to the Petrarchistic style as well. The elegies to Genèvre and Ronsard's work with Theocritus and Marullus had prepared him progressively, if perhaps unconsciously, to manage the deceptive mode. And armed with new content, Ronsard was able to make the Petrarchistic style conform with amazing ease.

Ronsard's example basically upholds the sixteenth cen-

3. Desonay, *Ronsard, poète de l'amour*, 2, 120.
4. See p. 104.

tury's faith in the Italian style but indicates that the Petrarchistic tradition is no lyric vehicle unless imbued with some spirit of direction and emotional orientation. Without Petrarch's moral doubts and Laura's function in the "In Morte" poems, epigones transmitted a massive void. Ronsard's semi-abandonment of the tradition in the middle years represents a search to escape this void, but the continuing presence of Petrarchistic material in the works of 1555–60 attests to the weakness of this revolt. Undecided about the direction of his efforts, Ronsard retained the essence of the traditional style of the love cycle. His so-called "return" to Petrarchism in 1578, on the other hand, is a true triumph over the Italian mode. The void is filled; the style, rendered the servant of a new and very different vision.

The poet's adherence to the Petrarchistic style is but one aspect of the sixteenth-century belief in the necessity of models. Without them, the "illustration" and "deffense" of the French language would have appeared impossible. However, at the same time that the Pléiade manifesto invoked the masters to be followed liberally in the new language and literature, the *Deffense* also warns against a facile view of imitation. Thus the word "translation" would hardly suffice as a synonym for Du Bellay's "immitation": "Se compose donq' celuy qui voudra enrichir sa Langue, à l'immitation des meilleurs Aucteurs Grecz & Latins, & à toutes leurs plus grandes vertuz, comme à vn certain but, dirrige la pointe de son Style: car il n'y a point de doute, que la plus grand' part de l'Artifice ne soit contenue en l'immitation. . . . Mais entende celuy qui voudra immiter, que ce n'est chose facile de bien suyure les vertuz d'vn bon Aucteur & quasi comme se transformer en luy. . . ."[5] This ambiguity regarding the exact meaning of

5. Du Bellay, *Oeuvres Françoises*, ed. Marty-Laveaux (Paris, 1864), *I*, 17.

"immitation" reappears throughout the works of the
Pléiade, and insofar as imitation, ranging from translation
to mere suggestion, is present in virtually all their works
and those of the period, it would be useless to seek a hier-
archy of Renaissance poets with originality as the criterion
of distinction.

For the Renaissance, the word "originality" simply did
not have the implications with which Romanticism in
particular has endowed the term. Its equivalent would be
more likely "poetic craftsmanship," best expressed by the
sixteenth-century word "artifice," generally considered as
synonymous with the modern French word "art." [6] This
surely is what Du Bellay is attempting to point out when he
considers imitation as a means to a specific end ("dirrige la
pointe de son Style"). The poet must learn his art through
imitation; for, as Du Bellay takes care to inject, "la plus
grand' part de l'Artifice ne soit contenue en l'immitation."
When imitating, the poet pits his knowledge of versifica-
tion and language against the original, attempting to reproduce in French the quality of the original and, at best,
to surpass it. The manifold translations of Du Bellay in
L'Olive could well illustrate the former intention. The

6. Although it is traditional to translate "artifice" as it appears in
sixteenth-century texts by "art," this practice, in truth, solves little.
"Artifice," as studied by Huguet, *Dictionnaire de la Langue Française
du Seizième Siècle* (Paris, 1946), *1*, 324–25, means "travail," "habileté,"
"art consommé," and is translated by Huguet as "art" only in the expressions "d'artifice," "par artifice." Moreover, the distinction between
"travail" and "art consommé" or "habileté" seems rather arbitrary,
judging by the very quotations given by Huguet himself. For example,
in this quotation. "Ils feirent . . . representer la bataille des geants contre les Dieux en grands personnages de sculpture dont l'artifice estoit
excellent," "artifice" means "travail" according to Huguet, while in
"Louant ce grand Architecteur, facteur de toutes choses, qui a fait et
composé avec un si indicible et incomparable artifice toutes les parties
de nostre corps," we should read "habileté" and "art consommé." However precise we try to be, I do not see how it is possible to ignore the
very basic idea of work (cf. "facteur") present in "artifice" and thus,
ultimately in "art."

manner in which Ronsard manipulates in his hymns Folengo's rather crude description of the seasons might illustrate the latter. The distinction is always just a bit artificial, however, and the important distinction is not between intentions but between executions.

With rather similar intentions, Du Bellay and Ronsard produced two Petrarchistic cycles that are strikingly different with regard to imitation. *Amours I* is not a work of wholesale translation as is Du Bellay's *L'Olive. Amours I* is laden with Petrarch, but in bits and tatters; its piecemeal execution fails for many reasons and yet reveals at the outset, when compared with Du Bellay's cycle, a greater sense of "art" and of the poet's determination to recast the model in a personal fashion. This sense of "art" is mentioned here, even in association with an abortive effort, because we have seen it present throughout Ronsard's handling of his sources. It may take diverse forms—the general search for more successful models in the middle years, the superb handling of precise texts and techniques in *Sonnets pour Hélène*—but it must stand with the broader aim of a "defense and illustration of the French language" as one of the guiding principles behind Ronsard's evolution.

A constant preoccupation in this study has been the quantity of imitation in each of the major works treated. The results dovetail significantly with the guiding principles of "art" and "illustration." Large amounts of imitation from Marullus and Theocritus appear at the critical moment in the craftsman's development. He has been disappointed in his initial attempts with the sonnet cycle; more than a little confused as to the next major direction of effort, he is understandably in need of new material for experimentation. When he seems to comprehend that the fault is more conceptual than stylistic and formulates his own ideas, the amount of imitation drops conspicuously. In the seasonal hymns and finally in *Sonnets pour Hélène,* imitation becomes a judicious assimilation of suggestive and pregnant material with a personal creation. From this study's many pages of confrontation of text and source, Ronsard emerges as much more than the mass imitator, who, to use Vianey's expression, rarely stooped to plagiarism. His imitation is rarely gratuitous. Even in the crisis of the middle years, his sources bear the mark of the craftsman, for he seems to see in Marullus the ambivalence, in Theocritus, the escape needed at different moments to solve his various problems. Moreover, considering the bulk of Ronsard's production in the realm of the sonnet cycle and the span of years during which he worked with this genre, his imitative efforts are not overwhelmingly numerous, and, clearly prompted after 1552 by the poet's desire to realize his potential as an artist, they become very useful to the critic as a guide to Ronsard's development. It is unfortunate that to the mind of the modern age, emotion and poetry are so closely associated. Ronsard learned of poetry from Daurat through reading and imitating the classics. That he should develop in the same way is not surprising. Heretofore, sighting the parallels and repetition of clichés, critics of the Renaissance interested only in identifying sources have often failed to note the nuances that distinguish text and original. But for the poet of that day all the value of the production was in the nuance; there the poet aimed at showing his "artifice," and there we must look for it.

Finally, imitation has its role in tracing Ronsard's development as a person. Let us think back to the material used in fashioning the seasonal hymns and *Sonnets pour Hélène*: it is not all of the same order. In the case of Folengo, the source bears only the most distant relationship to Ronsard's finished work; with Propertius, however, Ronsard shows a deep affinity in both his understanding of the poet's situation and his expression of that situation. Although we cannot carry a discussion of Folengo beyond the slim resemblance, there is a wealth of similarity between Ronsard and Propertius. Barely lexical, it nonetheless is far more strong than the tie between Ronsard and Petrarch, to whom Ronsard seems to show an unequaled lexical bond. Ronsard's affinities with Propertius—the woman as inspiration, poetry as a value in itself, growing detachment from love—appear in a context, moreover, that has a Petrarchistic cast, but prove to form the true conceptual essence of the cycle.

Lexical imitation, then, must never alone be used as an index to conceptual affinity. However much Ronsard wished to rival and duplicate Petrarch's art, he had no intention of doing so at the expense of becoming like Petrarch. He uses Propertius in order to remain himself. This is the paradox of imitation and a point too seldom made in criticism of Ronsard's works, that through imitation Ronsard often found the patterns and poses which fitted his personality as well as his pen. *Amours I* proved that no artificial ideal equals the portrait of a woman and the *Continuations*, that roses alone cannot offset chaos in the poet's vision. During this time Ronsard was using elements from Propertius freely, yet never as he was to use them in *Sonnets pour Hélène*. Granted, the problems of 1555 were not the same as those posed by the choice of Hélène de Surgères to be the Muse of 1578, but, then, the poet's frame of thinking was not the same either. The work of the seasonal hymns is an essential sounding of the personality and only after realizing what he believed in a context which included love, poetry, and nature, did Ronsard see how much he shared with a poet like Propertius, and, conversely, how little in him reacted to the Petrarchistic portrait and vision.

This evolution, in its essence, is quite representative of the great writers of the Pléiade. Much that has been written concerning the Renaissance emphasizes now its affinity with antiquity, now its reaction to medieval modes. The two need not be fully separated, as appreciation of classical literature undoubtedly made contemporary offerings appear inferior, and contemporary poetry was not always attempting to improve upon the past. Yet much in the *Deffense's* string of models is bravado, not to mention undigested enthusiasm. The Pindaric odes of Ronsard attest well to this. The Pléiade comes of age when it discovers not simply models, but images of itself. When Du Bellay exhibited his affinity with the satirists, when Ronsard recognized the essence of Propertius' devotion yet detachment, so similar to his own final sentiments vis-à-vis Genèvre, they wrote two of the literary masterpieces of the sixteenth century. In the case of so skillful an imitator as Ronsard, the traces of affinity may not be immediately apparent, and close study of imitation can alone highlight the relationship between poem and source.[7] Yet the rewards of source-hunting cannot be denied. The analysis of source and imitation, undertaken with a positive goal in mind, leads us far from smug finger-pointing, as if the poet had been caught in a criminal act, to a full appreciation of his struggle to be one with himself and his art.[8]

Yvor Winters, writing of the poet and the difficulties he faces, concludes: "The poet who suffers from such difficulties instead of profiting by them is only in a rough sense a poet at all."[9] Insofar as this entire study has shown that the evolution of Ronsard's sonnet cycles is inseparable from his desire to surmount the difficulties of an attempt to rival the canzoniere of Petrarch, we have a sufficient reason for

7. See, for example, the excellent article of A. Noyer-Weidner, "Die innere Form des Imitatio bei Ronsard," *Romanistisches Jahrbuch*, 4 (1958), 174–93.

8. For a more detailed discussion of the problem of imitation and the Pléiade, see Grahame Castor, *Pléiade Poetics* (Cambridge, 1964).

9. Yvor Winters, *In Defense of Reason* (New York, 1947), p. 17.

claiming Ronsard to be a great poet. It is so fundamental a justification, moreover, that any other must ultimately derive from it, for it alone places Ronsard's greatness in the mastery of his art.

Generations of critics after Sainte-Beuve have elected to praise in Ronsard's love poetry the evocation of nature and the portrait of passion, although this praise falls short of the total picture of his poetry and reveals more about what modern centuries like in Ronsard than about what is at stake in a general appreciation of his claim to greatness. Yet to follow the course of Ronsard's love verse, to gather a sense of the love traditions of the period and to see what Ronsard finally was able to create of them cannot fail to underline the scope of his conquest. And, had we examined the odes, our conclusions might well have been the same: that the portrait of nature, the welling up of emotion, and the creation of the plot all form a carefully constructed poetic triumph. The many pages devoted to textual analysis throughout this study repeatedly point up Ronsard's poetic ambitions. They remind us also of how direct an impact upon the poet's writing was made by Ronsard's more exterior preoccupations during this evolution—imitation, philosophizing, revolt—so that when the initial and final products of Ronsard's sonnet cycles are juxtaposed, the advances of each step in his development fall into place, as they must have done for the poet. Those who place intuition above craftsmanship may feel that I have given little space to the spontaneous creation of the poet in love as distinguished from the poet of love. Judging by the framework of Ronsard's final love cycle and especially by the Hélène poems "Quand vous serez bien vieille" and the "Stances," however, the poet himself counted for little his sources of inspiration as long as the immortal, poetic monument was secure. I might quote the letter to Scevole de Sainte-Marthe, in which poetry again is seen as the domain

of the poet alone and a discipline of which women kr.
nothing: "C'est un grand malheur de servir une maistress
qui n'a jugement ny raison en nostre poësie, qui ne sçait
pas que les poëtes, principallement en petis et menus fatras
come elegies, epigrames et sonnetz, ne gardent ny ordre ny
temps, c'est affaire aux historiographes qui escrivent tout de
fil en aguille." [10]

Yet I would be the first to admit that Ronsard did not
place his art above the expression of the self. The seasonal
hymns, the elegies to Genèvre prove quite the contrary:
the two demands of art and self were always present and
often heeded. Ronsard is a great poet not only because he
overcame problems of form and technique but because he
saw in his desire to write great poetry a demand to write as
the needs of the self dictated. His contemplation of technique alone destroyed the *Franciade*, but when, in the
domain of his love cycles, he accepted the challenge to find
the starkest chords of his own voice and yet perfect them
within the sonnet form, he assured his place in Elysium.

10. Ronsard, *Oeuvres Complètes*, ed. Gustave Cohen (2 vols. Paris,
1950), 2, 1047.

Appendix: The Edition of 1584

ALTHOUGH the development of Ronsard's love cycles ends with *Sonnets pour Hélène* and the edition of 1578, the story of *Sonnets pour Hélène*–1578 does not. When Ronsard published a new edition of his works in 1584, *Sonnets pour Hélène* had become quite a different cycle through the addition of thirty-five sonnets from *Amours Diverses*, a division of poems that first appeared in 1578.[1] This new *Sonnets pour Hélène* is of particular importance because, while I have elected to analyze the earlier edition of Ronsard's final love cycle, other critics without exception have based their remarks on the edition of 1584.[2] Even Desonay considers the thirty-five sonnets as having doubtless been written for Hélène, since they were finally placed with the other sonnets to her in 1584, and he makes no distinction between the two versions of the Hélène story. Recent studies of the cycle such as those by Chadwick and Pelan also treat the edition of 1584 with no attempt to entertain the possibility that a basic change in conception had taken place since 1578.[3] This attitude is all the more surprising since to my knowledge the changes effected by Ronsard

1. This count undergoes a strange metamorphosis to thirty-six in Desonay's last volume. In his introductory 'Note bibliographique" he correctly lists ten *Amours Diverses* sonnets inserted in *Sonnets pour Hélène*, Book One and twenty-five in Book Two, making a total of thirty-five. The number "thirty-six" appearing on page 185 is clearly an oversight.

2. Cf. Desonay *Ronsard, poète de l'amour*, 3 and Lavaud's introduction to his critical edition of *Sonnets pour Hélène* (Paris, 1947).

3. M Pelan, "Ronsard's 'Amour d'Automne,'" *French Studies*, 7 (1953) 214–22 and C. Chadwick, "The Composition of the *Sonnets pour Hélène*," *French Studies*, 8: (1954) 326–32.

have never been studied closely, nor the supposition behind such a choice of editions brought to light. If, for example, in 1578 Ronsard, having at his disposition the same sonnets as in 1584, preferred to distribute them differently between *Sonnets pour Hélène* and *Amours Diverses*, some explanation may be found in a comparison of the content of the two cycles. Moreover, if our past observations concerning the careful execution and arrangement of *Sonnets pour Hélène* are correct, it is possible that Ronsard's conception of *Sonnets pour Hélène* in 1578 excluded certain material which he relegated to *Amours Diverses*.

The tendency of past criticism to analyze the edition of 1584 is a tacit suggestion that the later edition represents not only a careful reconstruction of *Sonnets pour Hélène*, but, indeed, the creation of a new sonnet cycle. This point of view is supported by a second supposition on the part of those few critics who have mentioned the change in the cycles: Ronsard supposedly did not want to compromise Hélène de Surgères in 1578 by publishing poems which might suggest that their relationship was not Platonic. He originally transferred to *Amours Diverses* thirty-five sonnets intended for Hélène and did not place them in their rightful context until six years later. According to such a theory the early edition must be considered an incomplete version of what in 1584 was revealed as a total unity. Ronsard appears hesitant in 1578 and betrays the truth of inspiration for a moral concern.

It is hoped that the following analysis of these questions and suppositions will reverse this prevailing interpretation and cast new light on the value of the original edition. A preference for *Sonnets pour Hélène*–1584 as the cycle where Ronsard cast aside his moral qualms, cannot be upheld before a confrontation with the texts, and there is no trace of any intricate refashioning of the Hélène cycle in 1584. Not only moral but literary considerations must be

Sonnet 28 is an elaborate series of metaphors by which the poet suggests that he has been mistaken in believing it was impossible to frequent beauty and not be affected by its power. His reasoning depends upon the "pointe" that he must, indeed, be wrong as his beloved remains unmoved "if not by a great fire, at least by a spark." This last line shows how the poet seeks to use the image of fire to transmit his thought. But this is not the metaphoric vein in which the poem opens: "Aller en marchandise aux Indes precieuses/ Sans acheter ny or ny parfum ny joyaux," the speaker says, like courting and seeking ladies without feeling love's arrows and torches, is a monstrous thing. The opposition Ronsard creates here is between a deliberate effort to seek a priceless object and the "pointe"—the lady is insensitive— which destroys the poet's argument. The cases are not at all equal, as nowhere does the poet suggest that the woman is looking for love. She is young, beautiful, but this does not suffice to put her in the same situation as the merchant or the speaker. Ronsard tries to make his imagery flow from merchants to torches to fires and sparks, but whether from the point of view of the metaphors or the central argument, the sonnet fails to hold together.

Sonnet 32 is similarly lame. As in the preceding example, the quatrains maintain a certain unity of presentation. The woman, on seeing the speaker bled, remarks on the blackness of his blood. He answers that love has been the cause. The first tercet seems to begin the poet's final turn by showing the speaker in a bid for youth. Become Medea and "Colorez d'un bon sang ma face ja ridee," he says. Verse 12 prolongs the movement by mentioning Medea's effect on Aeson. Then suddenly the sonnet veers a third time: "Nul charme ne sçauroit renouveller la mienne:/ Si je veux rajeunir, il ne faut plus aimer." While there is a vague continuity, the ending is disconcerting. The main idea is even left unsaid, and is quite poorly prepared by the preceding lines. The conversational element is done away with and

the reader is forced to accept this *à part*, not only as an e.
ment of the poem's natural flow, but as its conclusion. To.
sudden to be a natural movement and too elliptical to summarize the work, the lines fail on each count.

The sonnets in *Amours Diverses* are often inferior to the
poems to Hélène in another way: the treatment of their
subject matter.[5] Sonnet 22 and I/50 offer an excellent comparison.

Quoy? me donner congé d'embrasser chaque femme,
Mon feu des-attizer au premier corps venu,
Ainsi qu'un vagabond, sans estre retenu
Abandonner la bride au vouloir de ma flame:
Non, ce n'est pas aimer. L'Archer ne vous entame
Qu'un peu le haut du coeur d'un traict foible & menu.
Si d'un coup bien profond il vous estoit cognu,
Ce ne seroit que soulfre & braise de vostre ame.
En soupçon de vostre ombre en tous lieux vous seriez:
A toute heure, en tous temps, jalouse me suivriez,
D'ardeur & de fureur & de crainte allumee.
Amour au petit pas, non au gallop vous court,
Et vostre amitié n'est qu'une flame de Court,
Où peu de feu se trouve, & beaucoup de fumee.

(sonnet 22)

Amour est sans milieu, c'est une chose extrême,
Qui ne veult (je le sçay) de tiers ny de moitié:
Il ne faut point trencher en deux une amitié.
"Un est nombre parfait, imparfait le deuxiéme.
J'aime de tout mon coeur, je veux aussi qu'on m'aime.
Le desir au desir d'un noeud ferme lié,
Par le temps ne s'oublie, & n'est point oublié:
Il est toujours son tout, contenté de soymesme.

5. Nearly a third of the thirty-five sonnets are thematic doubles with
works in *Sonnets pour Hélène*: sonnets 15, 16, 18, 22, 27, 31, 49, 50, 51, 54,
and 59.

Mon ombre me fait peur, & jaloux je ne pius
Avoir un compaignon, tant amoureux je suis,
Et tant je m'essentie en la personne aimee.
L'autre amitié ressemble à quelque vent qui court.
Et brayment c'est aimer comme on fait à la Court,
Où le feu contrefait ne rend qu'une fumee.

(I/50)

Both condemn the woman's philosophy of love; the final lines are nearly the same. Yet the elaboration of the idea is noticeably on a higher level in the version of *Sonnets pour Hélène*. This poem maintains a unity of tone and expression because Ronsard has elected to present in the poem only his own ideas on love—its general nature (first quatrain), its manifestation in himself (second quatrain and first tercet), and how it makes him react to her ideas (second tercet). Even the initial generalizations are firmly attached to the self ("je le sçay"). This is what love is; this is how I feel, he says. When he arrives at the close, he has painted a personality which by definition cannot love otherwise.

The poem of *Amours Diverses*, on the other hand, has no central optic to stabilize it. Rather, the poet mixes the woman's philosophy and his own in a see-saw exchange of exclamation, exposition, and refutation. The first word "Quoi?" translates not only the rhythmic agitation but an emotional one as well. When the speaker tries to explain what the woman should feel, there is none of the simplicity of emotion we have seen in the other poem. Instead, Ronsard contents himself with clichés about the shallowness of love's blow: "Amour au petit pas, non au gallop vous court." Such lines compared with "J'aime de tout mon coeur, je veux aussi qu'on m'aime" or "Et tant je m'essentie en la personne aimee" leave little doubt that *Amours Diverses* was meant to preserve for *Sonnets pour Hélène* a relatively high aesthetic quality.

The omissions were also meant to prevent a thematic monotony. If certain new sonnets of the period did not reproduce the themes of the poems addressed to Hélène as exactly as sonnet 22, they often repeated common poses and arguments. Sonnet 50 reproduces an image used in I/24 of Achilles the healer in reference to the wounded lover. Sonnet 31 expresses in a new setting (he drinks from her cup) the famous shudder but in tired terminology:

> Ce vase me lia tous les Sens dés le jour
> Que je beu de son vin, mais plus tost une flame,
> Mais plus tost un venin qui m'en-yvra d'amour.
>
> (vv. 12–14)

Sonnet 49 is built around the symbols of a fig and the pomegranate, similar to the gifts in *Sonnets pour Hélène* of the orange and the lemon (I/26). It is filled out by such trite Petrarchistic verses as:

> Je suis pour vostre amour diversement malade,
> Maintenant plein de froid, maintenant de chaleur:
> Dedans le coeur pour vous autant j'ay de douleur,
> Comme il y a de grains dedans ceste Grenade.
>
> (vv. 1–4)

The poem also makes use of the "je faux" device. The technique is used in four poems published for the first time in 1578. Ronsard put only one example in *Sonnets pour Hélène* (II/30); all the others were banned from the love cycle. This fact seems to me to be more than a coincidence. I have insisted elsewhere on the careful structure of *Sonnets pour Hélène*. This discussion of certain sonnets in *Amours Diverses* adds another dimension to our observations. What we find is not simply a choice between good and inferior sonnets, but a selection of devices, symbols, techniques, all valid but valid only in a certain proportion.

Ronsard's desire not to overcrowd *Sonnets pour Hélène* with repetition is definitely an indication of his consciousness of the cycle as a structured work.

To this external confirmation of Ronsard's effort to structure Hélène's poems can be added a confirmation of his intention to present the love story in a particular light. If several sonnets in *Amours Diverses* would have been unacceptable in *Sonnets pour Hélène* for reasons of structure, others would have been incompatible with the vision of 1578. These poems establish a valuable point of reference concerning Ronsard's attitude in 1578 as these sonnets which were originally placed in *Amours Diverses,* too, will later find their way into *Sonnets pour Hélène.* In 1578, however, the line of demarcation was firm. All that is excessive, either in terms of the crude reality of the poet's desire or the crude reality of the affair (addressed after all to one of the ugliest women of the court), is relegated to *Amours Diverses.*[6] *Sonnets pour Hélène–1578* carefully avoids the blatant language of sonnet 25, where the speaker ends with his "pointe": "Si j'avois pres ma Dame un quart d'heure dormy/ Je serois non pas Dieu: je serois les Dieux mesme." He placed in *Amours Diverses* as well sonnet 20 with its verse "Qu'est-ce parler d'amour, sans point faire l'amour,"; sonnet 36, "Maintenant je veux estre importun amoureux/ Du bon pere Aristote . . . / Il est temps que je sois de l'Amour deslié"; sonnet 40: "Au vent aille l'Amour . . . / Vivre sans volupté c'est vivre sous la terre,"; and sonnet 39:

> Au milieu de la guerre, en un siecle sans foy,
> Entre mille procez, est-ce pas grand folie
> D'escrire de l'Amour?

Equally impossible were the two sonnets which suggest that the poet was loved by the woman (sonnets 42 and 48).

6. Sonnets 20, 24, 25, 26, 34, 36, 37, 39, 40, 41, 42, 48.

All these examples, whether dealing with construction, content, or expression, should suffice to show that in 1578 it is *Sonnets pour Hélène* which dominates the poet's arrangement of his new sonnets. With few exceptions Ronsard has reserved for this cycle the best of his poems; he has arranged them in a careful structure, telling a particular story, and what does not conform to these criteria Ronsard insists on separating from his masterpiece by forming *Amours Diverses*. The sonnets to Hélène were special, if only for a short while.

Between 1578 and 1584 a profound change in attitude must have taken place in Ronsard's mind regarding *Sonnets pour Hélène*. All the poems from *Amours Diverses* just analyzed were inserted in the world of Hélène and the vision, the structure, the tone of the cycle were radically altered. There is good reason to suppose that this revolution in attitude did not take place immediately after the publication of the 1578 cycles. On the contrary, Ronsard's first reaction seems to have been to rework *Sonnets pour Hélène* applying the same principles I have outlined in terms of the placement of the original *Amours Diverses* sonnets, but more stringently.

In 1584 five sonnets had disappeared from *Sonnets pour Hélène*: I/42, I/46, II/19, II/25, II/33. Sonnet I/46 repeated an image not only to be found elsewhere in the cycle, but in the very next poem! Sonnet II/19 suggested the Hélène had begun to reciprocate the poet's affections, and sonnets I/42, II/25, and II/33 all reproduce that harsh tone against love and lady of many *Amours Diverses* sonnets.[7] When these sonnets had been suppressed, the

7. A similarity of themes between these sonnets removed from *Sonnets pour Hélène*—1578 and the sonnets of *Amours Diverses* is not the only reason for suggesting that Ronsard decided upon these suppressions before inserting the thirty-five sonnets in *Sonnets pour Hélène*—1584.

weight of emphasis then moved from *Sonnets pour
Hélène*—which imposed an aesthetic of separation—to
Amours Diverses, and Ronsard's guiding principle became
a separation of sonnets, not according to suitability or unsuitability for the love cycle to Hélène, but according to
date of composition.

The sonnets from *Amours Diverses* inserted in *Sonnets
pour Hélène* present the following pattern: 20, 21, 22, 23,
24, 25, 26, 27; 29; 59; 41, 42, 43; 15, 16, 28, 54, 30, 39, 40,
46, 47, 48, 31, 32, 33, 34, 35, 36, 37; 18; 49, 50, 51, 52.[8] At
first glance, the order seems complicated and indicative of
much rearrangement. In fact such an impression is misleading. Ronsard's technique was quite rudimentary. It must be
kept in mind that the transfer of the sonnets from *Amours
Diverses* represents but one aspect of a general trend the
mechanism of which is only too evident: Ronsard systematically removed from *Amours Diverses* before 1584 all
poems first published in 1578 under this title and transferred them to whatever of the new 1578 divisions was best
suited to receive them. Since he maintained the division of
Amours Diverses, he preserved its introductory sonnet.
The poems already suppressed from earlier cycles, sonnets
3, 5, 9, 11, 12, 13, 14, 17, 19, and 58, were naturally retained. Of the decasyllabic poems, all, sonnets 2, 4, 7, 8,
and 57, were moved to *Astrée* except two, sonnets 6 and
10, which referred to another woman, Renée de Château-

When this is accomplished, one of the added sonnets, 18, is placed between II/24 and II/26 (sonnets II/43 and 45 in 1584), which presupposes
the prior suppression of sonnet II/25. There is no evidence, as we shall
see, of Ronsard's removing sonnets from *Sonnets pour Hélène* to make
room for the added poems, and other single *Amours Diverses* sonnets
were, like sonnet 18, placed between sonnets of the original cycle,
never in place of them.

8. Numbers separated by commas are contiguous in the 1584 cycle;
those separated by semicolons are separated in the 1584 edition by original *Sonnets pour Hélène* poems.

neuf, by name or status as a prince's mistress. Sonnet 5
Ronsard sent to *Sonnets à Diverses Personnes*. Certain of
the remaining sonnets were by content undesirable for a
love cycle by any standards. Sonnet 38 began, "Chacun me
dit Ronsard, ta maistresse n'est telle/Comme tu la descris";
sonnet 45 spoke of a "vierge, humble & jeune maistresse,"
hardly possible in a cycle for so high-born a lady as Hélène
de Surgères, and sonnet 53, the "godmicy" sonnet, speaks
for itself. Sonnets 44 and 55, both suggesting intimacy between the speaker and his lady, were also refused entry into
Sonnets pour Hélène.

The mechanistic aspect of this selection process, which
accounts for the future exclusion from *Amours Diverses* of
every sonnet save the five sonnets whose content was unacceptable, is a prime indication of Ronsard's attitude toward
Sonnets pour Hélène at this time. The new poems to
Hélène are hardly favored or handled with special care.
The attack on *Amours Diverses* is general and all the sonnets are selected or rejected according to the same criteria
of date of publication and suitableness for the proposed re-
organization.

Here are the groupings of those sonnets which were to
be transferred to *Sonnets pour Hélène*: 15, 16; 18;
20–37; 39–40 [9]; 41–43; 46–52; 54; 59. The correspondence
between this series of divisions and the position of these
sonnets in *Sonnets pour Hélène*–1584 is quite amazing:
20–27; 29; 59; 41–43; 15–16, 28, 54, 30, 39–40, 46–48,
31–37; 18; 49–52. Only the two long series 20–37 and
46–52 are still to be broken up. It remains to be seen now
whether the placing of these sonnets was subject to similar
patterns of swift, sweeping movement. The latter chain
was simply divided 46–48, 49–52. In the former, Ronsard
singled out sonnet 29 to occupy the position of an original

---

9. Sonnets 40 and 41 were automatically separated by a long intervening elegy.

nnet to Hélène that had been suppressed. The singly
grouped sonnet, 54, took the place of sonnet 29, and the
chain was finally cut 20–28, (54), 30–37. Of the thirty-five
sonnets, a bare three, then, were placed singly, and two of
them, sonnets 18 and 59 were originally lone sonnets
among the group of poems to be placed in *Sonnets pour
Hélène*. The rest all fall into four large blocks varying in
length from seventeen sonnets to three with two groups of
four and eight sonnets each. Of these blocks, only one, the
longest, is not composed of a group of sonnets arranged
precisely as they appeared in *Amours Diverses* in 1578, and
even that one is but a string of small, continuous blocks remaining after the selection and breaking of the long chains.
Ronsard did not take careful steps to integrate the *Amours
Diverses* poems. They continue with insignificant exceptions to be bound one to the other in long groups that do
not even seek to conceal the original sequence of 1578.
Even the option for sonnet 29 to be placed singly from
among a large group points to such segregation and not integration. Not just any of the *Amours Diverses* works, but
one of the few *Amours Diverses* poems to stand on a par
with the Hélène poems [10] was selected be placed alone.
Finally, it is startling to realize that Ronsard arranged in a
single block more than half the sonnets transferred. The
reality of the new text presents the very opposite of assimilation. A mere ninth, at the very most, of the sonnets in
Sonnets pour Hélène taken from *Amours Diverses* can be
said to have been placed in terms of a consideration of content between added and pre-existing material. From beginning to end, the process belies any painful effort to recreate
Sonnets pour Hélène. Selection by general principles, insertion by pre-determined blocks, both techniques are coupled with the final fact, as exemplified by the string of sev-

10. See p. 229.

enteen sonnets, that while creating an amalgam of old and
new poems, Ronsard effectively preserved within the second edition of *Sonnets pour Hélène* strong distinguishable
barriers between the original sonnets and the poems he
superimposed.

The texts are equally eloquent in discrediting the supposition that the thirty-five sonnets were originally excluded
to protect Hélène's reputation.[11] In effect, the 1578 love
story does have a chaste aura. The poet but once (II/7)
exhibits physical frustration and the woman remains im-
passive except for two moderate indications of involvement: "en aimant tu me donnes . . ." (I/46) and "le feu/
Qui commençoit en vous à se monstrer un peu" (II/19).
On the other hand, among the sonnets relegated to *Amours
Diverses* in 1578 can be found a number of poems which
indicate that the woman reciprocated the lover's feelings
(sonnets 21, 31, 42, 48, 52). Sonnet 25, beginning "Sommeillant sur ta face . . ." could have been injurious to her
reputation, and Ronsard even excluded three sonnets (23,
24, 27) where he indicated his lady continued their relationship for the sake of poems he wrote—not a very flattering remark. Yet most convincing in the argument for a
moral concern is the fate of sonnets I/46 and II/19 just
mentioned. They alone trouble the chastity of *Sonnets
pour Hélène* in 1578, and they are among the five sonnets
suppressed from the 1578 edition, only, however, to be replaced in the cycle in the edition of 1587.

The problem with this moral argument is that it applies
to so few of the works involved. Even including sonnets
23, 24, and 27 with the poems which attack the lady's atti-

11. Cf. Desonay, 3, 185–86: "Mais de ces 62 pièces [in *Amours Diverses*] dix seulement doivent nous retenir un instant; les 52 autres,
en effet, sont ou bien des reprises (12), ou bien des sonnets composés
à l'intention d'Astrée (4) ou d'Hélène (36), [sic] mais que Ronsard,
pour des raisons qui sont souvent des raisons de scruple, n'avait pas
cru devoir attribuer à ces deux inspiratrices en 1578."

tudes would account for a mere fourth of the problematic thirty-five sonnets, and three other sonnets beside I/46 and II/19 were suppressed from the 1578 poems to Hélène. Moreover, the juggling of the texts is not consistent. Why should Ronsard have hesitated to include in *Sonnets pour Hélène*–1584 sonnets 44 and 55 from *Amours Diverses* at a time when he supposedly had no more scruples about adding a frank portrait of passion in the woman? A possible solution is that other criteria are involved.

With minor exceptions, the remaining twenty-six *Amours Diverses* sonnets have already been discussed as being unsuitable for the cycle to Hélène in attitude, subject matter, or expression. What is important to recall here is that few (the quarrels over philosophy aside) even deal with the woman at all. Their unsuitability for *Sonnets pour Hélène* as the cycle was conceived in 1578 stems not from moral questions but from questions of presentation. The string of sonnets 35–37, 39–40, for example, which deprecate love and threaten abandonment of the Muses, could hardly participate in the 1578 cycle without upsetting totally the structure of gradual and intensified separation from the woman. Again, the sonnets suppressed from *Sonnets pour Hélène*–1578 reveal the poet's prejudices. In addition to the moral complications, there is precisely this disrespectful tone to love (II/33). And sonnets II/25 and I/42 rather rudely attack Hélène's philosophy, the third obvious category for exclusion. The final category, repetition of themes, has been closely studied above.

In conclusion it is hard to see how the nature of but one category, the moral question—hardly the most numerous —could define Ronsard's practice with his sonnets in 1578. He was evidently sensitive to much more than a moral problem, for each of the other categories of rejected sonnets deals with basic aethetic considerations: structure, treatment of various themes, unity of tone, and propor-

tioned variety in devices and techniques. The clear abandonment of these considerations in 1584 forces us to reject
the un- or ill-justified preference for *Sonnets pour Hélène–
1584.* The poet permitted tones of bitterness, disgust,
frankness, and sensuality to define a love formerly disturbed but momentarily. It is no wonder that in 1587 certain poems suppressed from the cycle to Hélène after 1578
(sonnets I/46 and II/19) returned. In a cycle which now
contained poems such as:

> Prenant congé de vous, dont les yeux m'ont donté,
> Vous me distes un soir comme passionnee,
> Je vous aime, Ronsard, par seule destinee,
> Le Ciel à vous aimer force ma volonté
> > (*Amours Diverses*–1578, sonnet 42)

there could be no opposition to such a line as "le feu/Qui
commençoit en vous à se monstrer un peu" (II/19). And
the problems of recurring images (I/47 and I/46) are hardly
problems any more.

If we stop to consider why Ronsard should in the first
place have created the limbo of *Amours Diverses* for out-
casts from *Sonnets pour Hélène,* we may begin to arrive at
an answer to his motives after 1578. Is it not strange that a
poet who realizes the unsuitable quality of a number of his
creations, should arrange a special place for them and not
suppress them all? Perhaps in an absolute sense it is, but
judging by Ronsard's relative position in 1578, we must admit the existence of a perfect justification: his rivalry with
Desportes. Every poem suppressed was a poem unread by
the older poet's public, who had already come to prefer the
young favorite of Henri III. Ronsard, though old, did not
want to appear poetically sterile, and the poems which
were unsuitable for the special world of Hélène's love
story were not necessarily unacceptable as love poetry in

general. In order to show the continued virulence of his pen he suppressed as little as possible. After the publication of his complete works in 1578, he continued to work his verse as in the past, correcting, switching poems from one cycle to another, and suppressing others. He seems to have worked on *Sonnets pour Hélène* with the same attitude that had directed its original creation. Then something made him change his entire orientation toward the production of 1578. Desportes' acquisition in 1582 of more lucrative abbeys did not serve to calm Ronsard's feelings.[12] But the major crisis may well have been Desportes' collective edition of 1583. Previous reimpressions of his edition of 1578 had added little to the number of works already published,[13] but the edition of 1583 added 224 new poems to the production.[14] One can only speculate as to Ronsard's reaction, but for those who know of his fierce pride and jealousy, the desire to effect a rapid counter-attack does not seem at all impossible. The few recorded dates, moreover, do not contradict this hypothesis. The privilege for Desportes' edition of 1583 is dated 3 January,[15] which suggests that the work appeared early in that year. Ronsard's famous letter to Scevole de Sainte-Marthe about proposed work with his poems that Hélène does not appear to appreciate is dated July 1583, and his edition appeared the following January.[16]

Conscious of his poetic evolution, he no longer dared permit some of his earlier poems to appear beside his latest works. The reader was less likely to notice the stylistic and conceptual gaps that separate the various periods of his development if they were no longer to be found in close

12. Jacques Lavaud, *Philippe Desportes* (Paris, 1936), p. 259.
13. Ibid., p. 262.
14. Ibid., p. 263.
15. Ibid., p. 263.
16. See, Chamard, *Histoire de la Pléiade*, 3, 368.

proximity, as was the case in *Amours Diverses*–1578. The lesser poems of his late period, grouped now among the *Sonnets pour Hélène*, were perhaps expected to share their perfection. If we shall probably never know the particulars of his intent we can definitely say that in 1584 the esthetic force which created *Sonnets pour Hélène* was directed away from the intention of 1578 to display an artistic showpiece. The individual poems retain their fine quality, but the structure of the story, the story itself, can never be the same. In 1578 style, structure, vision, tone transcend the poetic effort. In 1584 one can only be aware of the particular successes as the intimate relationship of the parts can never be reworked to admit the divergent aspects of tone and vision inserted after 1578.

Ronsard may well have sought by these myriad individual successes to combat a crumbling popularity. Certain beauties of *Sonnets pour Hélène* were probably too subtle to impress the dilettante courtisans. Ronsard may have known they would not be missed by his general public, which was more eager to find the well-turned "pointe," the pithy hyperbole, and the witty exaggerations the poet had put aside and then revived because of Desportes, yet relegated most often to *Amours Diverses*. We can pardon Ronsard his willingness to cater to the public's poor taste when we understand the importance of favor at the courts of the period. But, more important, we must acknowledge the genius of the poet which, early in the struggle with Desportes, gave all to the poetic spirit and banished from the cycle to Hélène, if not from the general edition of Ronsard's works, all that did not contribute to make *Sonnets pour Hélène*–1578 Ronsard's finest artistic achievement.

Index

(Ronsard's works are listed under his name, the major collections chronologically and individual poems within those collections alphabetically by title.)